AF552705

Brendan Fernandes

SKIRA

Re/Form

edited by Alhena Katsof

Graham Foundation for
Advanced Studies in the Fine Arts

The Isamu Noguchi Foundation
and Garden Museum

Without the generous financial support of these individuals this book would not have come into being. With heartfelt gratitude to:

Ellen-Blair Chube
Tad Freese + Brook Hartzell
Alida + Christopher Latham
Abby Pucker
Rennie Collection, Vancouver

Since its founding in 1956, the Graham Foundation has supported individuals across many disciplines whose work aligns at the intersection of architecture. Our mission, to foster the development and exchange of diverse and challenging ideas about architecture and its role in the arts, culture, and society, is realized through making project-based grants to individuals and organizations and producing exhibitions, events, and publications. Working with Brendan on what became *The Master and Form*—in collaboration with the design practice Norman Kelley—marked an exciting evolution within the Graham Fellowship program, which provides support for the development and production of a new body of work and the opportunity to present these projects in an exhibition at the Foundation's Madlener House galleries in Chicago.

The Fellowship program extends the legacy of the Foundation's first awards made in 1957 and 1958. Initial fellowships provided a diverse group of practitioners a platform to pursue experimental ideas in the field. Recipients included Pritzker Prize winning architects Balkrishna V. Doshi and Fumihiko Maki, designer Harry Bertoia, photographer Harry M. Callahan, sculptor Eduardo Chillida, experimental architect Frederick J. Kiesler, and painter Wilfredo Lam, among others. Recent Fellows include architect Tatiana Bilbao, curator Mark Wasiuta, and the artists Nelly Agassi, Torkwase Dyson, David Hartt, Sergio Prego, Barbara Stauffacher Solomon, Martine Syms, and Anna Martine Whitehead.

As a Fellow, Brendan continued this tradition of exploring new perspectives on spatial practices and design culture, encouraging us to think about architecture as the lens through which to consider other disciplines such as dance. This continuity references the Graham's engagement with performance including our 2014 exhibition, *Experiments in Environment: The Halprin Workshops, 1966–71*, which presented the experimental cross-disciplinary workshops on environmental awareness by American landscape architect Lawrence Halprin and avant-garde dance pioneer Anna Halprin originally staged in northern California. Our long-standing partnership and performance series with Lampo—an organization that presents work by experimental sound and interdisciplinary artists—paved the way for interdisciplinary engagement of performance at the Graham.

It was at the culminating Graham residency performance of *Kjell Theøry* with ATOMr—a performing collective that explores queer embodiment through performance, language, and emerging technologies—that the idea of what could be possible for Brendan at the Graham begin to germinate.

Though we could not have foreseen the development of *The Master and Form* at the beginning of Brendan's Fellowship, the collaborative nature of the work was foundational from the outset. We are grateful for the collaboration of the Whitney Museum of American Art and the thoughtful expansion of *The Master and Form* in the 2019 Biennial, curated by Jane Panetta and Rujeko Hockley. Early conversations also included discussions of storied partnerships in design and performance, chiefly that of sculptor Isamu Noguchi and choreographer Martha Graham—one of the many reasons it was so exciting to see the beautiful presentation of *Contract and Release* at the Noguchi Museum. We are thankful to Brett Littman, Director of the Noguchi Museum, and staff, for their collaboration to bring these projects together in this publication.

Collaboration made *The Master and Form* at the Graham Foundation possible and created opportunities for future realizations of the work. We specifically acknowledge the contributions of Norman Kelley; the Joffrey Academy of Dance, particularly dancers Satoru Iwasaki, Yuha Kamoto, Andrea de León Rivera, Antonio Mannino, and Leah Upchurch; the work of Alex Inglizian, Jason Lewis Furniture, Navillus Woodworks, and Karsten Osterby; Monique Meloche Gallery; and the Graham Foundation staff, especially Ellen Alderman, and Ava Barrett, Tom Leinberger, Zoe Kauder Nalebuff, Carolyn Kelly, Ron Konow, Claire Morton, James Pike, Alexandra Small, and Rachel Spek. Finally, none of this would be possible without the Graham Foundation Board of Trustees and their unwavering support of experimental ideas that expand our understanding of architecture. It is thrilling to see this publication go to print as an embodiment of these collaborations continued. May there be more to come!

Sarah Herda
Director
Graham Foundation for Advanced Studies in the Fine Arts

Brendan Fernandes: Contract and Release and *Body–Space Devices*, both curated by our senior curator Dakin Hart in 2019–20, were exactly the kind of integrated exhibitions that I wanted to see at the Isamu Noguchi Foundation and Garden Museum when I became director in 2017. The question of how we could continue to keep Noguchi's ideas, legacy and influence dynamic and relevant to younger creatives working in many fields, not just in the visual arts, is probably the issue that has taken up most of my energy and thinking during my tenure so far. What attracted me to Isamu Noguchi was his protean and fluid approach to applying sculptural values to the worlds of dance, architecture, and industrial, garden and landscape design. His steadfast, insistent, and fearless multi-disciplinary gambits into various aesthetic realms always pushed the boundaries of his own knowledge and understanding of how sculptural ideas and the role of the artist could be expanded in positive ways into the lived world. I want to take Noguchi's lead and have our program follow in this path as a series of collaborative, outwardly radiating concentric circles that constantly investigate and absorb new ideas and create space for a multitude of interpretations of his life work.

One facet of Noguchi's oeuvre that I have been very interested in are his collaborations with Martha Graham. Not to say that these haven't been explored in depth before, but in my opinion, given the preponderance of interest in movement and dance in the contemporary art world in the past decade, they still hold many important lessons for artists and art historians. I have personally spent the last three years seeing as many performances of Graham's repertoire with Noguchi's sets as I can, in order to experience first-hand the relationships between the dancers' bodies and his scenography. Noguchi states about his work with Graham: "The theater of dance in particular adds the movement of bodies, in relation to form and space, together with music. There is joy in seeing sculpture come to life on the state in its own world of timeless time … Theater is ceremonial; the performance is a rite. Sculpture in daily life should or could be like this."[1]

It was an incredible opportunity for the museum to work with an artist like Brendan Fernandes to develop not only a Noguchi collection show curated by an artist but also a new body of sculpture

1
Isamu Noguchi, *Isamu Noguchi: A Sculptor's World*, rev. ed. (New York: Harper & Row, 1968), 143.

and performances. Brendan comes to the visual arts from the world of dance—he was trained as a ballet dancer and studied Graham technique during his BFA in Toronto—so his unique training and background gave us special artistic insight into the interplay of dance, the stage and the set. Brendan's work, like Noguchi's, is also imbued with social content. His firmly centered, honest and unflinching exploration of what it means to question and understand identity, race and sexuality through sculpture, space, fashion and movement extend Noguchi's own ideas on these issues. His deep understanding and respect for Noguchi's work made his interventions at the museum both profoundly revelatory and insightful. Watching his performers interact with his own sculptures *Still Release I–VI*, which were spread throughout our second-floor galleries and were based on the Rocking Chair Noguchi designed for Graham's Appalachian Spring, and Noguchi's own *Play Sculpture*, was to me a salient example of how our museum could intertwine past and present to create new interpretive methods for the future. I want to personally thank Brendan for providing the platform for us to see this complex braiding of Noguchi's sense of "timeless time" clearly.

Brett Littman

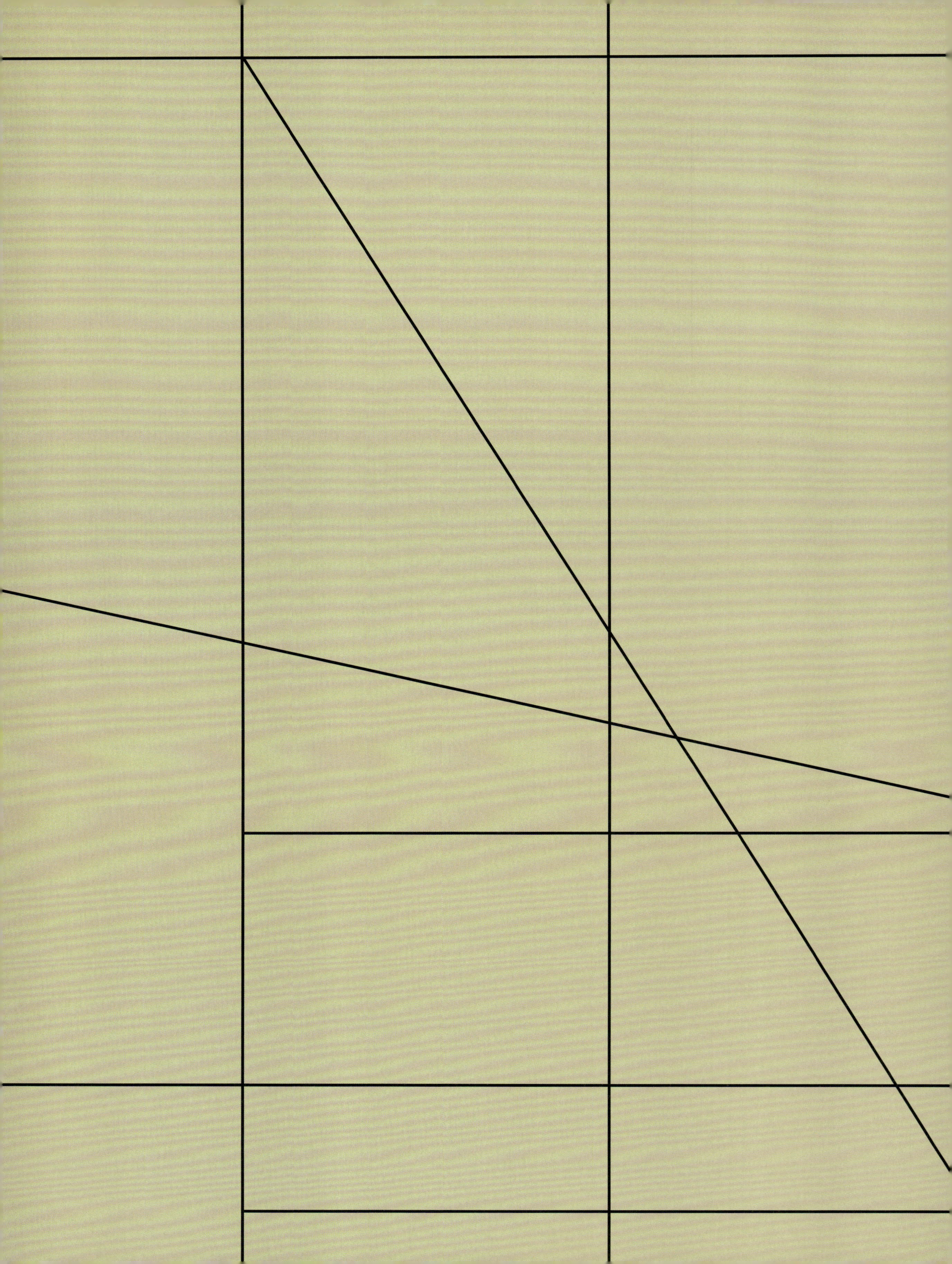

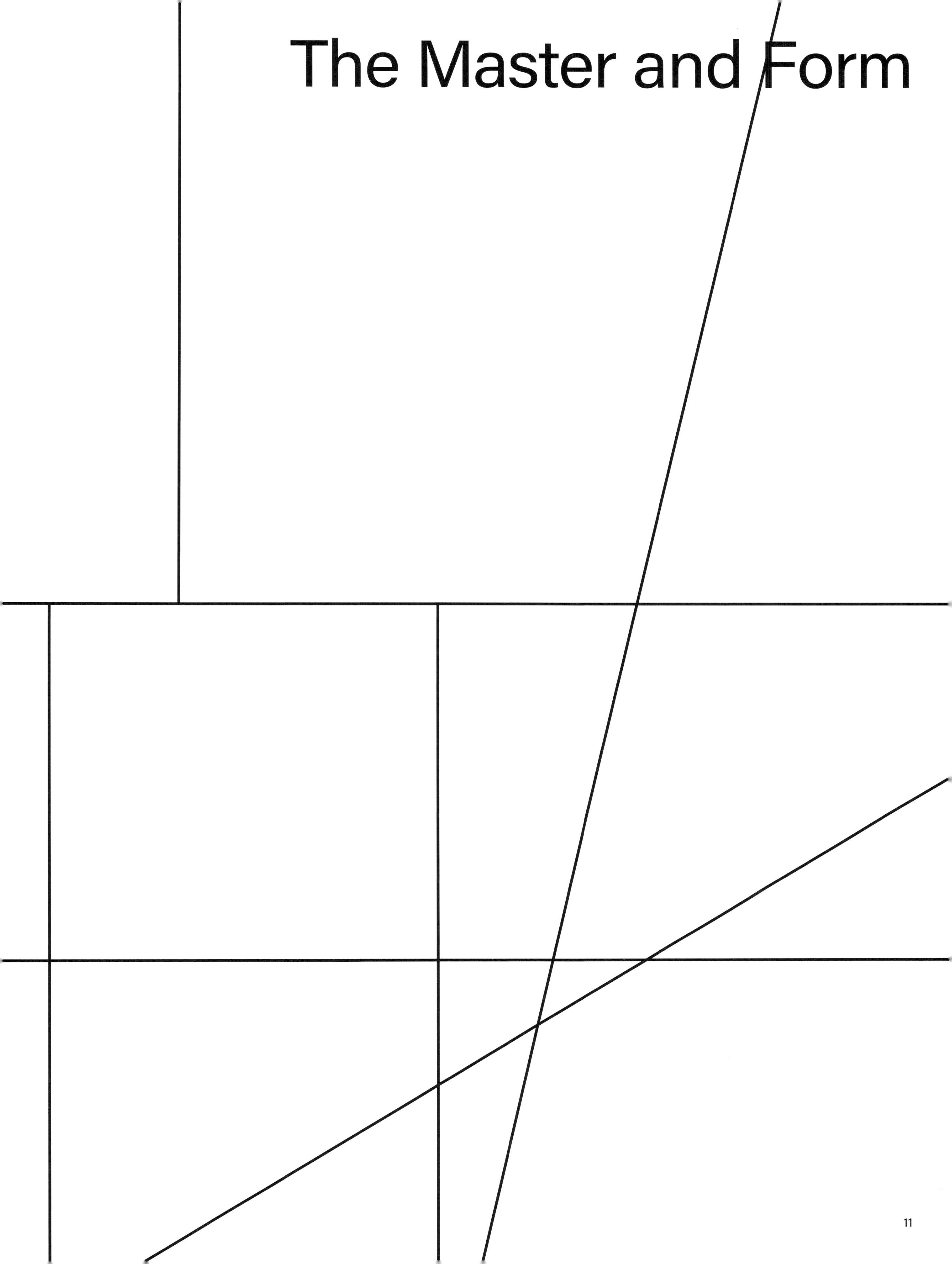

The Master and Form

Score

Enter

(Walks)

00:10:00

Dance Devices

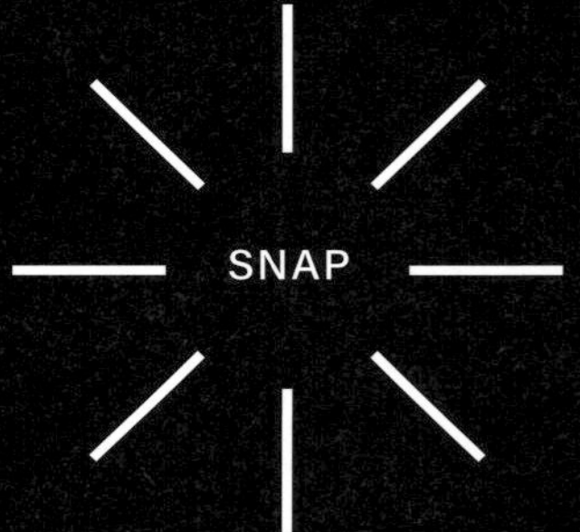

Device 1 Leads Transition

00:20:00

Cage: Improvised Motifs

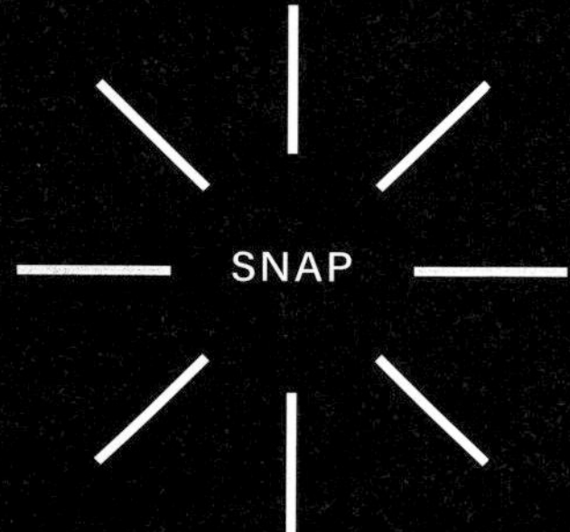

Device 1 Leads Transition

Device 5 Calls Barre

1

Plié en croix, two demis and a grand, port de bras in each position

2

Two tendus in plié to first position, two tendus w/o plié to fifth position. En croix

3

Eight dégagés in each position en croix — use of arms in each corresponding position

4

Four ronds de jambe à terre, two ronds de jambe with plié and port de bras. Reverse from back

5

Two grands battements en croix

Device 5 Ends Barre

00:30:00

Dance Devices

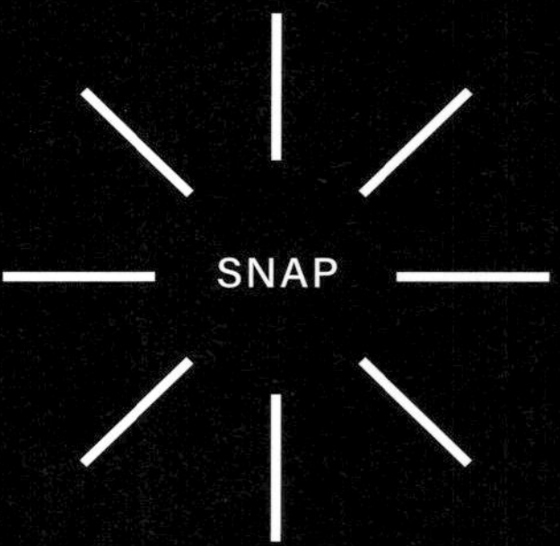

Device 1 Leads Transition

00:40:00

Cage: Improvised Motifs

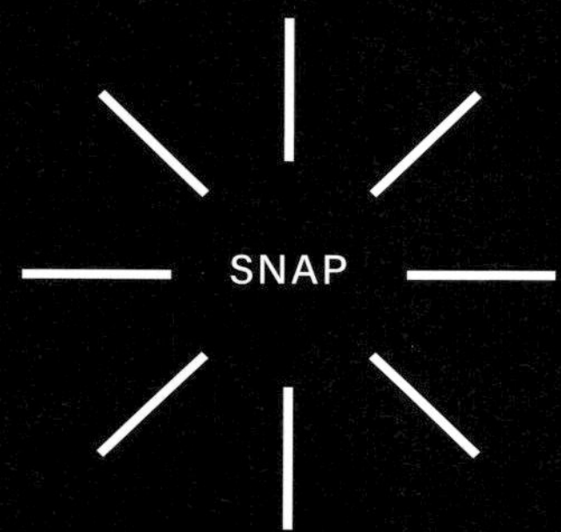

Device 1 Leads Transition

00:48:00

Ropes: Improvised Motifs

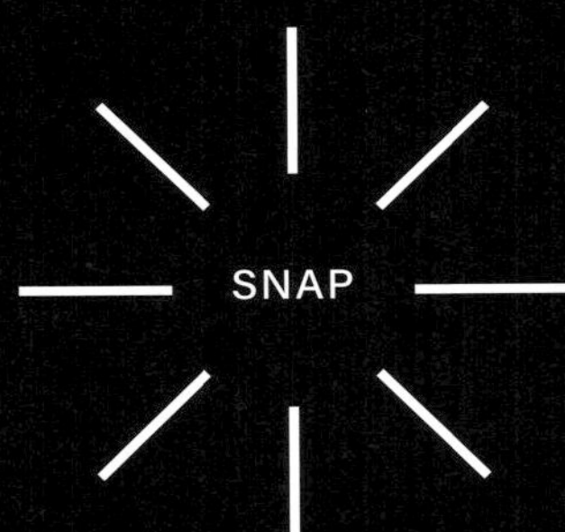

Device 1 Leads Transition

Exit

(Walks)

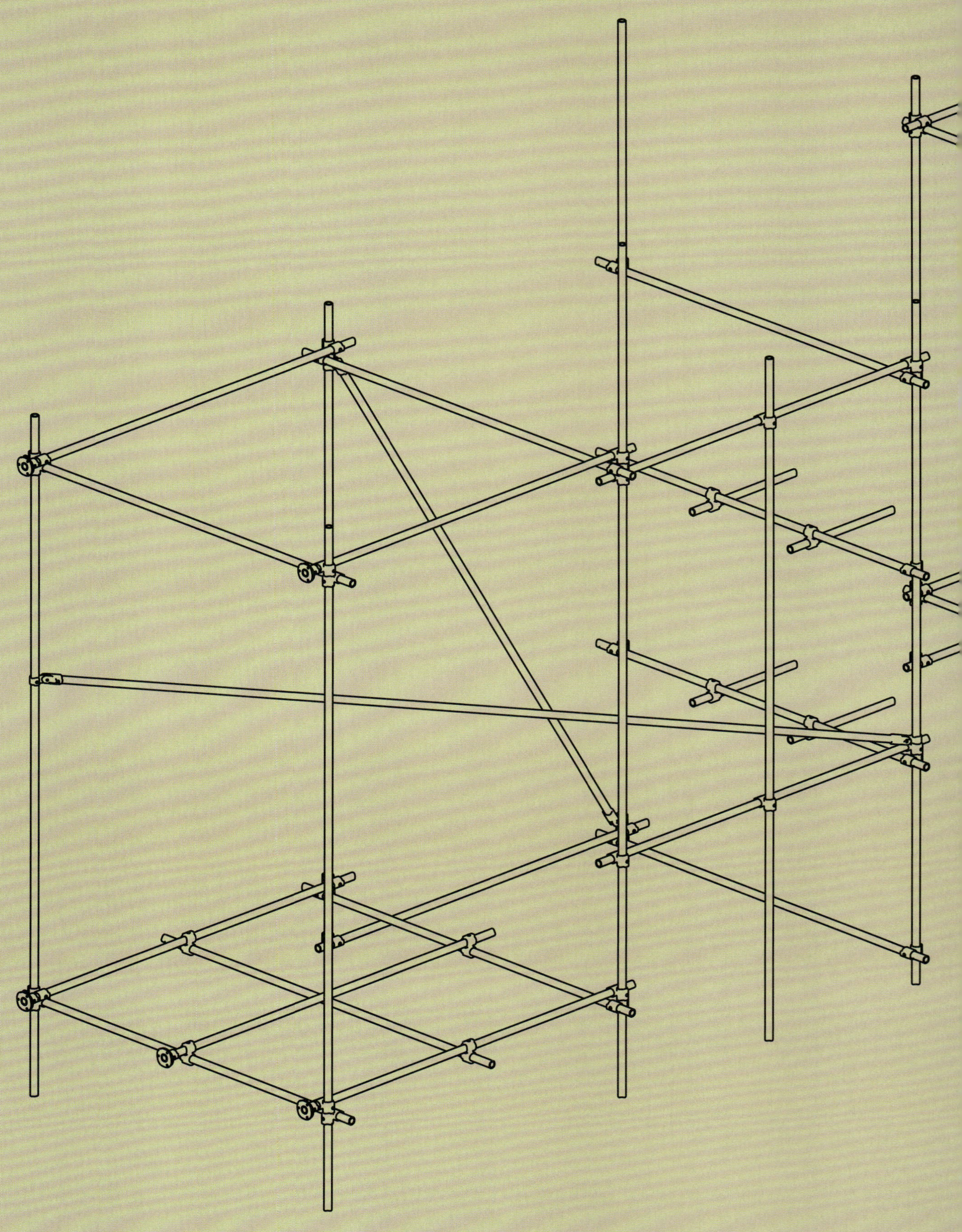

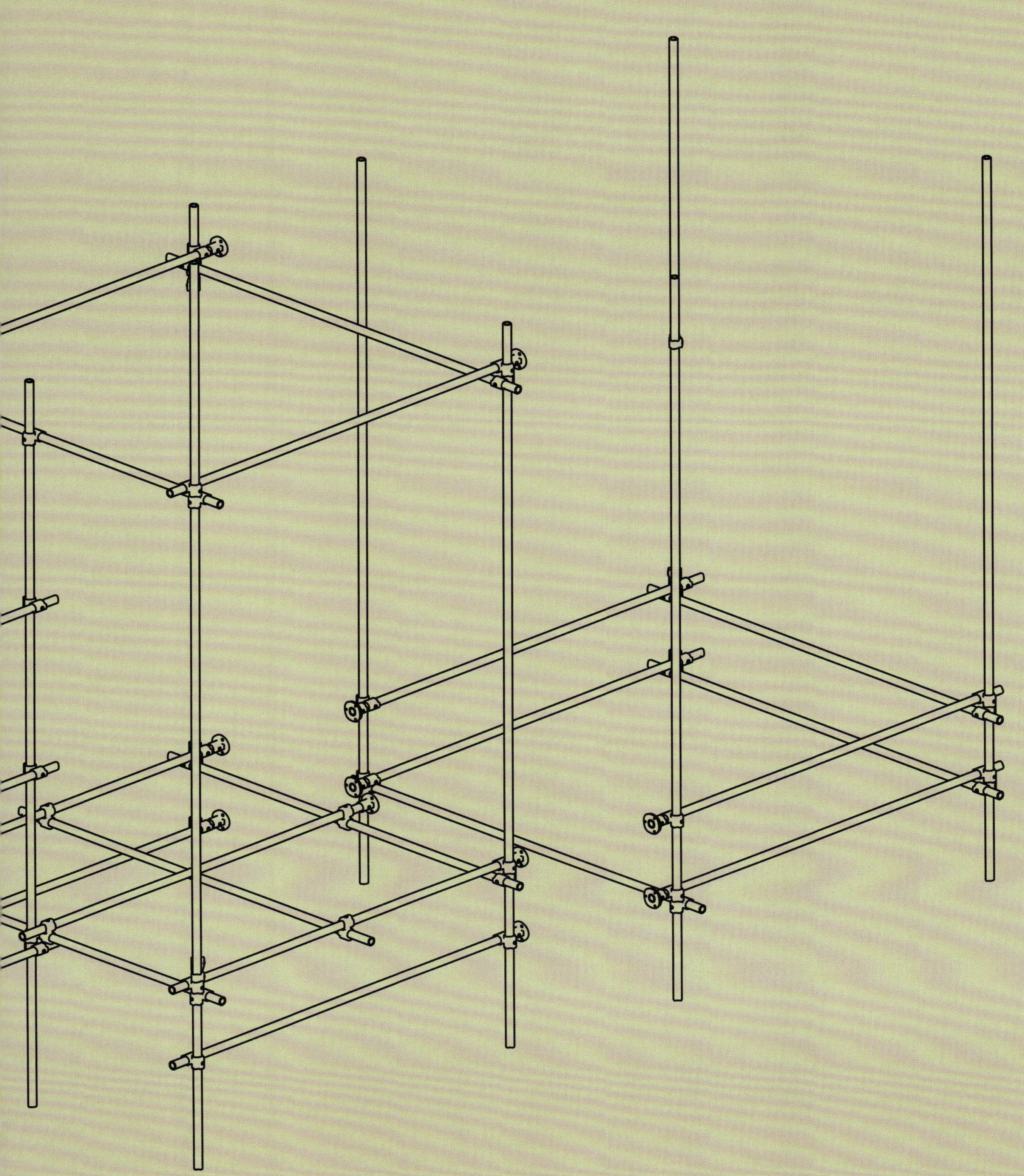

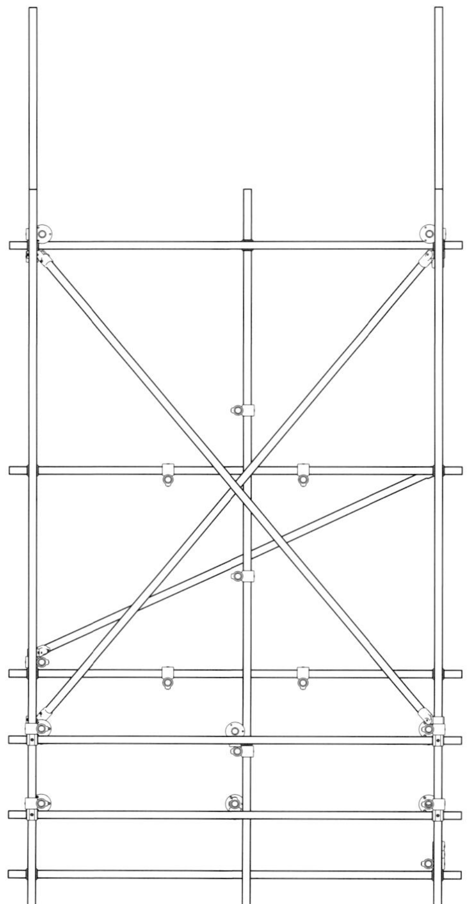

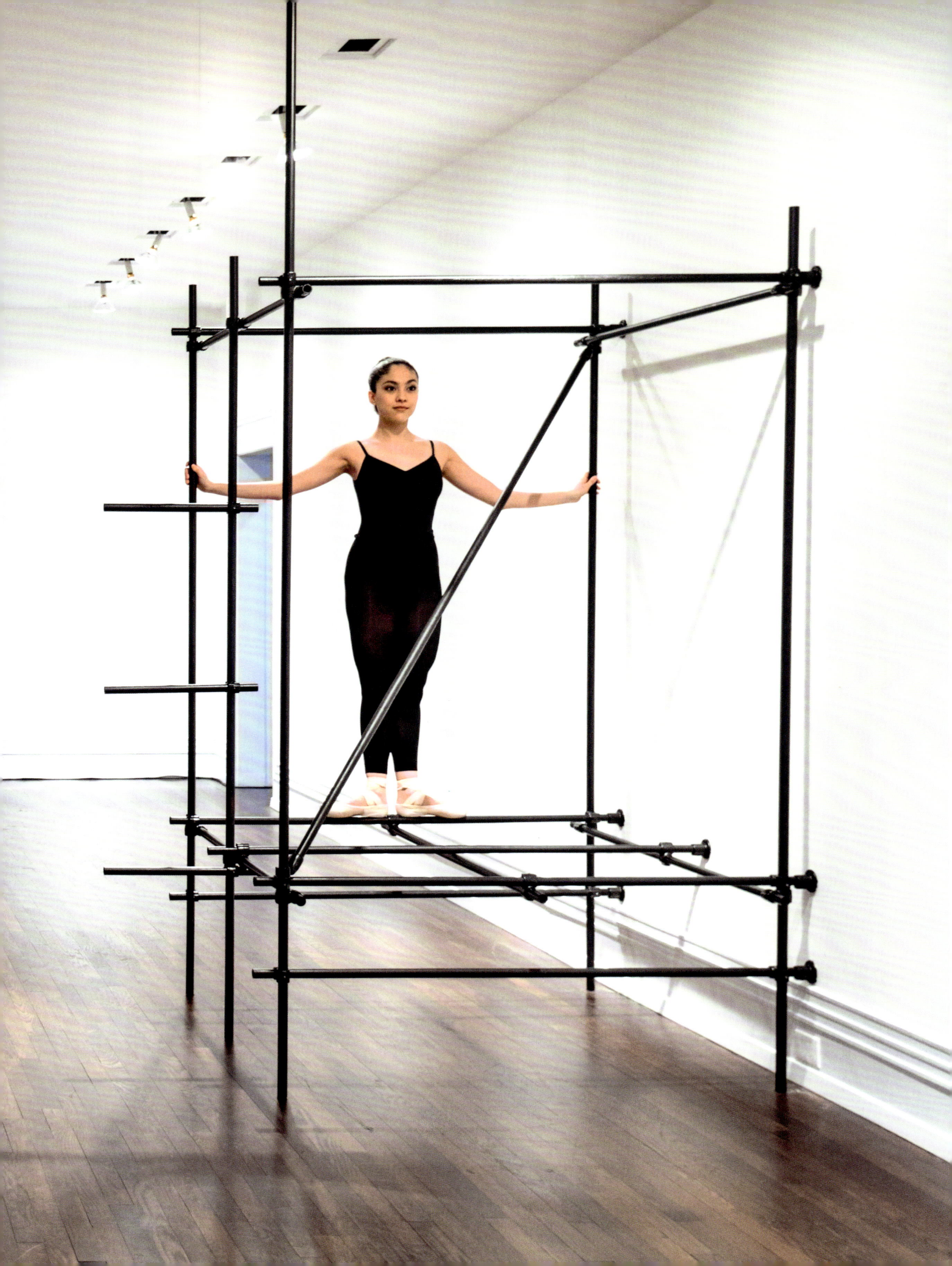

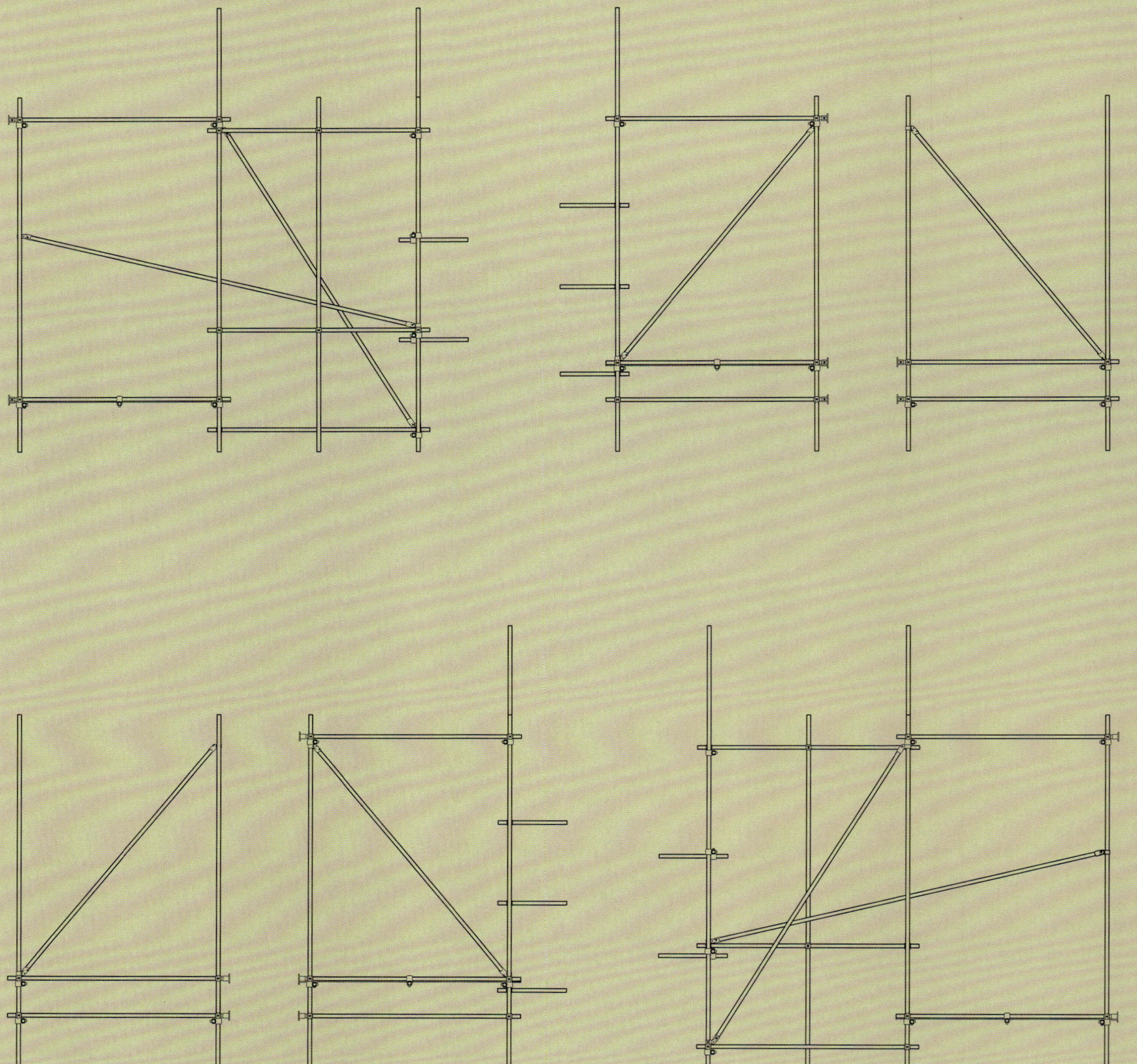

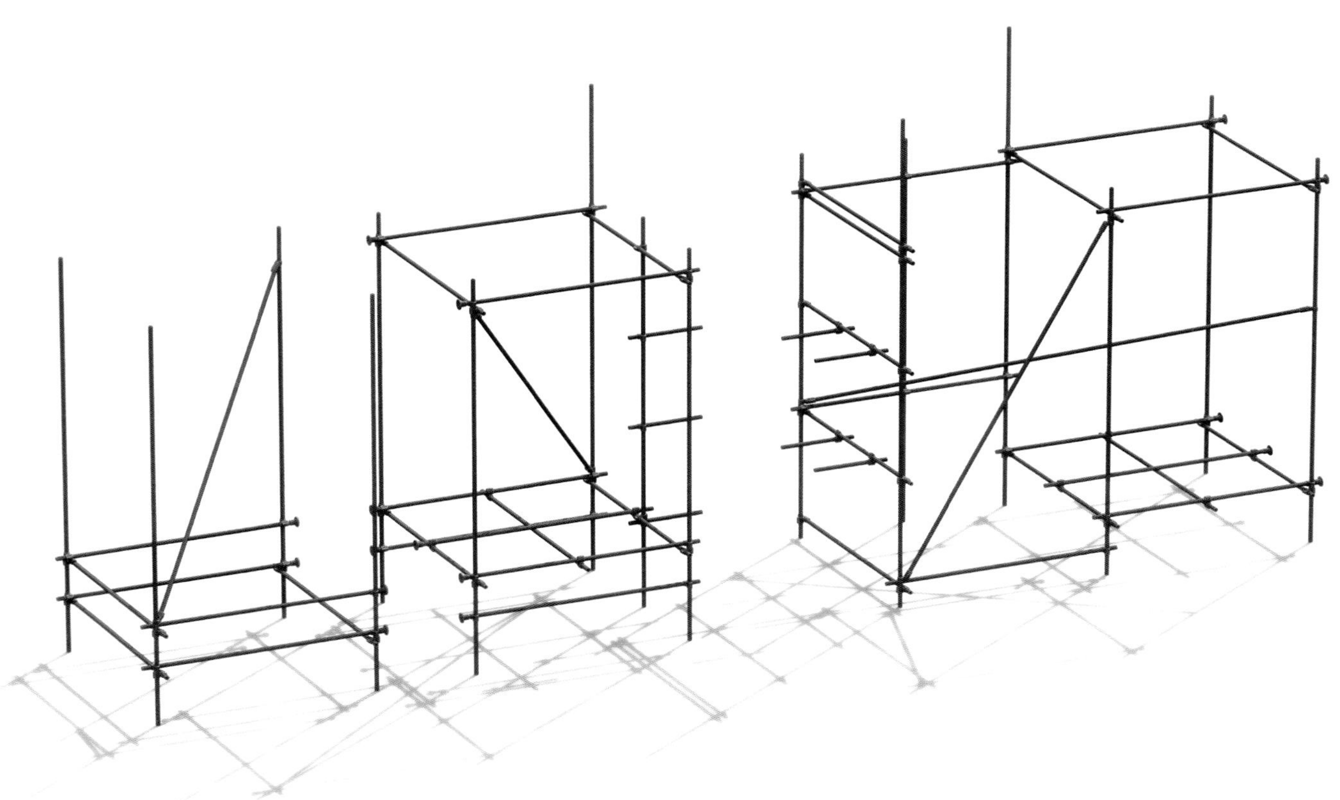

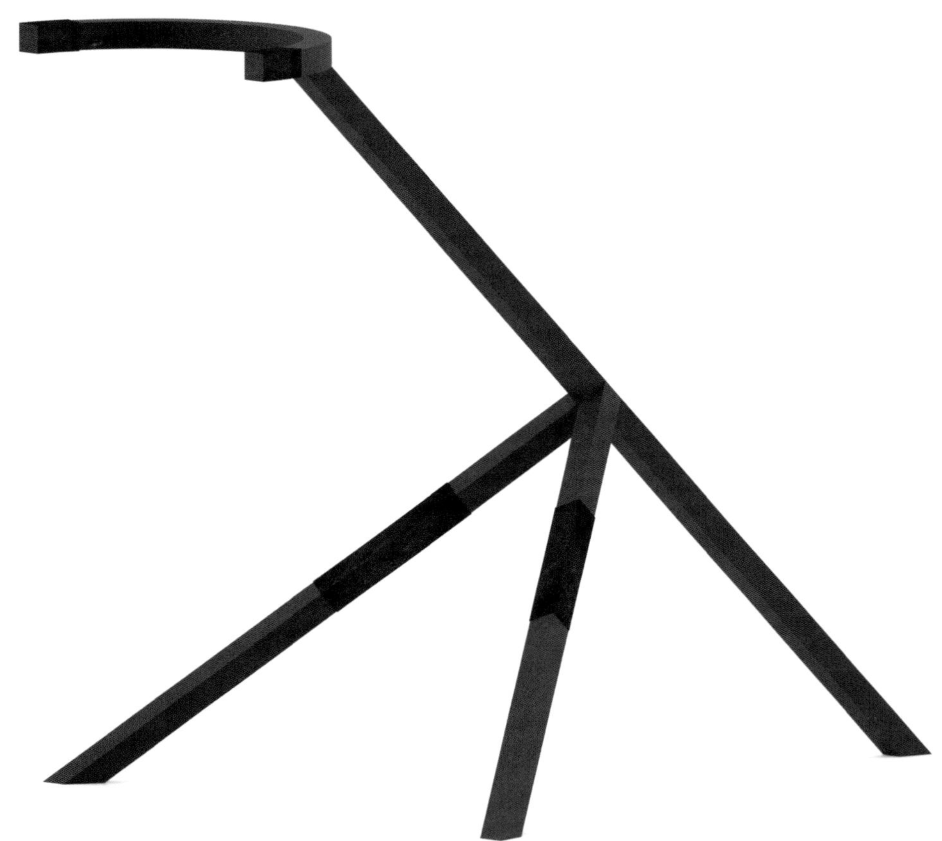

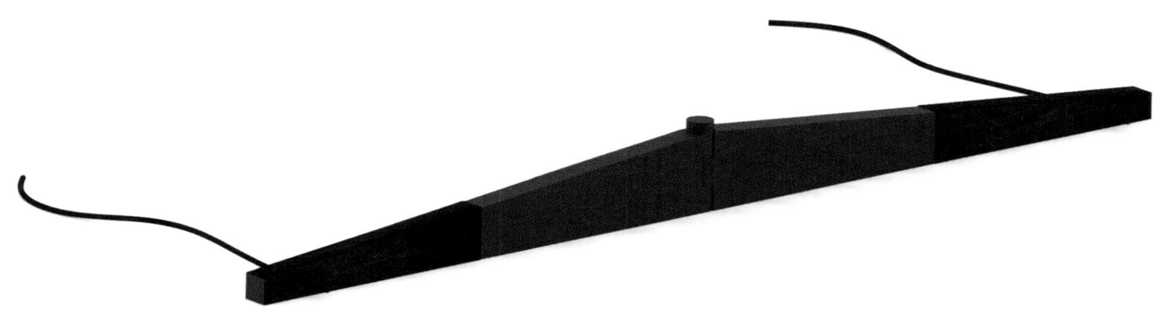

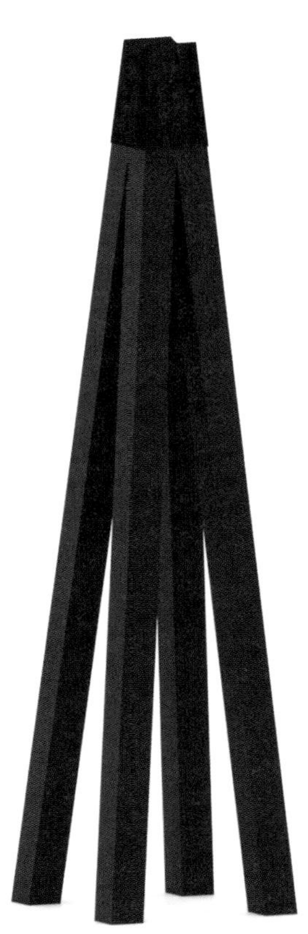

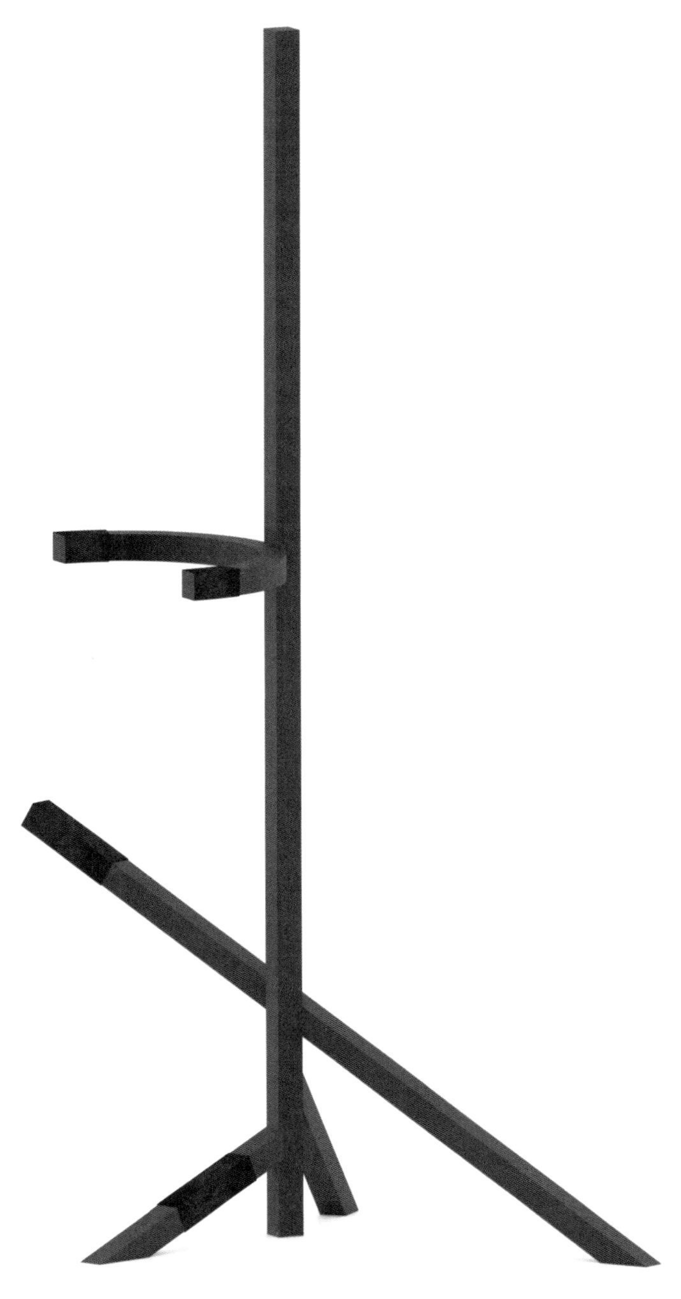

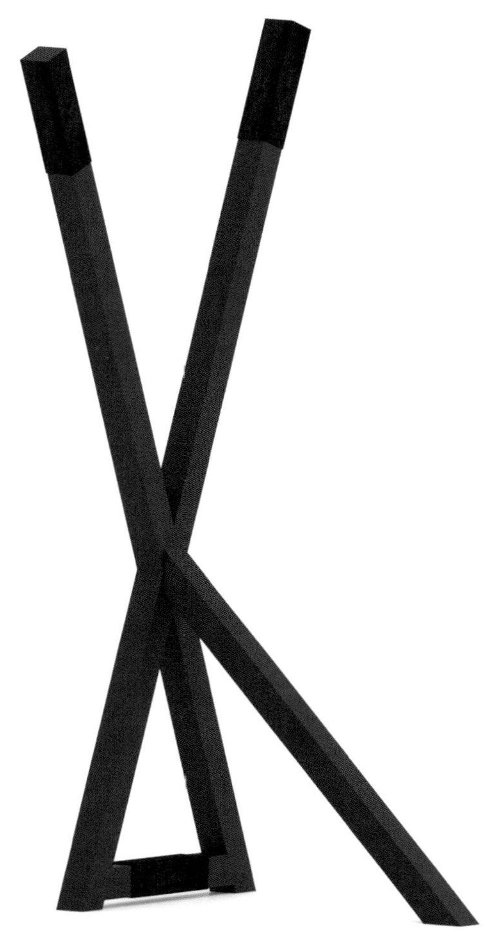

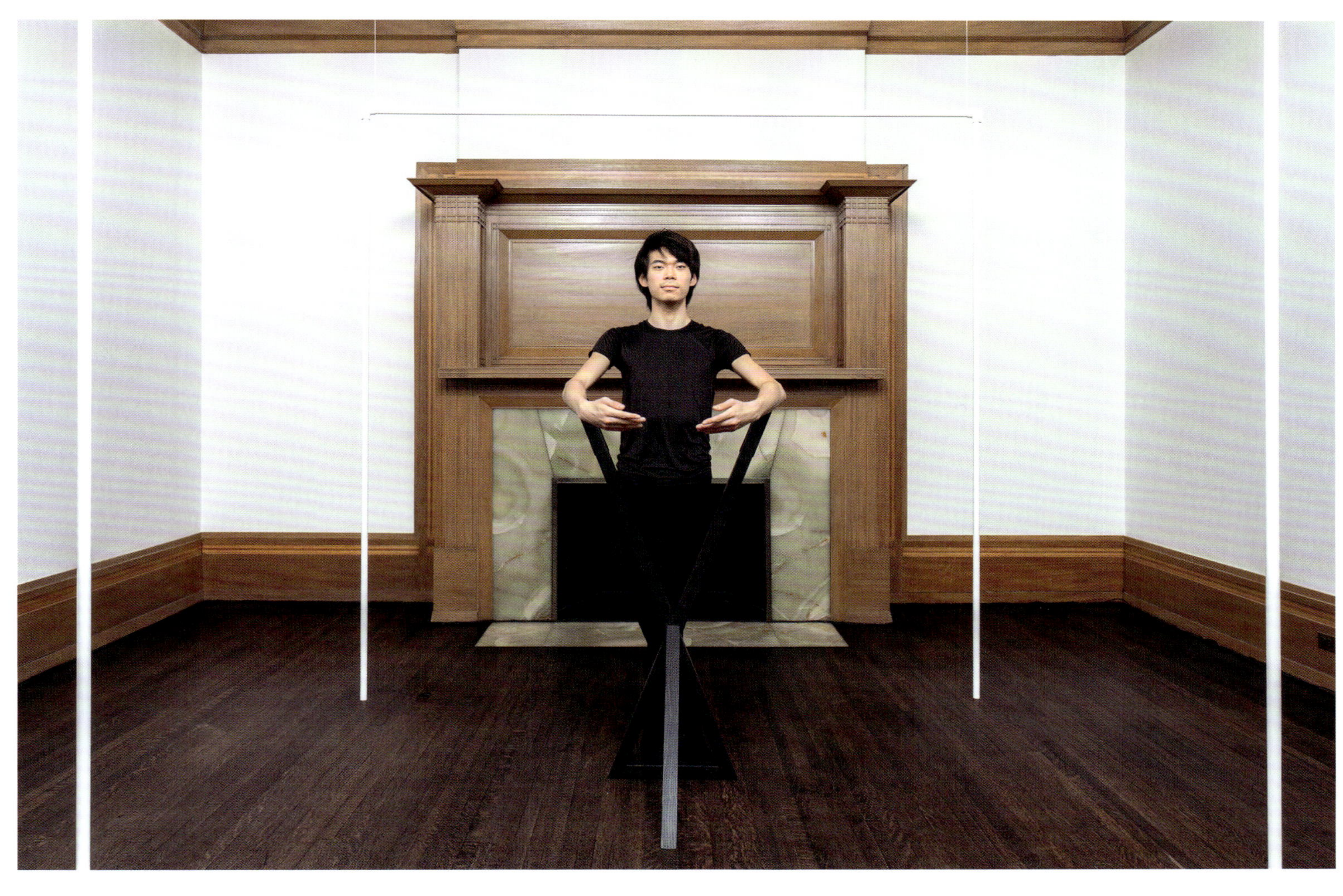

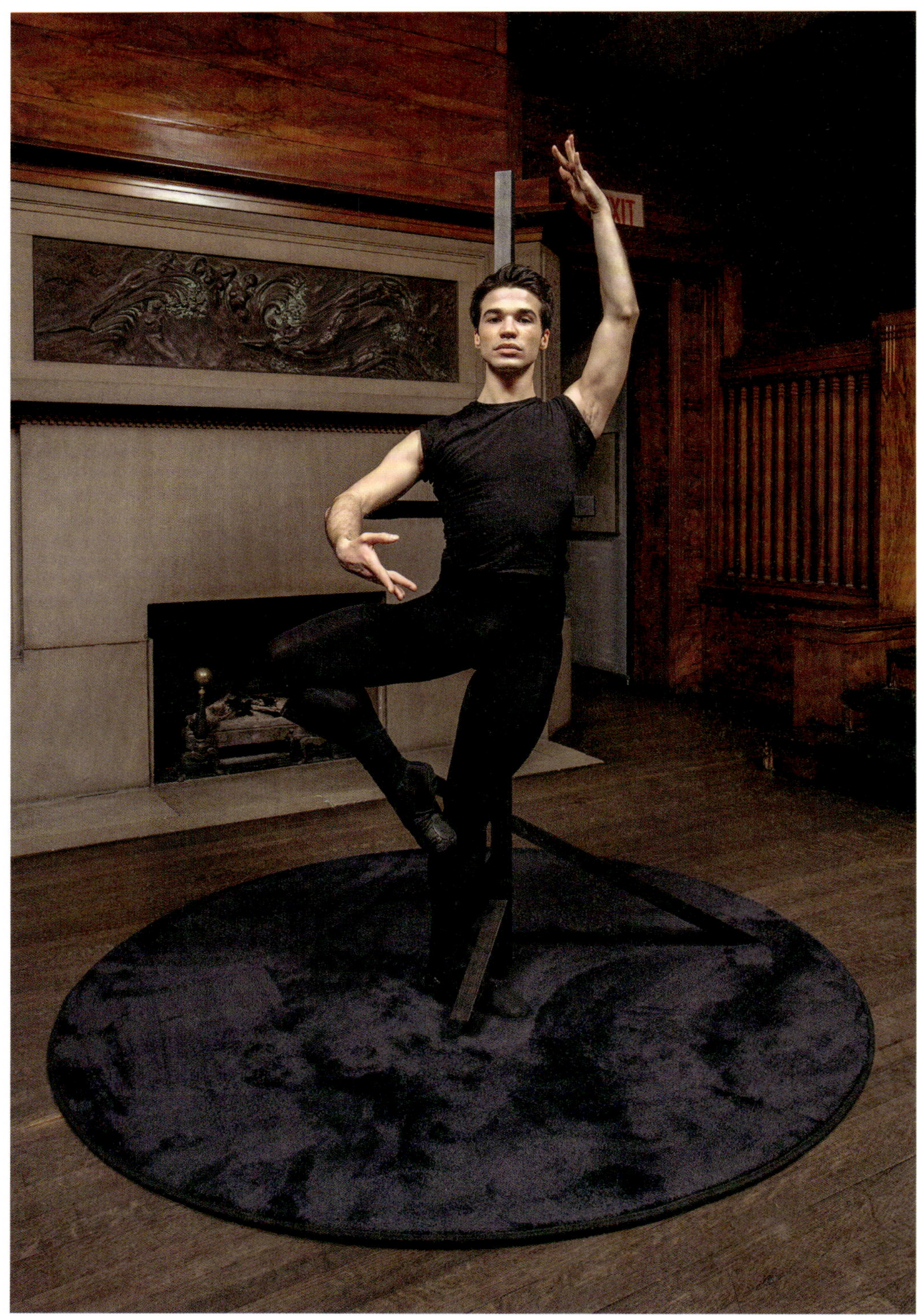

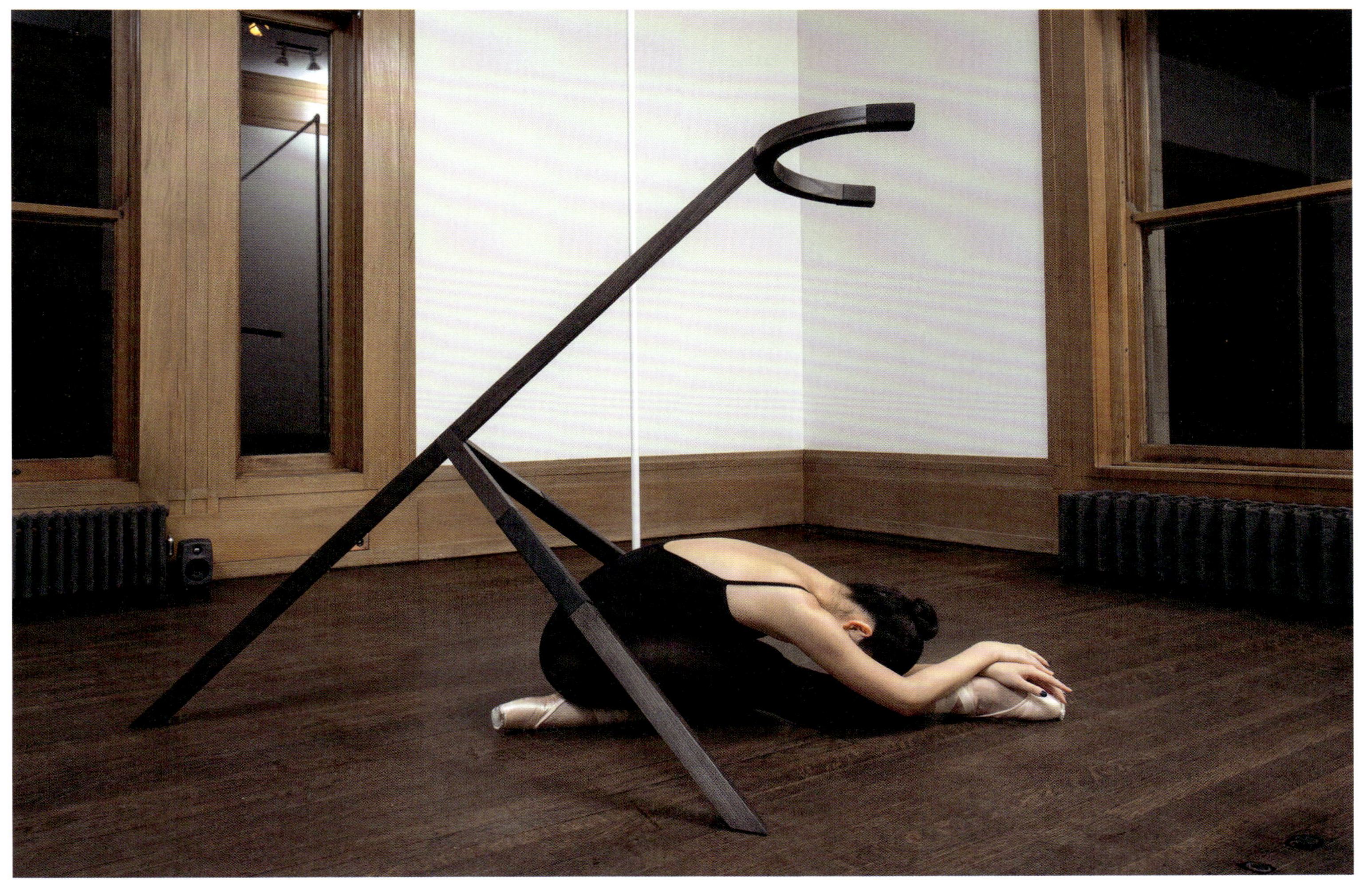

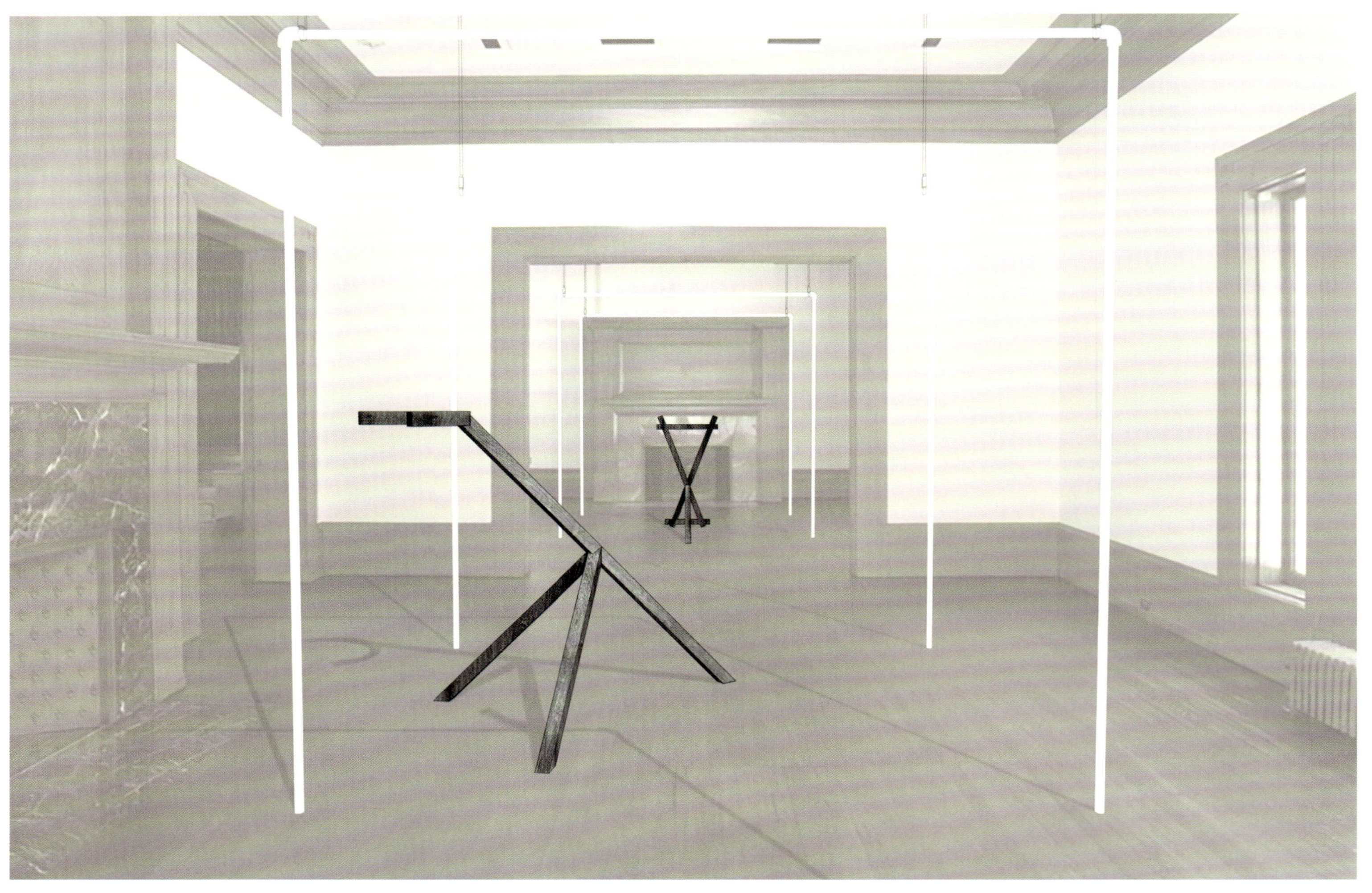

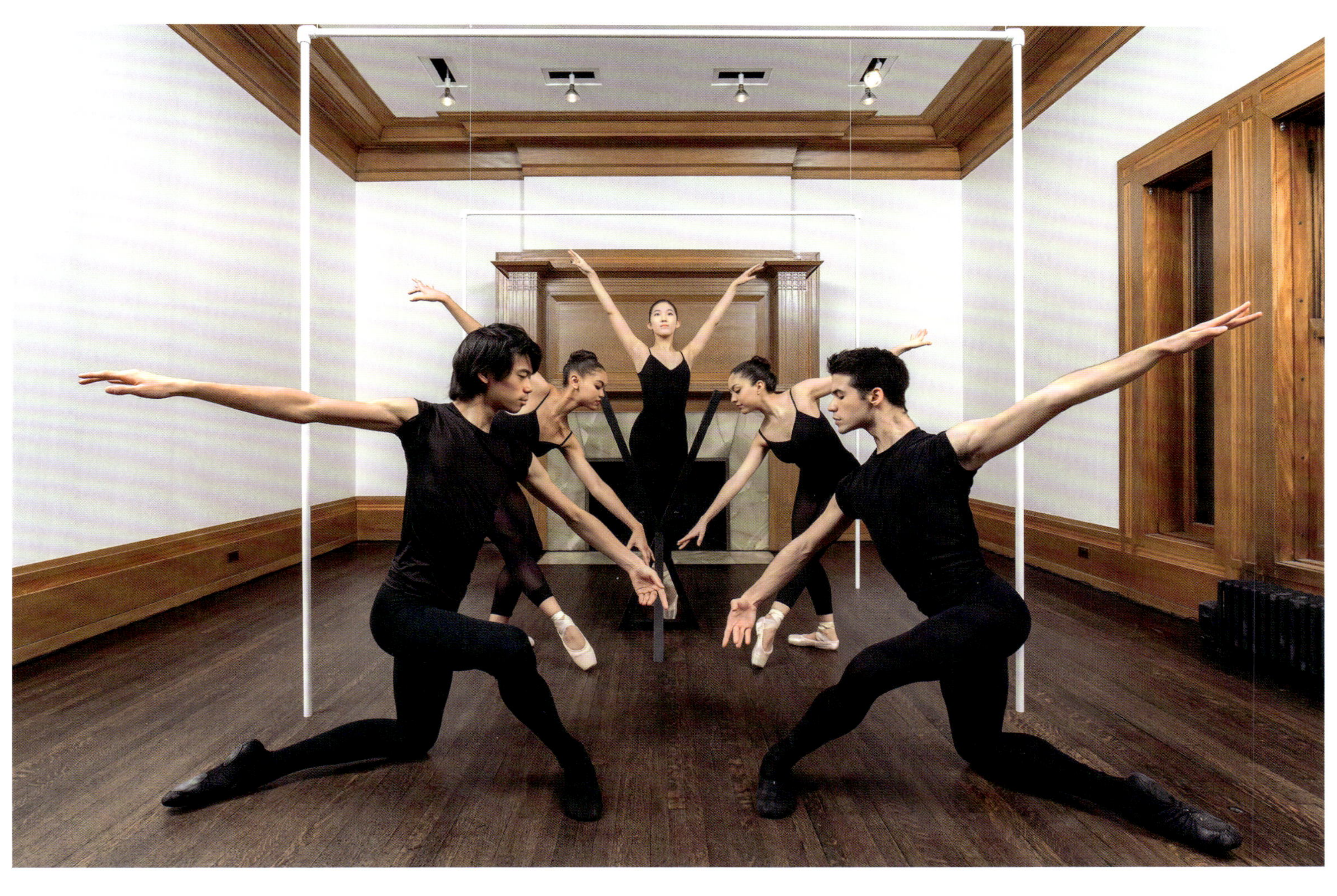

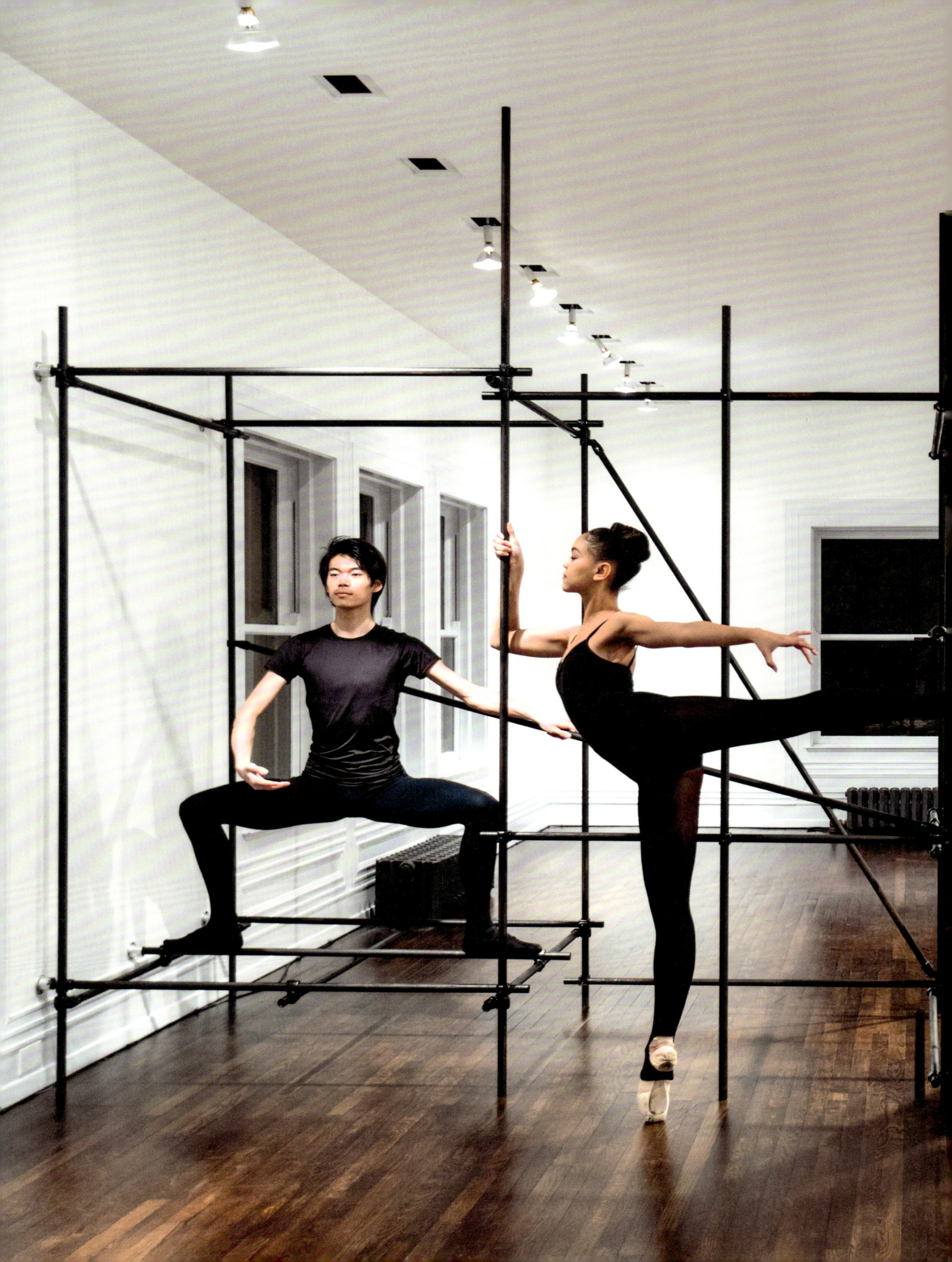

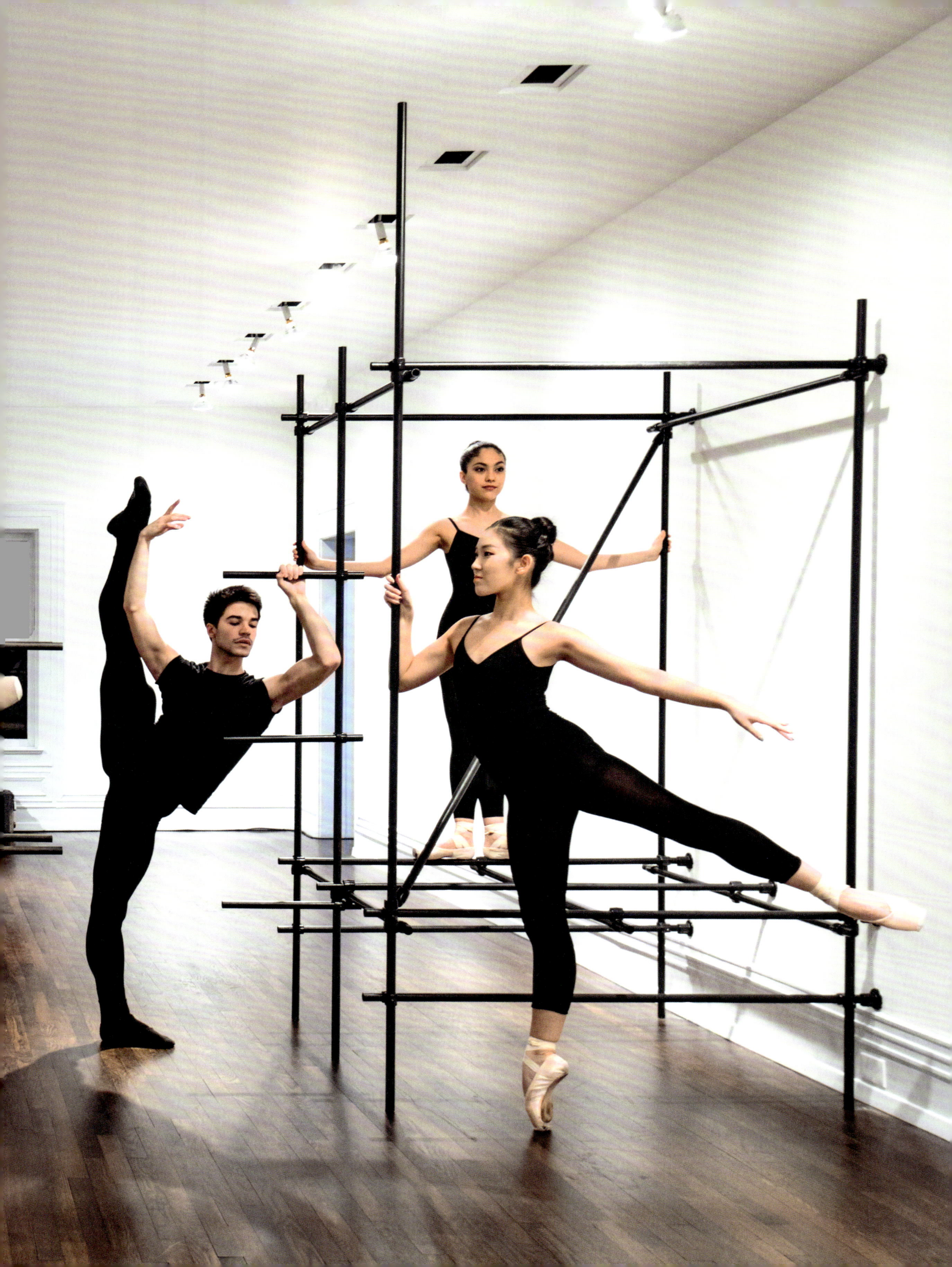

Forming the Master/ Mastering the Form

Juliet Bellow

Five dancers clad in black leotards, opaque tights, and ballet slippers approach a light-filled gallery on the fifth floor of the Whitney Museum of American Art, where a group of sculptural objects awaits them.[1] Walking single file with the leader snapping to keep time, the dancers wend their way into the gallery. At the center of the room looms a black steel cage measuring thirteen feet square and ten feet high. With its network of metal bars irregularly spaced along varied vertical, horizontal and diagonal axes, it resembles both a playground jungle gym and a construction scaffold. Flanking this ominous structure are five smaller sculptures fashioned of wood and leather that sit atop circular, spotlight-shaped matte black rugs.[2] Each of these devices is named for a different ballet position: *In Passé, in Fourth*; *In First, in Fifth*; *In Second*; *In Cambré à Terre*; *In Arabesque*. Ten long, thick ropes, each with a knot at the bottom end, hang down from the ceiling along the expansive window at the back of the gallery with intervals of just over six feet between them.

As the dancers circle around the room, they each station themselves at one of the five devices. At the snap of a museum staff member standing in a corner of the gallery as timekeeper, they use the wood and leather object to assume the position named in its title. After the dancers attempt to hold their respective positions for ten minutes, another snap sends them to the central cage for ten minutes of improvisation. As they move around and through the metal bars, their bodies form a series of lines and curves that are interwoven with the structure's stark geometries. A third snap calls the dancers to the circumference of the cage, where one member leads the group in a barre routine, after which they disperse again to their assigned devices. Again, a snap brings the dancers back to the cage where they engage in a ten-minute cycle of improvisational poses, stretches, and movement; then another snap brings them to the ropes for further improvisation. With a final snap, the dancers leave the room. In their absence, the recorded sounds of their collective effort—the scuffling of pointe shoes, the smacking of hands to soothe cramping muscles, their heavy breathing—are projected from hidden speakers so as to haunt the now-empty sculptures.

With *The Master and Form* (2018–19), as this multimedia work is titled, Brendan Fernandes creates an apparatus and choreography that together test these dancers' endurance.[3] In so doing, the artist merges the vocabulary of ballet with the ethos of BDSM. As the dancers move through the circuit of ten-minute intervals, they oscillate between modes of restraint, discipline, freedom and release. By partnering with sculptural objects to hold their weight or to prolong a pose, they assume active and passive roles, alternating between the two and sometimes occupying both at once. In this process, Fernandes's devices become strangely animate, catalyzing subtle shifts of control that blur the boundaries between person and thing. The sculptures mutely instruct the dancers as to what to do with their bodies and the dancers, in turn, mold the objects to the performance they wish to render. This scenario resonates with David Getsy's characterization of the "sculptural encounter" as a "theater of power relations."[4] Getsy construes sculpture's immobility as a performative act through which it acquires an unnerving, quasi-human agency that provokes in the spectator a desire to control, violate, or destroy it. *The Master and Form* invites this power dynamic into the gallery, unsettling each dancer's relationship to their audience, their fellow performers, and their own bodies; to ballet as a technique and a tradition; to their physical surroundings and to the museum as an institution.

By bringing ballet and BDSM into public conversation with one another, Fernandes draws our attention to their common origin in the French *ancien régime*. In her essay, "Must We Burn Sade?," Simone de Beauvoir construes sadomasochism as a response to the decline of aristocracy: their loss of power and prestige provoked the Marquis de Sade and his ilk to act out the part of the "lone and sovereign feudal despot" in sexual roleplay.[5] Taking de Beauvoir's analysis further, Elizabeth Freeman argues that Sade's symbolic reversal of the downfall of his class depended, somewhat paradoxically, upon a new concept of time inaugurated by the French Revolution in 1789. Dispensing with the Gregorian calendar, the Jacobins declared the moment of the monarchy's overthrow to be Year I of a new era, thenceforth to be measured in a reconfigured set of months, weeks, days, hours, minutes, and seconds. For Freeman, sadomasochism thus constitutes "a form of writing history with the body in which the linearity of history itself may be called into question," enabling participants to "recas[t] the future in terms other than those dictated by the past."[6] *The Master and Form* aims to rewrite ballet's injurious history through the decisions of performers and spectators in the present. In multiple ways, the piece offers participants the opportunity to reshape or to contest ballet's structures of power, thereby modeling a more ethical future for this art form.

In statements about his ballet-related projects, Fernandes often alludes to the genre's formative period in the palaces of Europe where it functioned as an expression of political power at the height of the Age of Absolutism, during the seventeenth and eighteenth centuries. Governed by rank and etiquette, ballets mapped out court society in spatial terms: the monarch's body served as the axis around which performances revolved.[7] As ballet moved into public theatres in the eighteenth century, this spatial hierarchy remained intact. For audience members seated at the center of the auditorium (the most privileged seat in the house), the proscenium stage perfectly framed the dancers' bodies, their limbs turned out to afford maximum visibility.[8] Fernandes does away with this ideal vantage point by staging his deconstructed ballet in the proverbial "white cube," the starkly blank museum gallery. *The Master and Form* therefore disrupts ballet's viewing conventions and their associated power dynamics. Without the proscenium stage, there is no clear boundary between the arenas of performance and spectatorship. Visitors,

Figure 1: Carlo Blasis, *An Elementary Treatise Upon the Theory and Practice of the Art of Dancing* (plate VIII), 1820

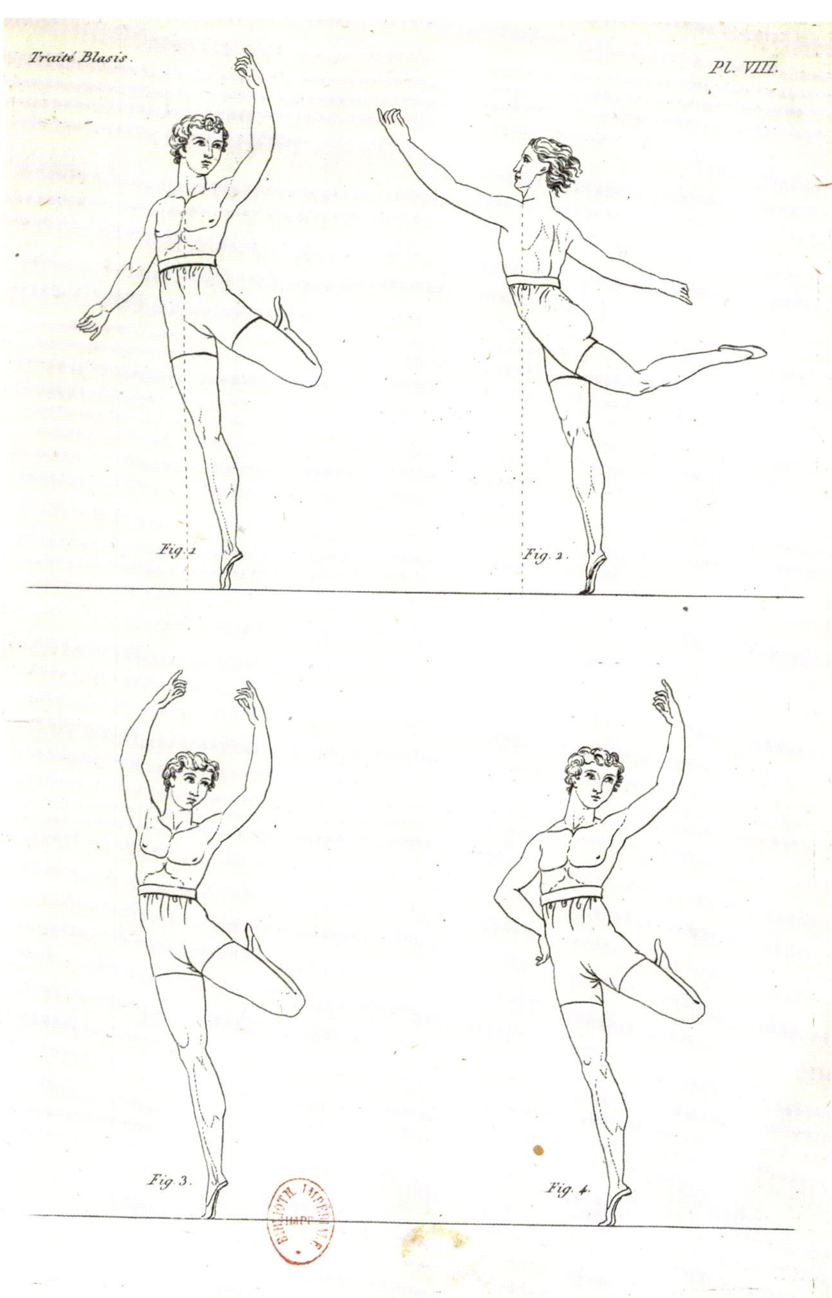

untethered from fixed seats and timed tickets, can roam around the gallery, snap photos, and come or go at will.[9] Under these circumstances, spectators have more mobility and choice, but they can never gain visual mastery over the performance. With activities occurring simultaneously in different parts of the gallery, the dancers constantly shifting place, and the sculptures impeding our sightline of the dancer's movements, *The Master and Form* offers no authoritative viewpoint.

With its incorporation of a guided barre routine, Fernandes confronts yet another key power dynamic embedded at the core of ballet history: that of the instructor and their pupils. In this regard, the artwork itself serves as the master disciplinarian who forms the dancer according to ballet's established codes of behavior. The founding of the Académie Royale de Danse in 1661, under letters of patent from Louis XIV, gave rise to a training system supervised by credentialed ballet masters, infamously strict in their pedagogical practice and enforcement of rules.[10] Over time, as choreographies increased in complexity and demanded a larger corps, ballet masters became responsible for developing dancers of ever-greater skill and promoting them through an ascending system of rank. An embodiment of institutional authority—that of a specific school or company as well as of ballet writ large—the ballet master assigns parts, leads class, and corrects dancers' form through verbal and physical cues. Here, too, *The Master and Form* disrupts the regimented structure of a typical ballet company. In one sense, Fernandes functioned as the ballet master: he determined the work's structure, wrote the score, and selected the poses that the dancers must assume. In other ways though, he consciously abdicated control over the scenario he created. He collaborated with the dancers in the initial phase of composition, gave them ample room for improvisation, and explicitly granted them the latitude to break position at times of their own choosing.[11] Unlike most ballet performances, the assignment of parts varied: dancers took turns leading and following, swapping these roles from one iteration of the piece to the next.

But it is perhaps the wood-and-leather devices that most insistently embody the disciplinary nature of ballet technique, which requires individual dancers to conform to an external ideal of aesthetic perfection. The proper execution of balletic comportment, which originally functioned as a marker of noble identity, came in the eighteenth century to signify the body's inherent trainability.[12] Early instruction manuals, such as Carlo Blasis's *Elementary Treatise Upon the Theory and Practice of the Art of Dancing* (1820), visualized this system as a network of lines imposed onto the body that distilled the correct form of a given pose (FIGURE 1). As Susan

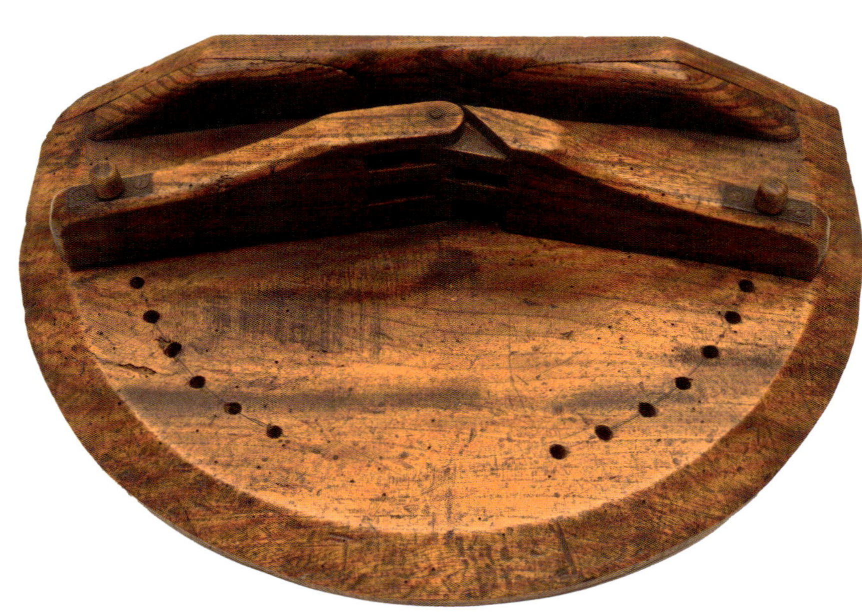

Figure 2: Tourne-hanche ("hip-turner"), c. 1800, Victoria and Albert Museum, London

Foster notes, such illustrations encouraged dancers to imaginatively absorb these geometric axes into their bodies, as if embedding them "within the flesh."[13] In order to perfect such techniques, dancers required additional external assistance from objects such as the barre, the blocked shoe, and, for some, turnout machines that nineteenth century caricaturists frequently portrayed as instruments of torture (FIGURE 2). Fernandes has explored these types of objects on multiple occasions, including his "endurance solo" *Standing Leg* (2014), where he submitted himself to a specially designed stretcher for an excruciating couple of hours to shape his own foot into the perfect balletic arch [Reference Images p. 128]. As in *The Master and Form*, Fernandes's use of these implements over an extended period of time throws the violence of balletic technique into vivid, painful relief and spotlights the dancers' willing participation in a system that subjects them to bodily harm.[14]

Finally, Fernandes's decision to cast dancers of color, including himself, in his ballet-related works prompts reflection about the genre's ontological entanglement with systems of white supremacy. Ballet's rise to prominence in European society coincided with the emergence of a colonialist project that conceptualized persons in occupied lands as uncultured and therefore sub-human, to be enslaved and exploited. Accordingly, the ballet masters of the period treated the dances of various cultures, both within and outside of Europe, as raw material to be subsumed into a movement idiom that they claimed as superior and universal.[15] Fernandes foregrounds these racialized dimensions of ballet in works like *Inverted Pyramid* (2014), whose title refers to the shape of the body in arabesque [Reference Images p. 128]. In this position, the dancer balances on one leg while extending their other limbs—raised arms and the other, elevated leg—in opposite directions.[16] The etymology of the term arabesque, which means loosely "of the Arabs" or "in an Arab style," and its prominence in works such as *La Bayadère* (1877)—one of many canonical works set in locations that European audiences deemed "exotic"—bespeak the dynamics of cultural appropriation endemic to ballet.[17]

In addition to this type of Orientalist appropriation, ballet masters of the period, and those of subsequent generations, frequently used the normative standard of a "classical body," premised upon stereotypically white physical attributes, to exclude dancers of color from the most prestigious, well-funded companies.[18] In response to these painful histories, Fernandes offers his cast the autonomy to make the ballet vocabulary more responsive to their own bodies, cultural backgrounds, and personal needs. When leading the barre routine, for example, each dancer can call out the steps in the language they feel most comfortable speaking (rather than French, ballet's ur-language). By communicating with one another before each iteration of the performance, the dancers may also choose to work with the device that best suits the way their body feels at that particular moment. Moreover, while the score is challenging for the dancers, because of the poses required and the duration of the work, Fernandes explicitly invited them to safeguard their bodies—thus bringing a strikingly atypical culture of self-care to ballet. As cast member Allison Walsh recalled in an interview, "I don't know if I've ever been asked [to do] that before as a dancer."[19]

In an evocation of the revolutionary calendar, *The Master and Form*'s ten-minute intervals both lay bare ballet's internal power structures and give participants the tools to reconstruct this art form in more egalitarian terms. This intervention in time is paired with a shift in space: the transposition from classroom and stage to the gallery allows us to see ballet's conventions and underlying ideologies anew. But does this move simply entangle ballet in another institution inherited from the *ancien régime*? *The Master and Form* was not only staged at the Whitney Museum of American Art, but as a part of that institution's notoriously controversial Whitney Biennial, which intensifies this question. The longest running survey of American art, this exhibition embodies the Whitney's cultural authority and its imbrication in larger structures of political and economic power.[20] As it happens, the six-month run of *The Master and Form* took place against the backdrop of protests regarding the composition of the Whitney's Board of Trustees, targeting the role of Warren B. Kanders, a military weapons manufacturer, as Vice-Chairman. Some artists chose to leverage the platform that the Biennial afforded them by boycotting the exhibition. Others, including Fernandes, chose to challenge the museum from within. Like most works of institutional critique, *The Master and Form* uses the infrastructure of the gallery to make its politics visible. By remaking ballet inside the museum, another "theater" of power, Fernandes shows us how these hegemonic institutions are inter-related, and how we might go about changing our relationship to both institutions, one gesture at a time.

1 The five dancers in each performance were drawn from a rotating cast of ten. All are classically trained dancers who have worked in a range of different genres, companies, and assignments. Most are currently working as freelancers. In researching this essay, I interviewed four cast members: Héctor Cerna, Tiffany Mangulabnan, Violetta Komyshan, and Allison Walsh. Those conversations, as well as discussions with Fernandes, provided crucial insight into the artworks.

2 The installation for *The Master and Form* was developed with architecture and design collaborative Norman Kelley.

3 *The Master and Form* was first conceived and performed in 2018 at the Graham Foundation in Chicago. It was then reconfigured and installed at the Whitney Museum of American Art as part of the Whitney Biennial in 2019.

4 David Getsy, "Acts of Stillness: Statues, Performativity, and Passive Resistance," *Criticism* 56, no. 1 (December 2014): 8. Getsy's argument focuses primarily on the effects of figural statues but does relate this phenomenon to some abstract sculptures as well.

5 Simone de Beauvoir, "Faut-il brûler Sade?," *Les Temps modernes* 74–75 (December 1951 and January 1952), reprinted and translated in The Marquis de Sade, trans. Annette Michelson (New York: Grove Press, 1953), 16–17.

6 Elizabeth Freeman, "Turn the Beat Around: Sadomasochism, Temporality, History," in *Time Binds: Queer Temporalities, Queer Histories* (Durham: University of North Carolina Press, 2010), 142. See also Richard Taws, *The Politics of the Provisional: Art and Ephemera in Revolutionary France* (University Park: Penn State University Press, 2013), especially the chapter entitled "Material Futures: Marking Time in a Revolutionary Almanac."

7 Marina Nordera, "Ballet de cour," trans. Jonathan Steinberg, in Marion Kant, ed., *The Cambridge Companion to Ballet* (Cambridge: Cambridge University Press, 2007), 20–21.

8 Tim Scholl, *From Petipa to Balanchine: Classical Revival and the Modernization of Ballet* (London and New York: Routledge, 1994), 8–9.

9 For more on dance in the museum see Mark Franko and André Lepecki, eds., "Dance in the Museum," special issue of *Dance Research Journal* 46, no. 3 (December 2014). During Fernandes's performance at the Whitney Museum of American Art, gallery attendants monitored the performances to protect the performers. According to Fernandes and the cast members interviewed for this essay, visitors at times came close to the dancers, but none walked directly into their space during a performance.

10 The Académie supplanted the existing minstrels' guild (founded in 1321); the role of dancing master was thus not new, but it was newly coupled with ballet technique. See Sandra Noll Hammond, "The Rise of Ballet Technique and Training: The Professionalization of an Art Form," in Kant, *The Cambridge Companion*, 65–66.

11 All of the dancers interviewed described the piece as giving them more opportunities for exploring their own creativity than most of their jobs.

12 Susan Leigh Foster, *Choreography and Narrative: Ballet's Staging of Love and Desire* (Bloomington: Indiana University Press, 1996), 9.

13 Susan Leigh Foster, *Choreographing Empathy: Kinesthesia in Performance* (London and New York: Routledge, 2010), 39.

14 Several of the dancers interviewed mentioned the pressure that they put on themselves to stay in poses as long as possible.

15 Foster, *Choreographing Empathy*, 23–24, 40–41.

16 Francesca Falcone, "The Evolution of the Arabesque in Dance," *Dance Chronicle* 19, no. 3 (1999): 71–117.

17 Juliet Bellow, "Drawing a Line with the Body," in Anne Leonard, ed., *Arabesque without End*, forthcoming from Routledge.

18 Lauren Erin Brown, "'As Long as They Have Talent': Organizational Barriers to Black Ballet," *Dance Chronicle* 41, no. 3 (2018): 359–92. During our interviews, several of the dancers discussed the racism and body-shaming they experienced during their classical ballet training.

19 Interview with Allison Walsh, December 12, 2020.

20 From its founding, the Whitney Biennial has come under intense criticism for its curatorial decisions, including its history of marginalizing artists of color as well as racial insensitivity—the latter most recently evident in the decision to include Dana Schutz's painting *Open Casket* in the 2017 Biennial. That painting appropriated and aestheticized the photograph of Emmett Till's lynched body, an image originally published in *Jet* magazine in 1955 at the behest of Till's mother, Mamie Till-Mobley. On this controversy, and the protests of artist Parker Bright as well as others against it, see Aruna D'Souza, *Whitewalling: Art, Race & Protest in 3 Acts* (New York: Badlands Unlimited, 2018). For a historical perspective, see Susan E. Cahan, *Mounting Frustration: The Art Museum in the Age of Black Power* (Durham: Duke University Press, 2016).

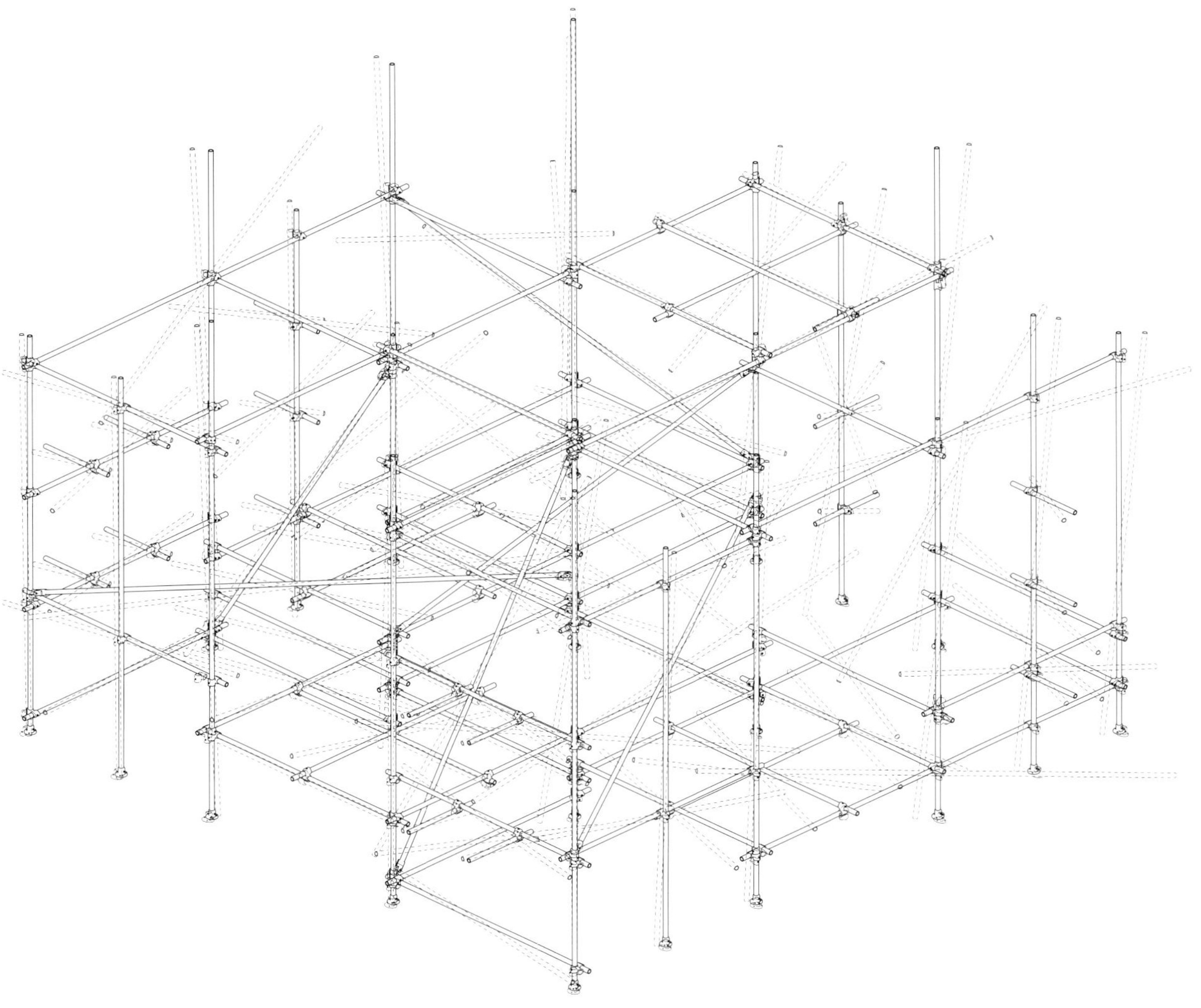

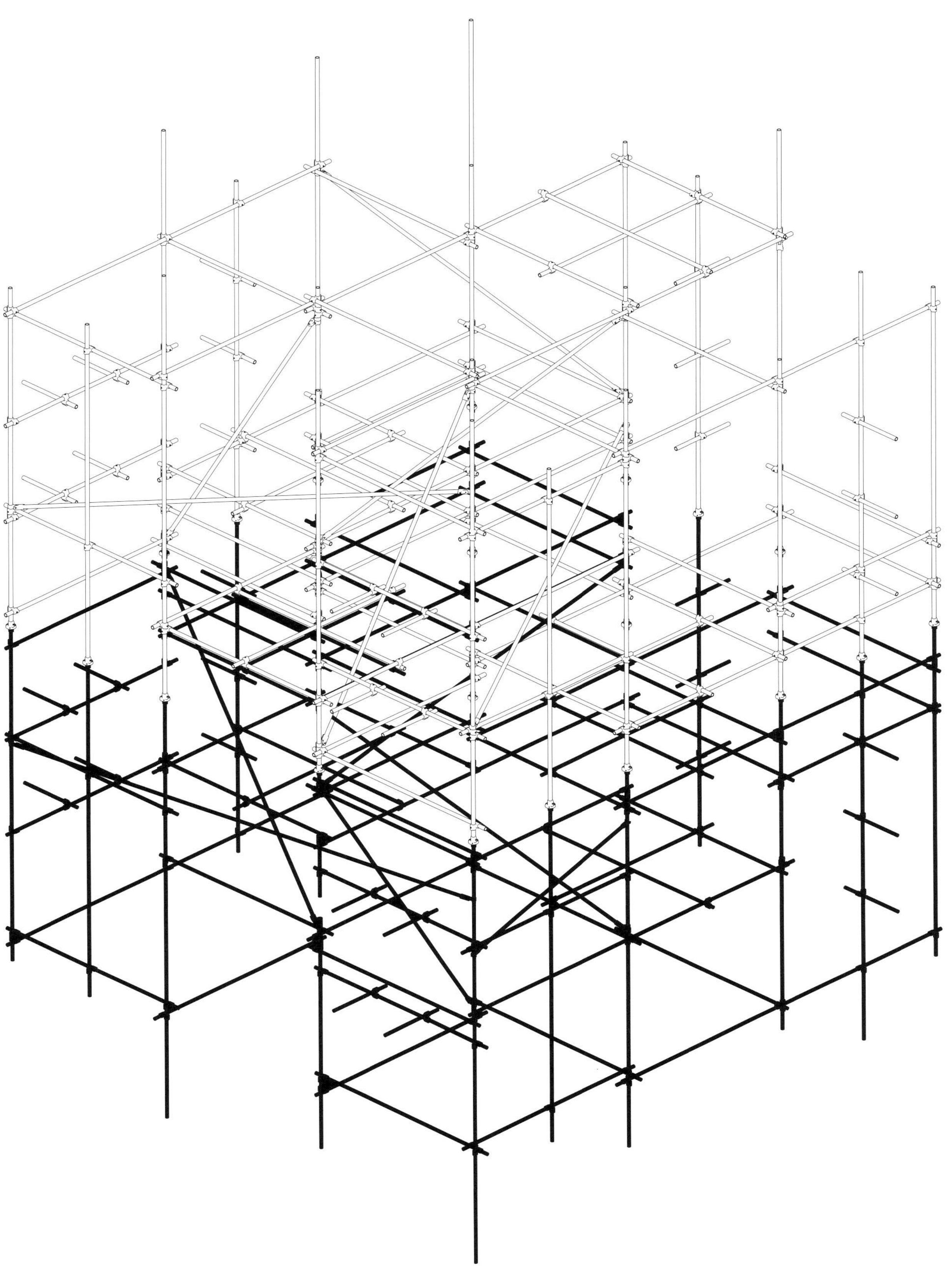

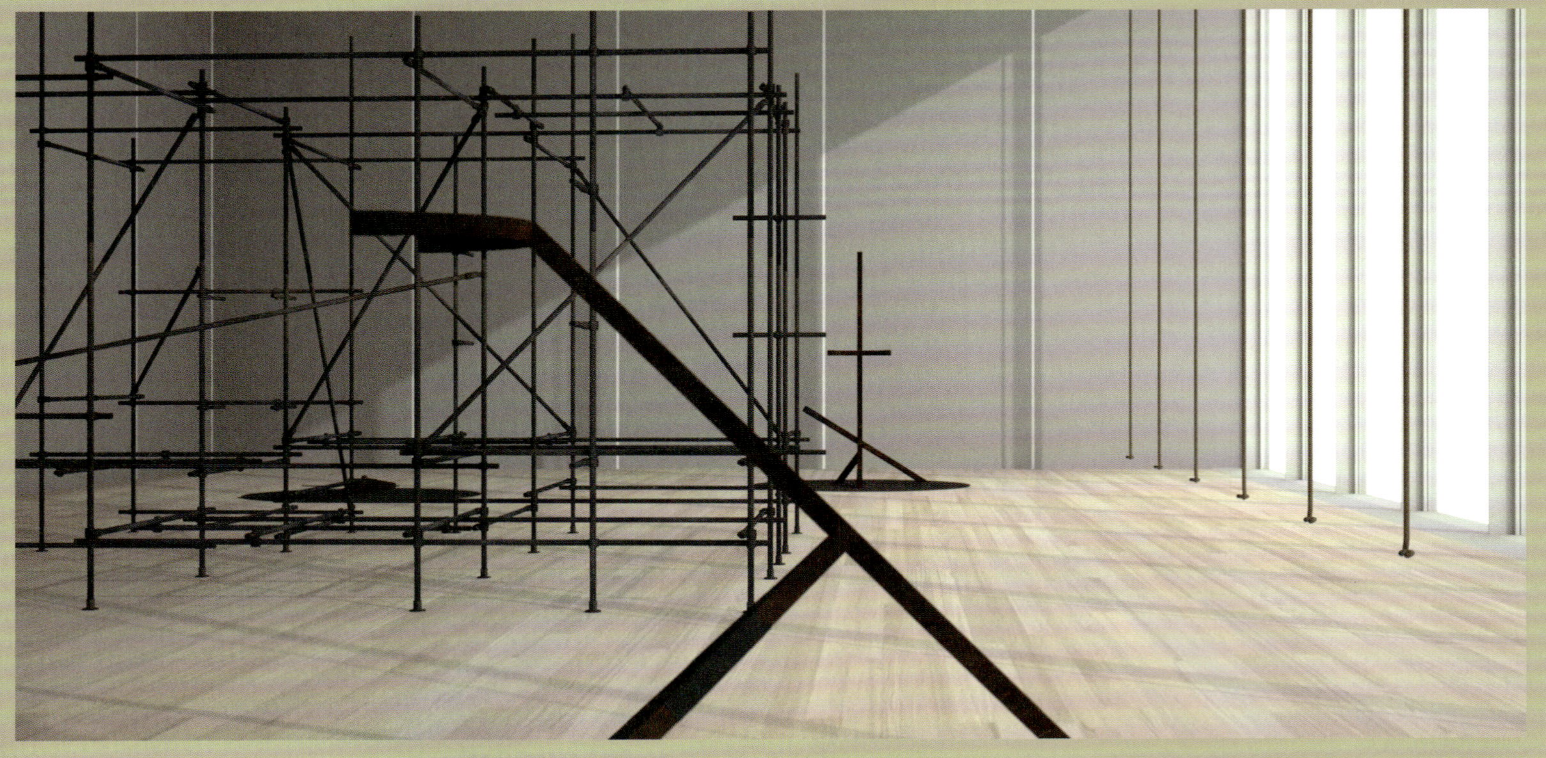

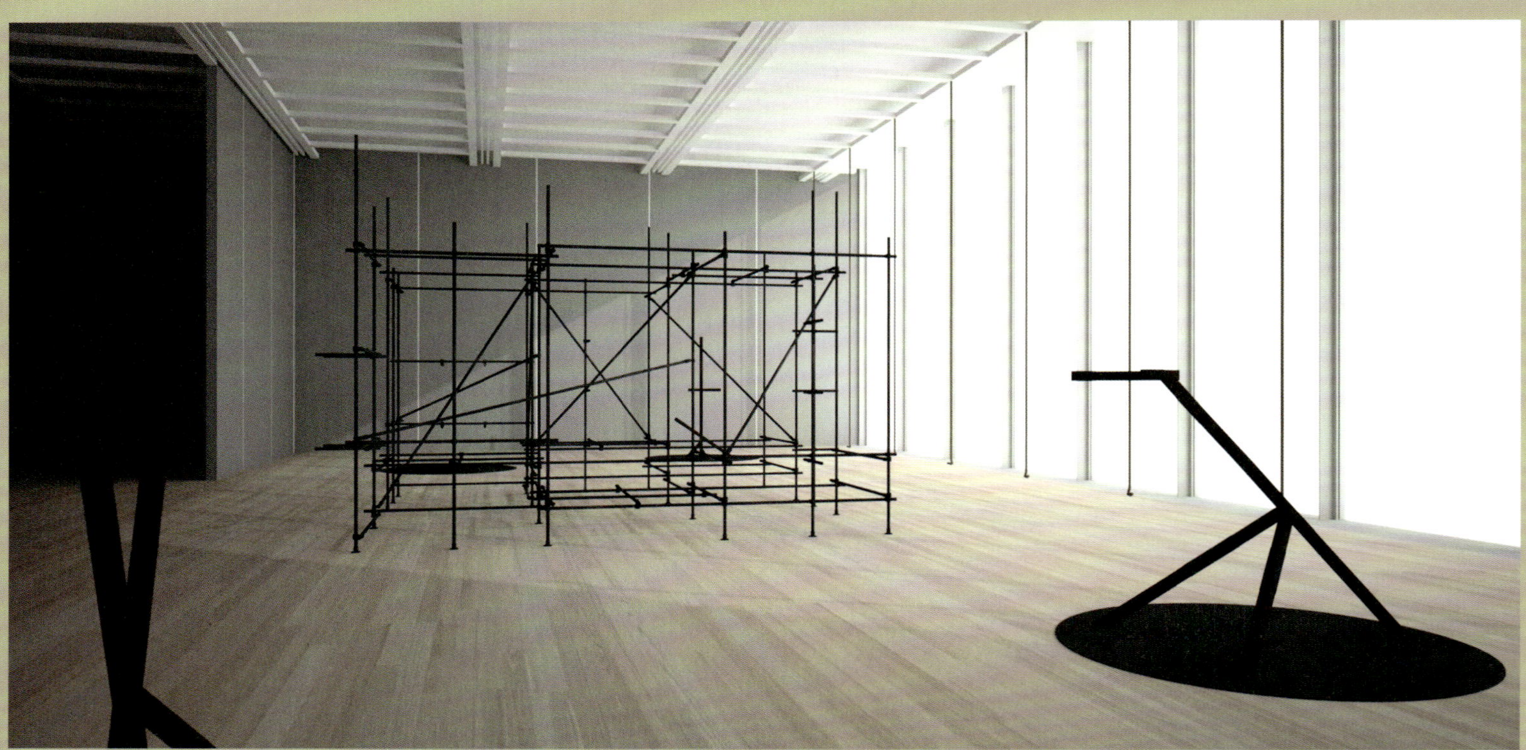

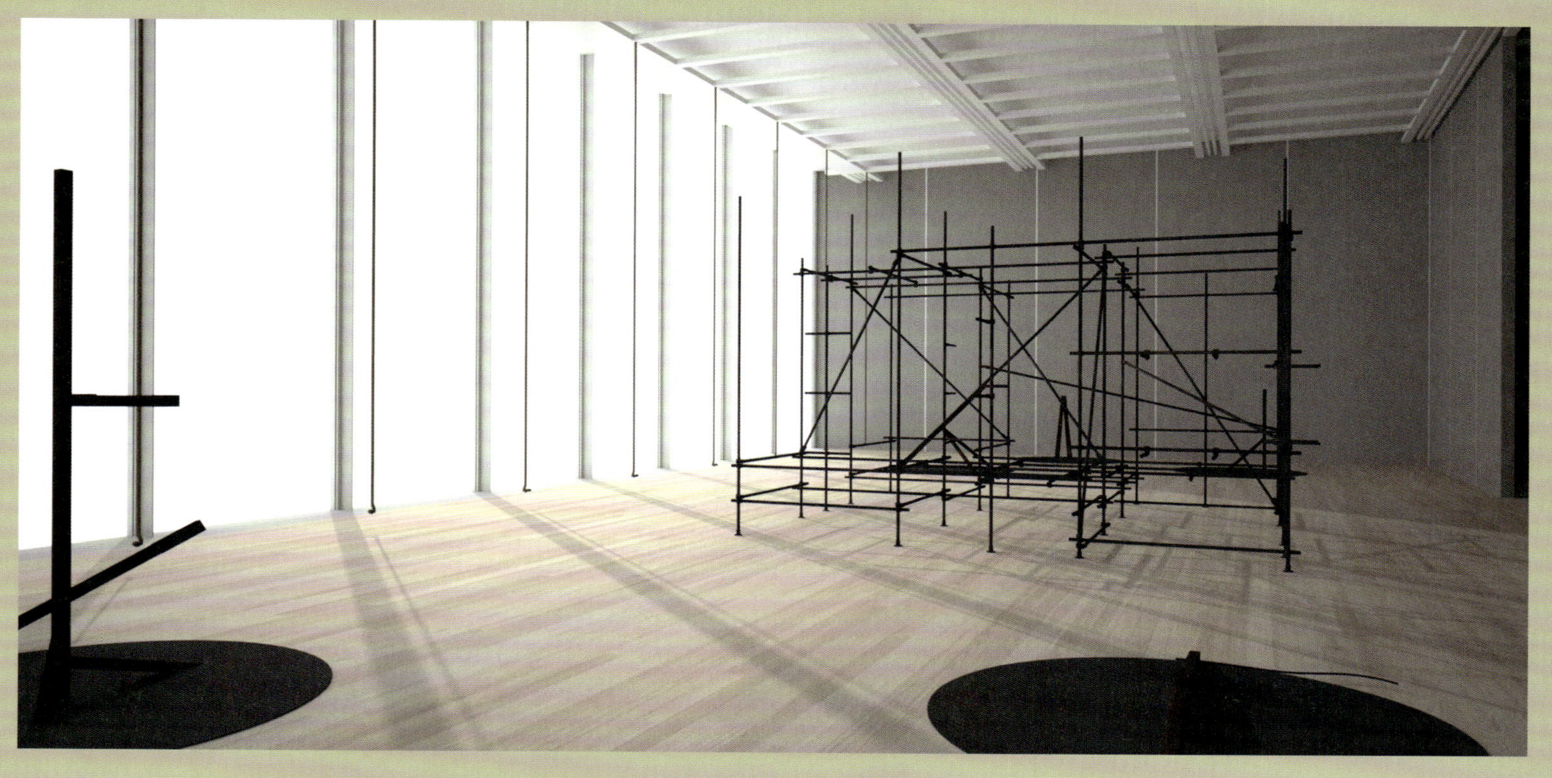

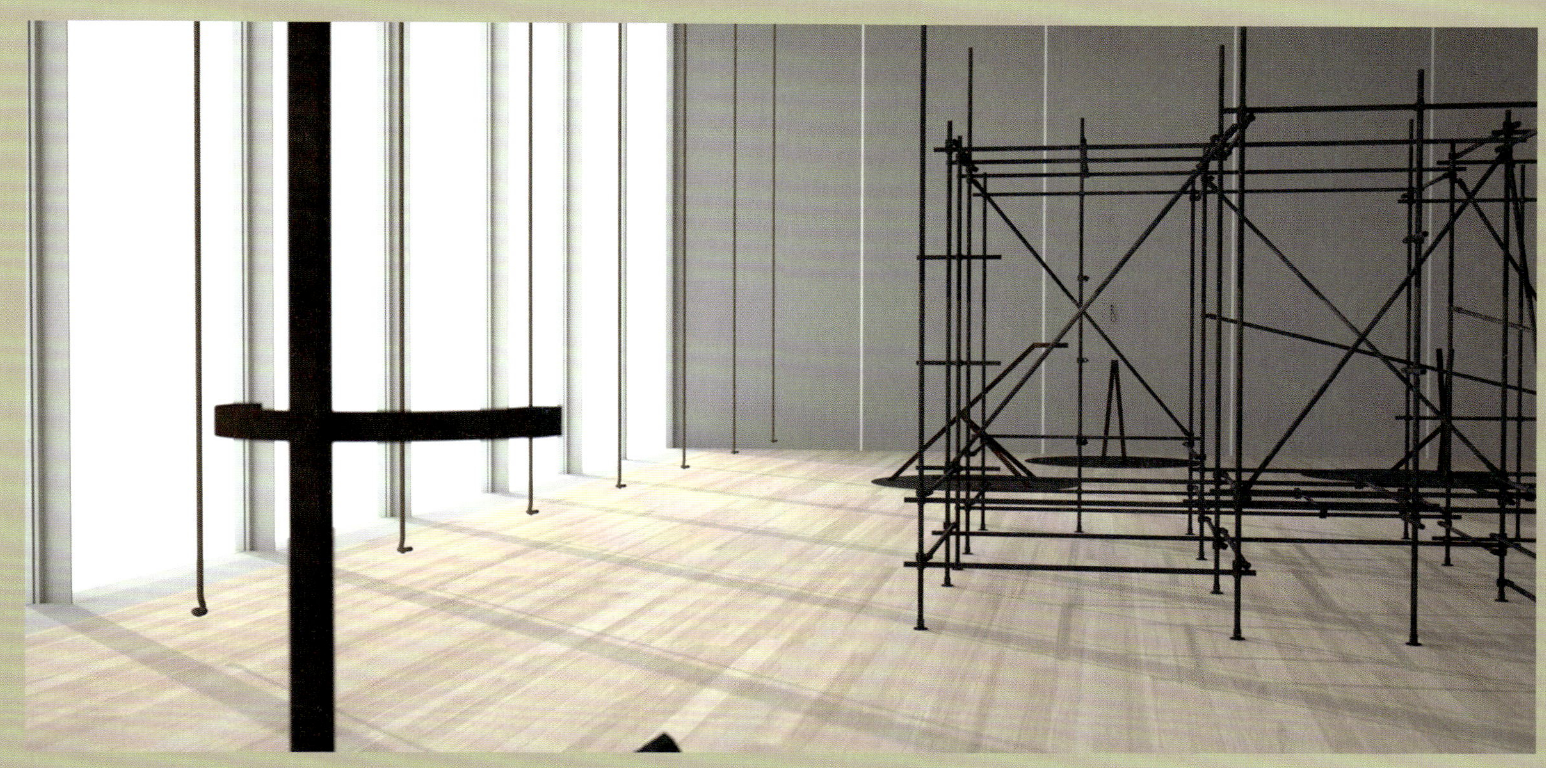

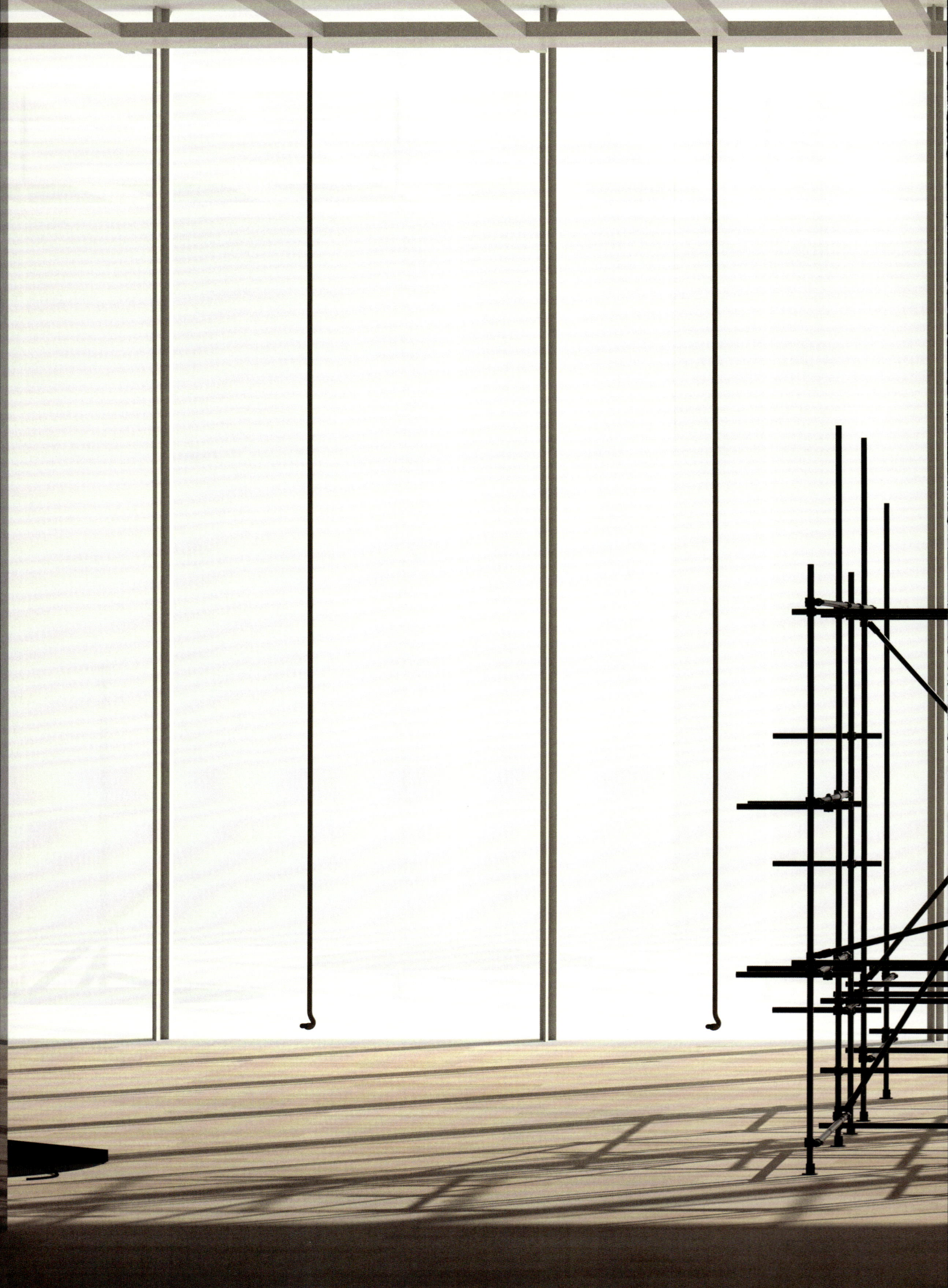

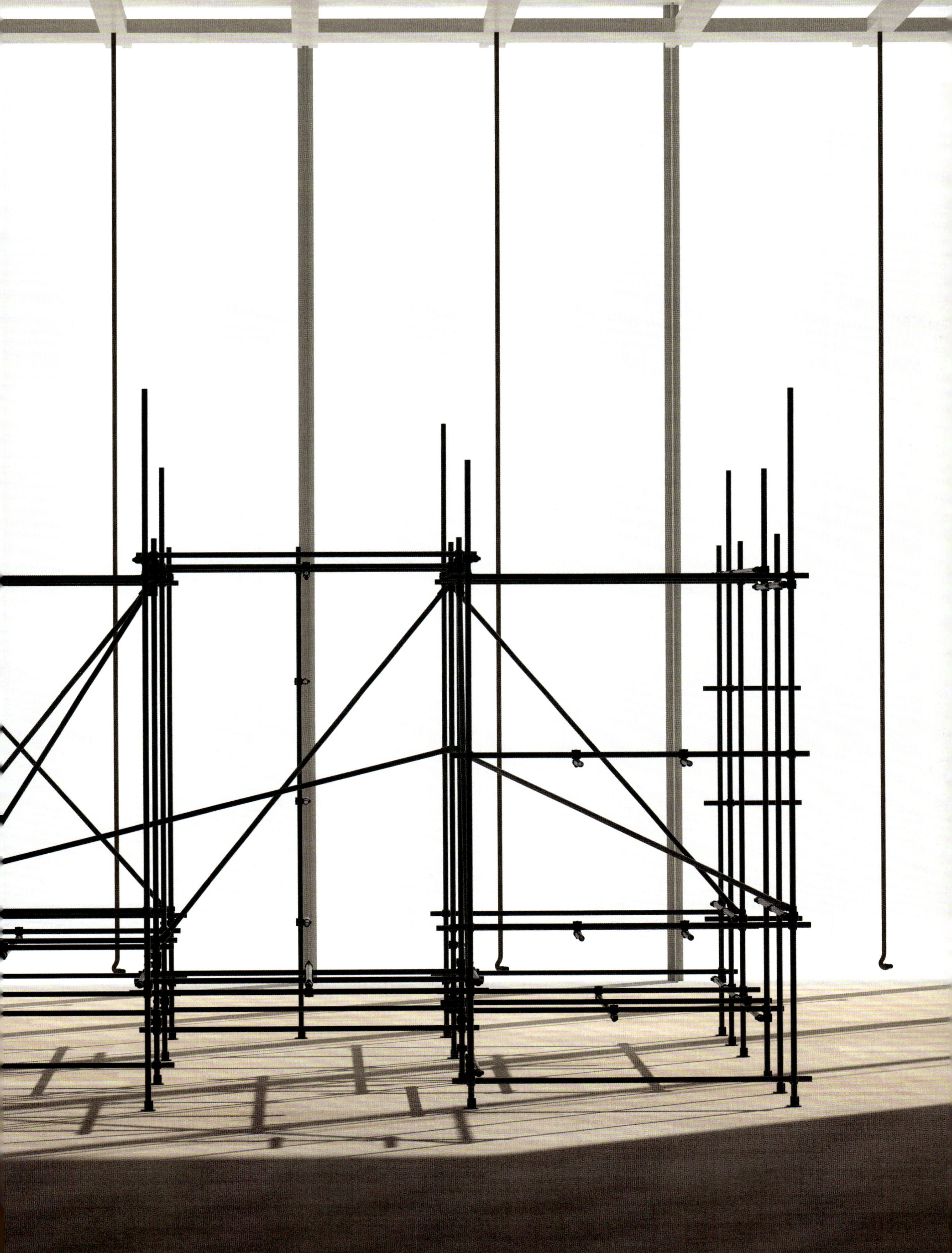

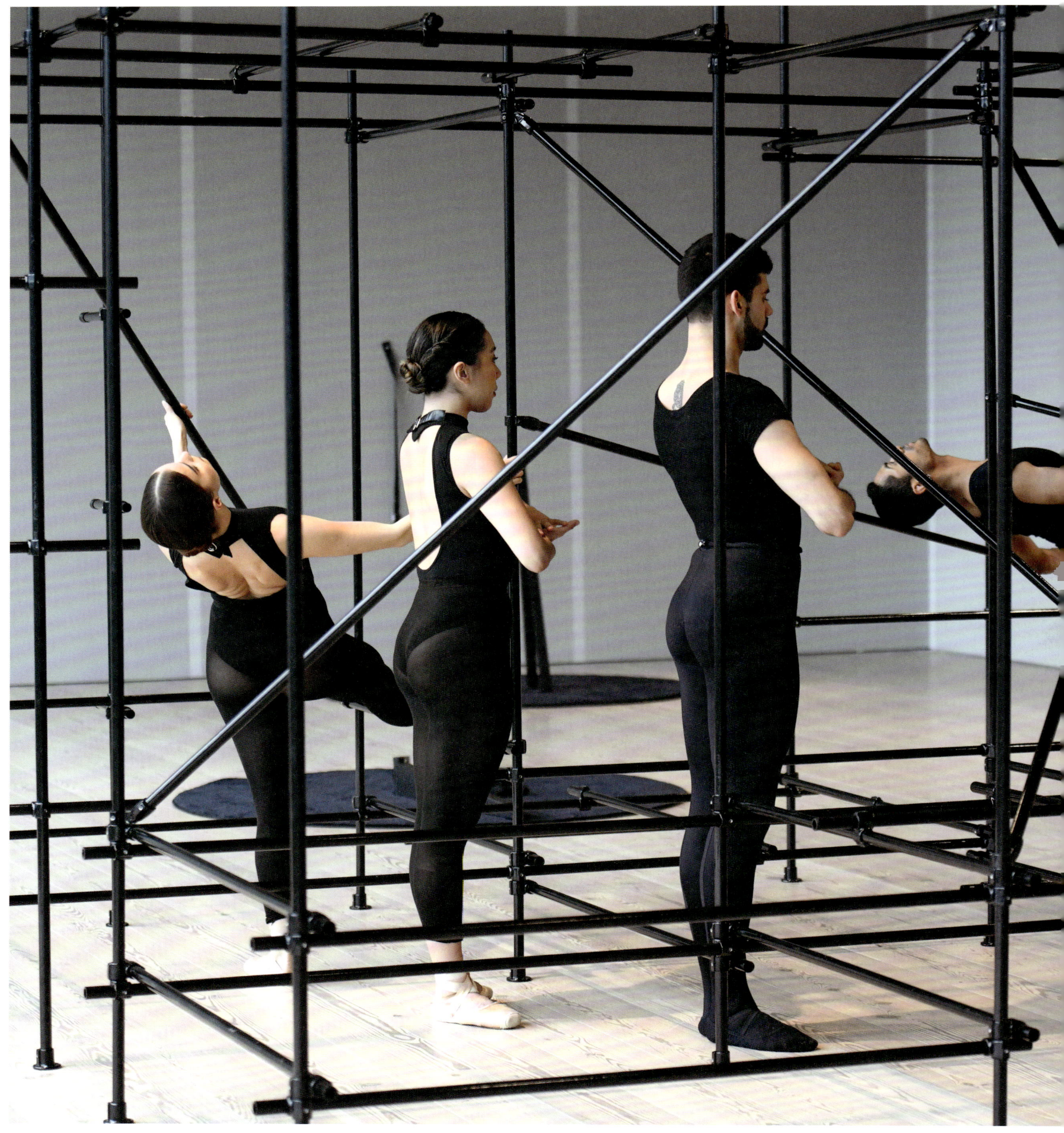

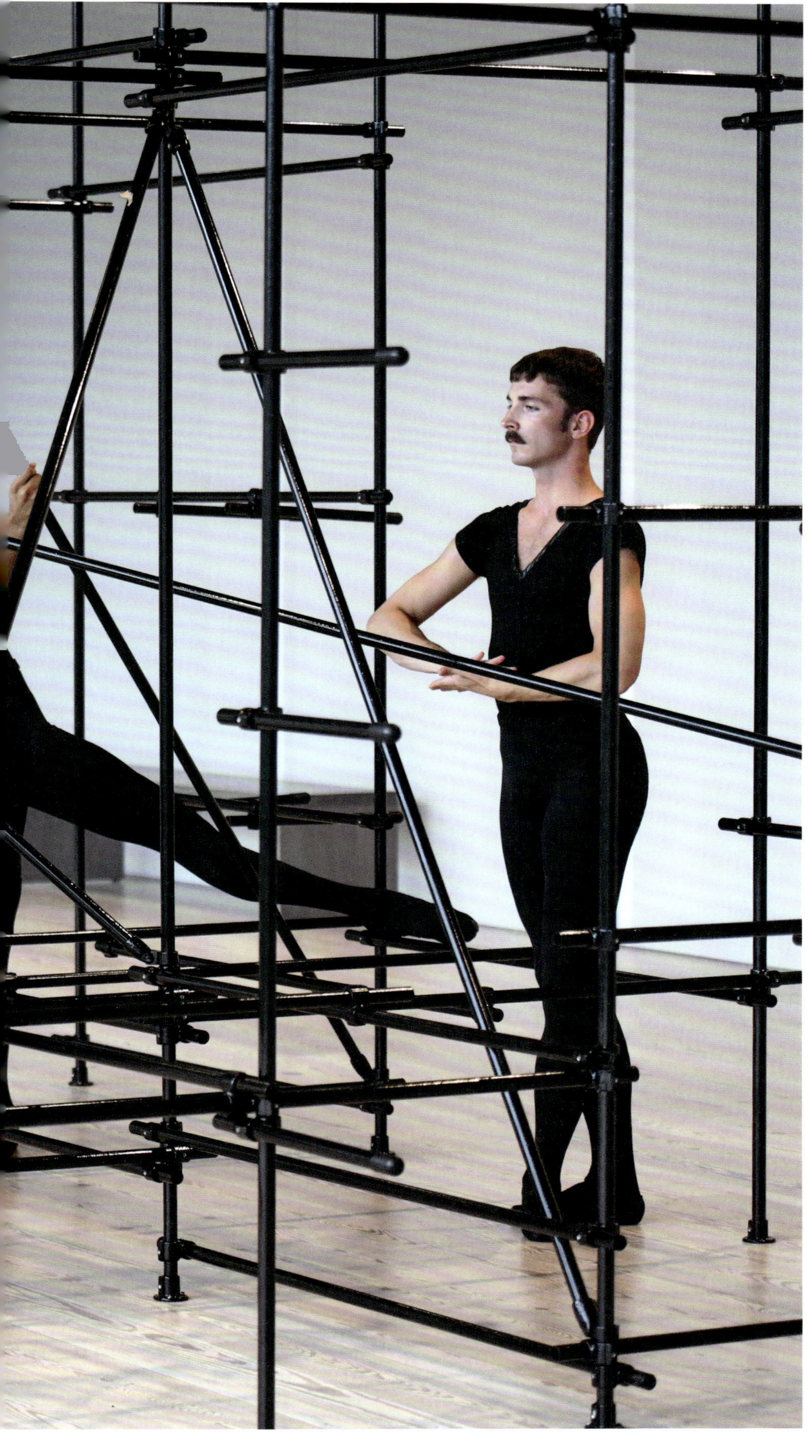

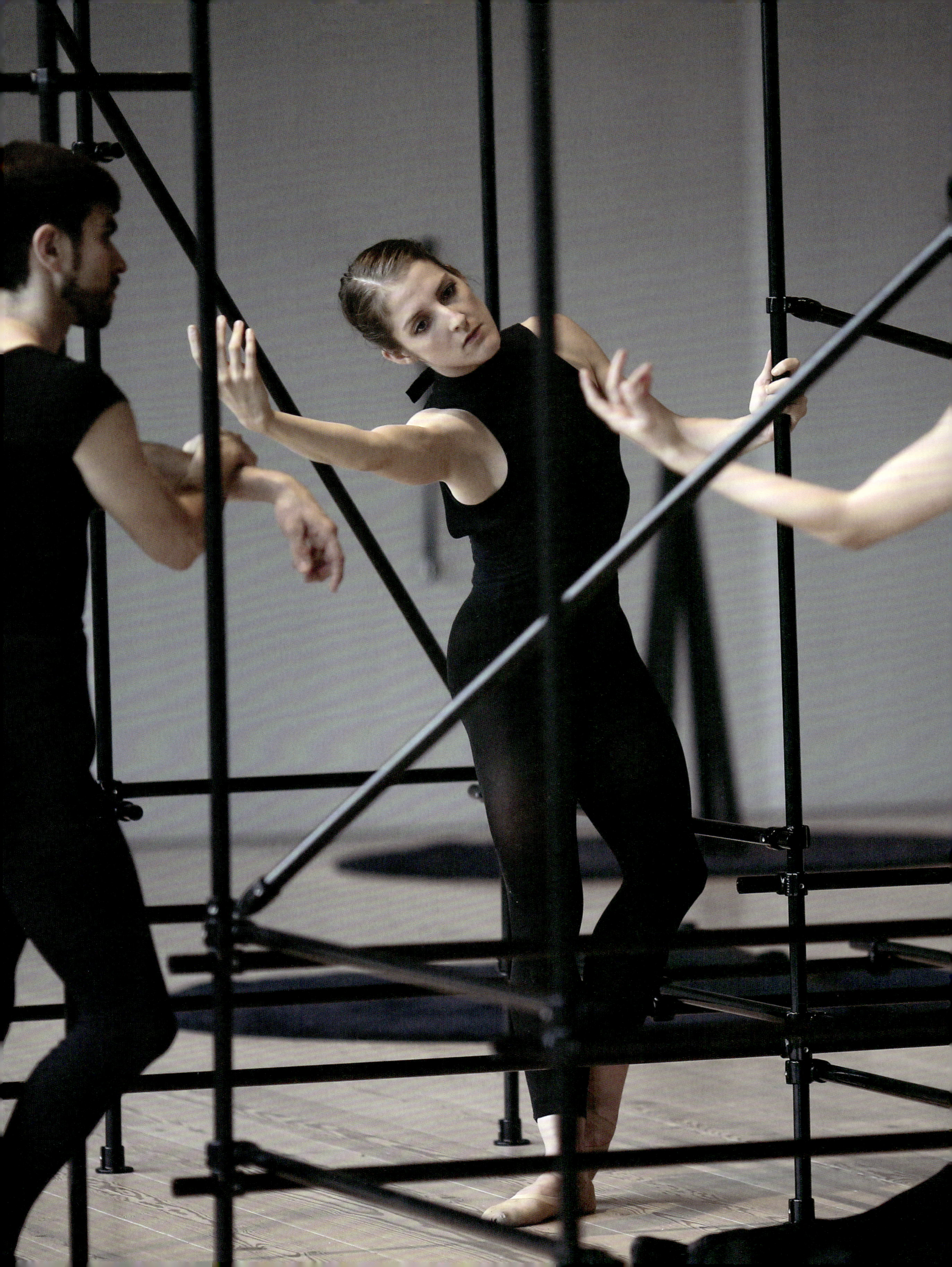

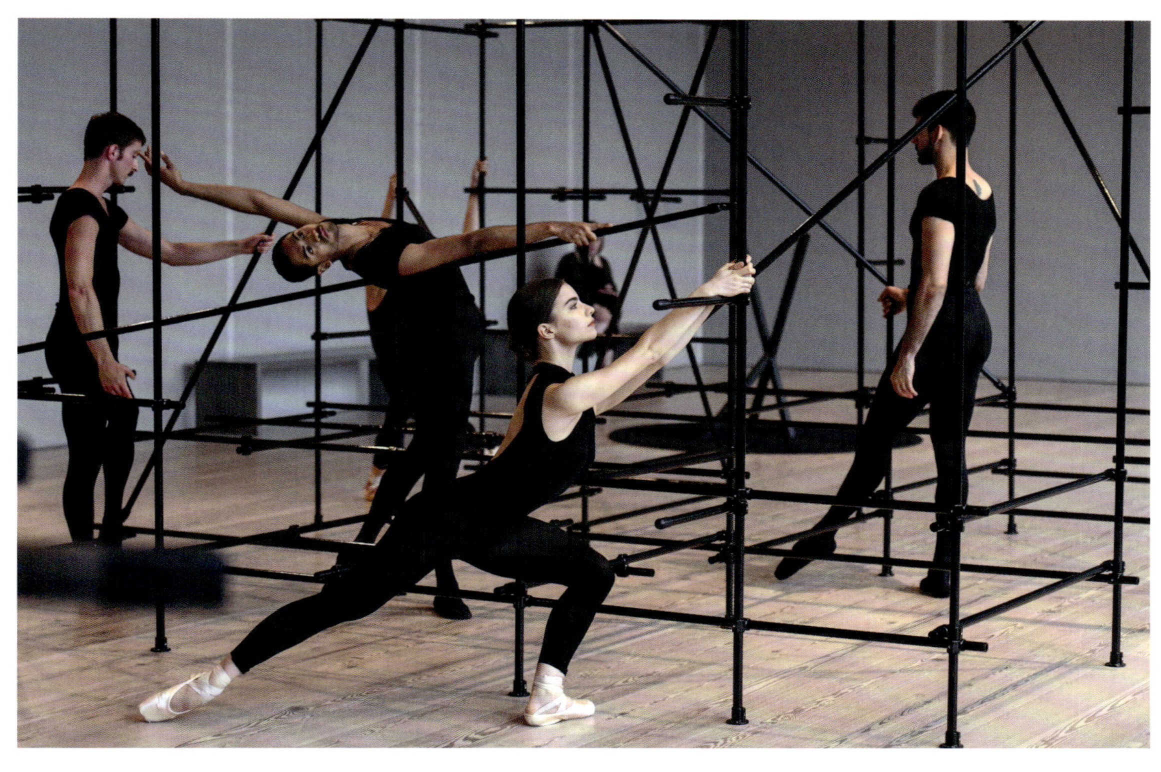

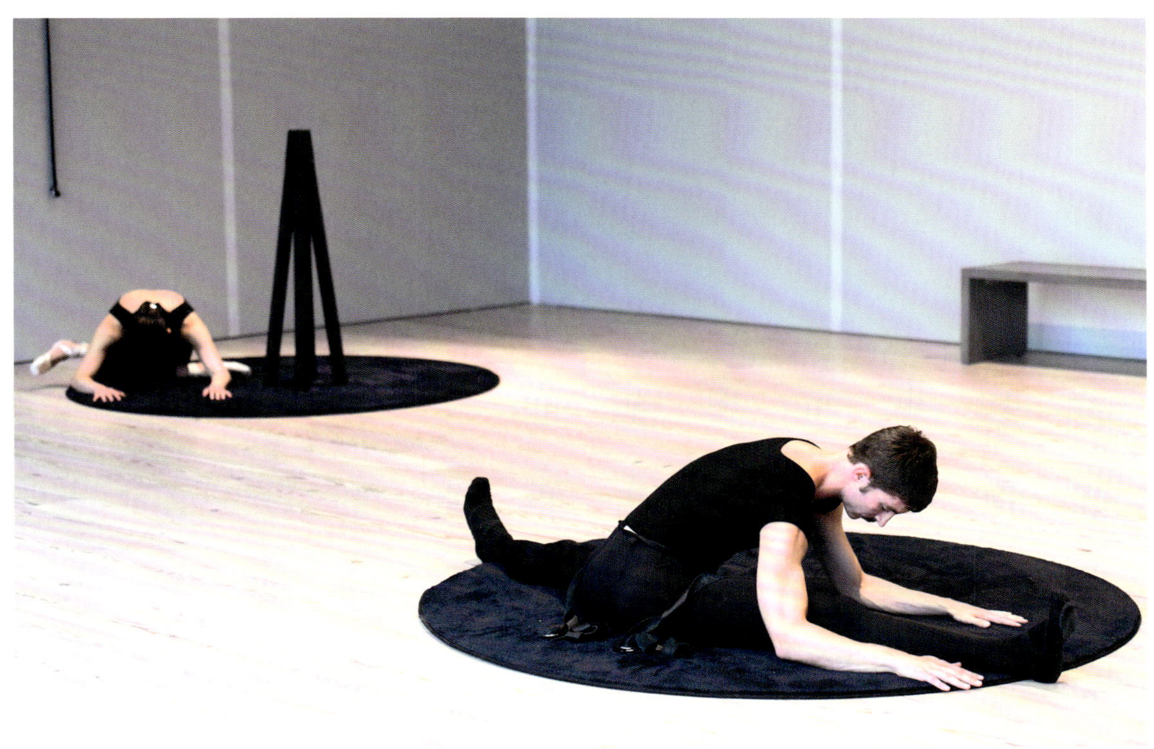

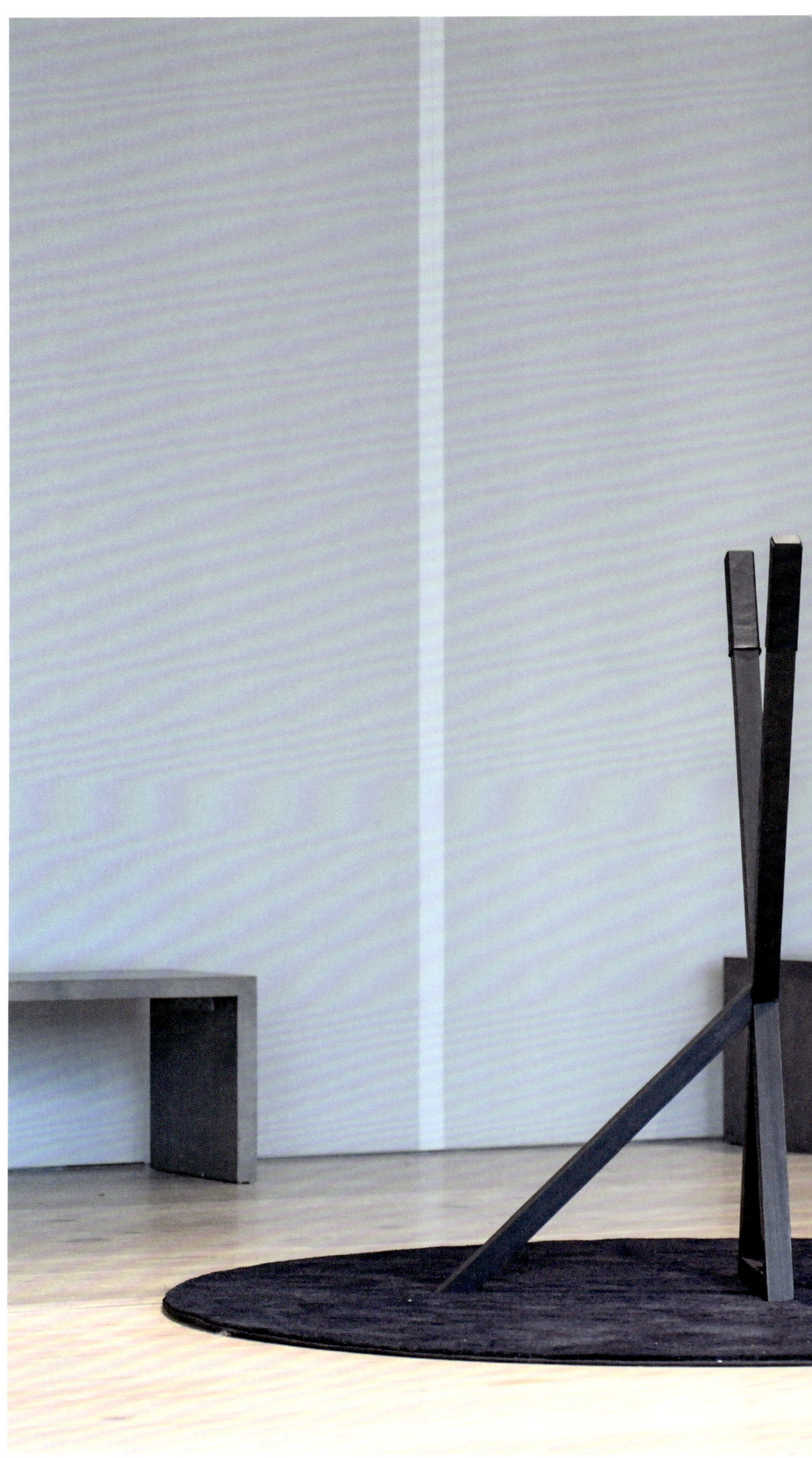

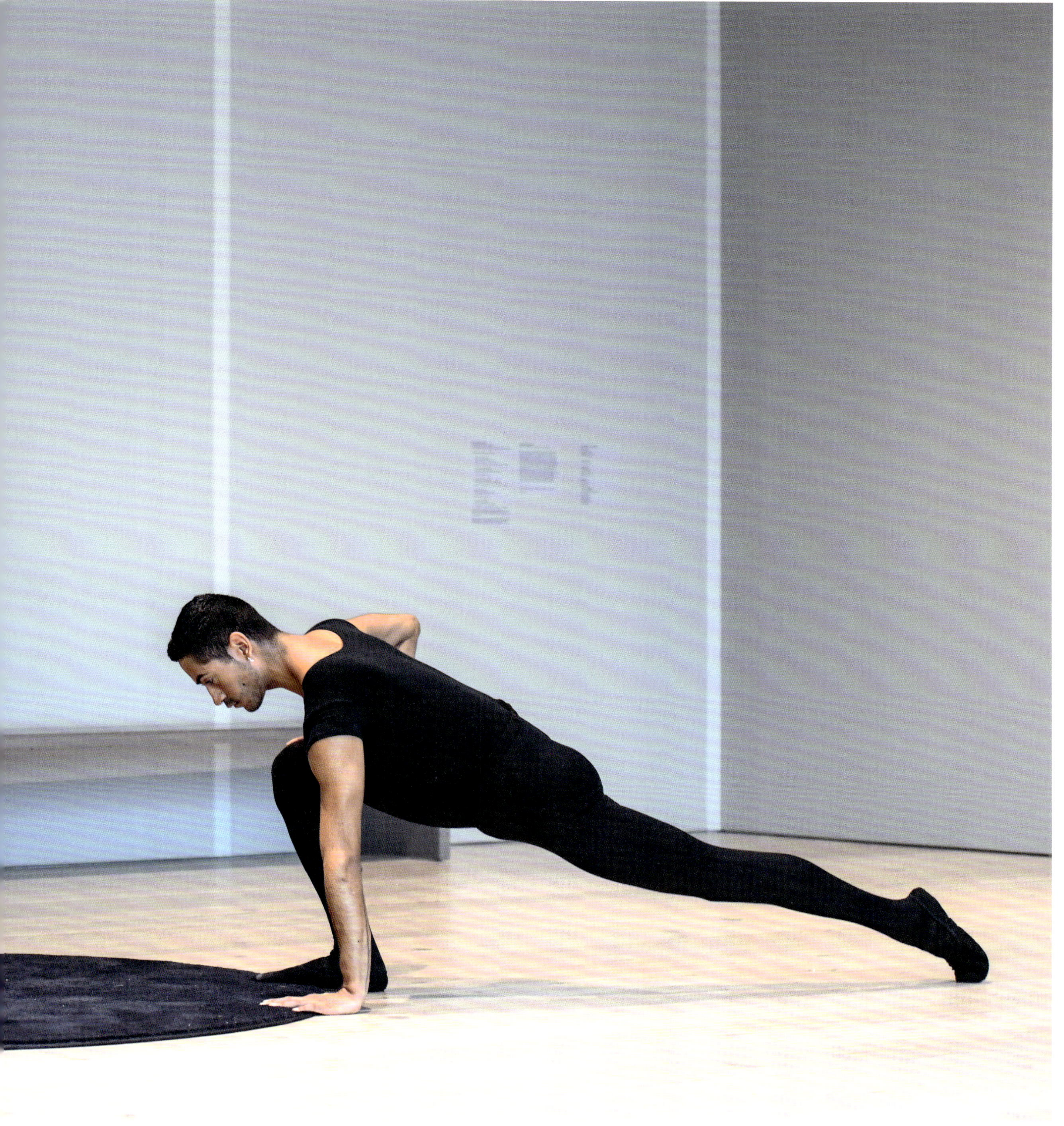

Pas de Deux: Fernandes and Orejudos

Andy Campbell

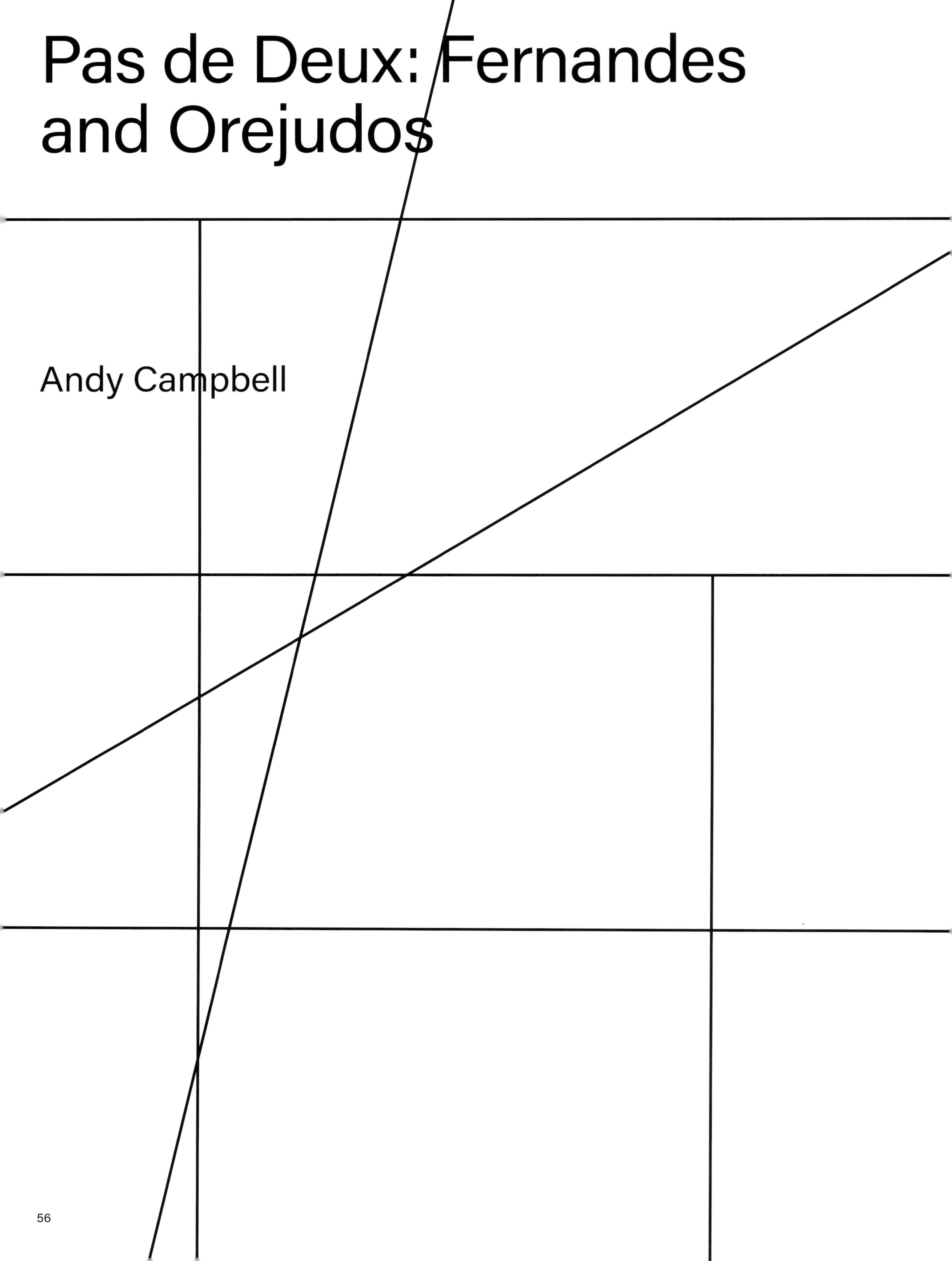

If, as performance theorist and historian André Lepecki suggests, we take "the formation of choreography as a peculiar invention of early modernity, as a technology that creates a body disciplined to move according to the commands of writing," how then might we site kink within dance's most entrenched, conventional, and legible forms?[1] In other words, how might we understand kink as another form of writing onto the body and what does Brendan Fernandes mean when he designates, even titles, some of his recent performance work "ballet kink"?

In the pages that follow, kink refers to that suite of practices loosely organized around the psychic-somatic willed exchange of pleasure and power, whose appearance and/or apprehension is marked as somehow outside of normative conceptions of sexual behavior (conceptions which are perforce always changing). In this essay, I use "kink" as a general term that refers to BDSM (bondage and discipline, dominance and submission, sadism and masochism), SM (sadomasochism), and leather: these terms share a disciplinary set of erotics and codes, each with their own histories and subcultures.[2] Elsewhere in the essay, when talking about historical gay communities invested in sadomasochism, I use "leather" because the synecdoche was much more pervasive at the time. While each of these terms encapsulate a wide range of activities, at their core are practices that have to do with bodies, pleasure, and power. Above all else, kink points to the negotiated exchange of such power. Especially since kink deploys a set of signifiers that both draw upon and are too often glibly elided with historical traumas such as chattel slavery, it is crucial to underscore the primary distinction between *nonconsensual* and *consensual* exchanges vis-à-vis practices of kink.

Illuminating the disciplinary relation to the body that many forms of dance instantiate and rely upon, as well as the pain and perverse pleasures they produce for dancers and viewers alike, is a key ambition of Fernandes's performances. At first this critique was directed squarely at the hierarchized and colonialist realities undergirding the production of Western dance—specifically, for the purposes of this essay, ballet.[3] Take, for example, *Inverted Pyramid* (2014), which dynamically positions the arabesque (a classical ballet posture that shares its name with an ornamental design originally found in Arabic or Moorish decoration) as an enduring Orientalizing technique of colonial control [Reference Images p. 128]. Or *Standing Leg* (2014), which demonstrates how a dancer's body is sculpted and exhausted by the demands of ballet technique [Reference Images p. 128]. During this durational solo performance, Fernandes manipulates a foot stretcher—an oblong implement (often wooden) that molds one's foot into an arched position. As the artist tensions his foot against the stretcher with a stocking, he struggles to hold the position over the course of the performance, variously extending his leg and bringing it in to cradle it in his arms. This visual oscillation, which we witness through a scrim of stretched fabric, both obscures and reveals the disciplinary process. It is arduous work, reshaping one's body to be

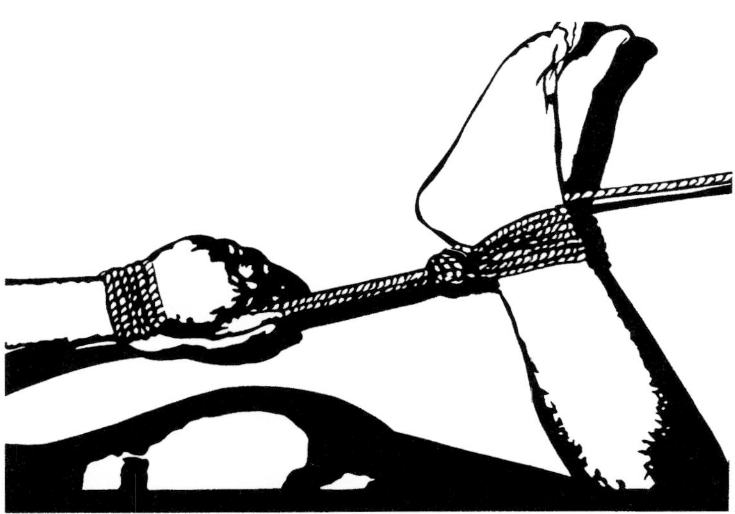

Figure 1: Wall label from the exhibition *Bondage Safety* at the Leather Archives & Museum, Chicago (2012), Photo by Brendan Fernandes

consistent with a set of artificial standards passed down orally and kinesthetically from the court cultures of sixteenth-century Italy and France. *Standing Leg*, like the more recent *The Master and Form* (2018–19), emphasizes haptic points of connection whereby order is internalized and pursued, implicating the foot stretcher in a history of disciplining objects (the inanimate Masters, if you will). Fernandes's performance also has an autobiographical dimension: in order to perform he must perversely contend with an injury which made his career as a ballet dancer no longer feasible. In this way, we can think of Fernandes's career as an artist as one of the many outcomes of the disciplinary system of ballet where obeisance to one's Masters is just as integral as it is in kink communities. This parallel between ballet's strict teachers and the dominatrices of kink is relayed in an anecdote that Fernandes shares about a dear friend and talented dancer who became a ProDomme (a professional dominant sex worker) when she retired from the world of ballet. As she once said to Fernandes, "We all call our teachers: Master!"[4]

Fernandes's engagement with master-teachers does not end there. For *Ballet Kink* (2019), a performance staged for the Solomon R. Guggenheim Museum's Young Collector's Party, Fernandes collaborated with *shibari* rope master Ming Chang (Master Ming) and Vincent Tiley, who uses *shibari* technique in his work as an artist (FIGURE 1). Inspired by *shibari* and *kinbaku*, the erotic rope bondage techniques pioneered in nineteenth- and twentieth-century Japan, Fernandes bound a group of dancers who performed movements, many based on ballet positions and sequences, inside and around a cylindrical stage made of metal trussing and theatrical lighting [Reference Images p. 128]. Fernandes's stage was designed to reflexively echo the museum's iconic lobby, an architectural void carved out by the spiraling sloped walkway that rims the museum's centrifugal galleries. His staging turned the museum's lobby into an operating theater of movement. "Under these binds," writes Fernandes about the trussed stage and the use of *shibari* and *kinbaku*, "the dancers must re-negotiate their agency. As such the performance embodies metaphors for contemporary situations in which we too might find ourselves redefining freedom, movement and solidarity under social and political restraints."[5] Thus, the kink practice of bondage—which involves restricting, tying, and framing a person's movements—is leveraged towards a broader critique of the actions and responses that make up our daily living under normative constraints and power dynamics like white supremacy and capitalism. It is an exercise in domination, submission, and the various exchanges of power that take place between the two. By enlisting the skillsets of Master Ming and Tiley (who makes prodigious use of rope bondage in his "bound" paintings), Fernandes creates work that is as cognizant of kink as it is ballet and its histories.

As much as Fernandes exposes how disciplinary standards (bodily, social, and otherwise) function as aesthetic and visual codes that are often tied to fantasy, pleasure, and fetishistic recreation, he also considers the effects of the internalization of body standards on a dancer's livelihood and labor. One way to understand this is via the term "delegated performance" coined by Claire Bishop, wherein "the act of hiring nonprofessionals or specialists in other fields to undertake the job of being present and performing at a particular time and a particular place on behalf of the artist, and following his or her instructions," parlays into imperatives, "to perform *their own socioeconomic category*, be this on the basis of gender, class, ethnicity, age, disability, or (more rarely) profession."[6] Although Bishop's theory is general, her understanding of the intersubjectivity of such delegations, which flow between the producing artist and the contracted performer (dancers and kink experts in Fernandes's case), are particularly useful.[7] Guided by Pierre Klossowski's writing projects, which include texts on the Marquis de Sade and Nietzsche as well as French translations of German critical theory, Bishop articulates both the "moral queasiness" and potential *jouissance* that such practices can instantiate. In doing so, she highlights delegated performance's inculcation within a neoliberal economic and political order. The result is that instead of interaction, delegated performances often align with market imperatives and encourage "interpassivity," or the degradation of "bodies into objects."[8] At the same time she holds open the possibility that art is a space where "norms are suspended and put in service of pleasure in perverse ways (to return to Sade, a space not unlike that of BDSM sex)."[9] Bishop's discussion of delegated performance only begins to address what is so striking about performances like *Ballet Kink* and *The Master and Form*, both of which bring two divergent movement systems into coordination—nearly unthinkable a couple generations ago.

The Master and Form, which premiered at the Graham Foundation in Chicago, is one of Fernandes's most intricate performances to date. It includes a cast of five dancers who activate an installation of sculptural elements and structures developed with architecture and design collaborative Norman Kelley. The equipment and restraints devised for *The Master and Form* are somewhat ambiguous, derived from dance and/or kink contexts. A good example is the stretcher (or spreader) bar activated by one of Fernandes's dancers during the performance, which, with the help of restraints, might be used to make the body more flexible and/or leave it strategically vulnerable in the scene of kinky sex. Such generative visual, utilitarian, and

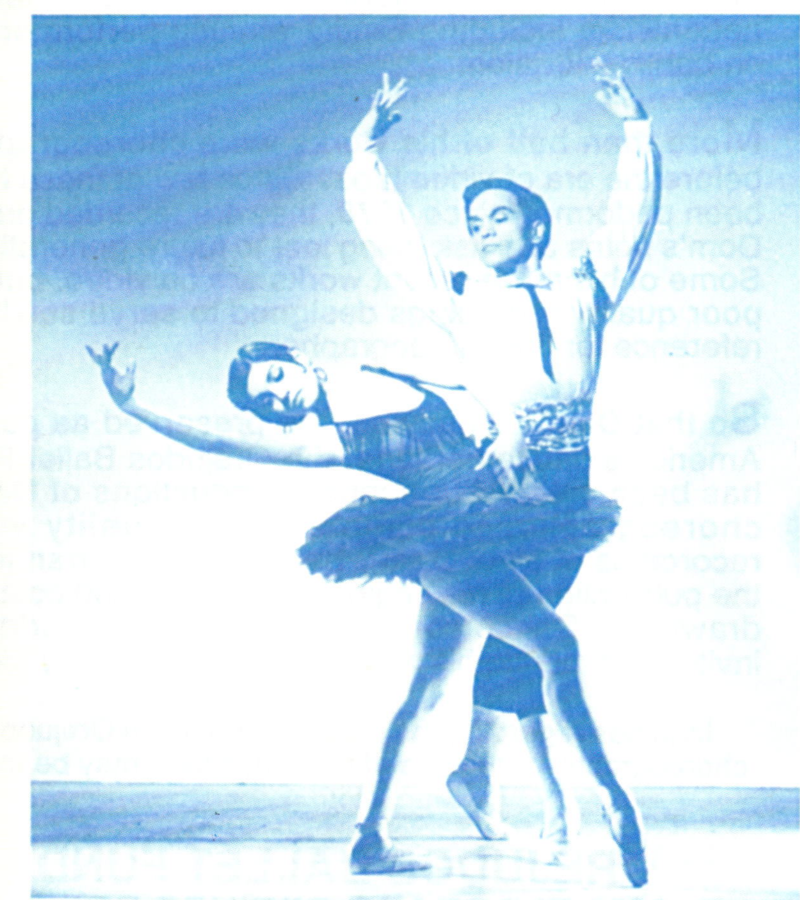

Figure 2: VHS released by the Orejudos Ballet Fund, 1993. From the collections of the Leather Archives & Museum, Chicago

somatic double entendres (which abound in *The Master and Form*) stem from Fernandes's research at the Leather Archives & Museum in Chicago, "a community archives, library, and museum of Leather, kink, fetish, and BDSM history and culture."[10] Images from magazines, drawings of kinky furniture and apparel from vintage catalogs, and other archival materials that he viewed there aided and informed *The Master and Form*'s development.

One of the items accessed by Fernandes during his visits to the LA&M was a VHS anthology of choreographic works by Domingo "Dom" Orejudos. The blue-tinted photograph on the cover shows the Chicago-born Orejudos soigné, upright and with arms raised; while his partner, conversely, bends her body back and outwards, presenting her torso for Orejudos's downward gaze (FIGURE 2). While the overdetermined gender performances on the VHS cover are hardly remarkable in the repertoire of ballet, the date range at the bottom (July 1, 1933 – September 24, 1991) indicates that the anthology has a special, memorial function. Orejudos's death is one of, if not *the* primary catalytic event leading to the founding of the LA&M later that year by his partner Chuck Renslow and leather editor and writer Tony DeBlase.[11]

Because of his deep and simultaneous investments in dance and leather in Chicago, Orejudos appears to this writer as Fernandes's most remarkable queer forebearer. As a ballet dancer and choreographer, Orejudos worked in Chicago, New Orleans, and with regional dance companies across the United States from the 1960s through the 1980s. He was also simultaneously well-known in gay male leather communities for his erotic graphic art, produced under the Europeanized mononymous pseudonym Etienne.[12] That Orejudos necessarily kept his pursuits as a dancer/choreographer and leather artist/business-owner separate points toward the real and perceived conservatism of the classical dance world, where involvement with kinky sex communities was, if not explicitly verboten, certainly not openly discussed with any frequency. At the time, being outed as a gay, much less a kinky person, would have posed a dire existential threat to his work as a mainstream dancer and choreographer. A nasty result of this strategic compartmentalization is that there is not yet a fulsome accounting of Orejudos's contributions to both leather and dance communities.[13]

Together with Renslow, who was already well-known as a homophile activist and photographer, Orejudos founded and maintained an astonishing set of businesses and community spaces. These included: an erotic photography studio that supplied a steady stream of carefully posed photographs for beefcake magazines such as *Man of Tomorrow* and *Mars* (also Renslow/Orejudos properties), leather bars catering to local club goers and out-of-town visitors (the most famous being The Gold Coast), bathhouses, gyms, a tattoo parlor, and an occult bookstore (named Bell, Book, and Candle after the Catholic act of excommunication by anathema). The pair were so successful in these endeavors that for a time they lived with other lovers and friends in the Francis J. Dewes House, an elaborate *fin de siècle* mansion in Chicago's swanky Lincoln Park neighborhood. Among their many endeavors, the International Mr. Leather Competition, often referred to as simply IML, was founded by Orejudos and Renslow in 1979—the year that Fernandes was born.[14] Inspired by similar events such as The Advocate's annual "Groovy Guy" contest that began a decade earlier, IML brought together competitors from bars and clubs across the United States and abroad, further sedimenting Chicago as an important site for national and international gay male leather communities.

Fernandes's melding of dance, art, and kink provides an occasion to think about how Orejudos, throughout his own life, made prodigious use of his skills as a dancer and choreographer in his work as an erotic artist and business owner and vice versa. He was adept at posing young men for the beefcake photographs he and Renslow produced and distributed, a fact that can be directly attributed to his understanding of body mechanics. The same might also be said of the way he drew figures in his erotic art, where he crafted dynamic stories populated with images of trim figures engaged in nearly-balletic sexual acrobatics. As leather writer and editor Jack Fritscher succinctly puts it,"[Orejudos's] talent for dramatic movement and story arcs, developed on stage in his choreography, informed his cartoon-strip narratives."[15] Yet, if leather writers and editors such as Fritscher could recognize and value his contributions across artistic media, the same was not true for those who knew and valued his work as a dancer and choreographer. Orejudos's obituary in the *Chicago Tribune*, for example, makes passing mention of his work in leather communities or businesses.[16]

Yet, whether they knew him by name or not, Orejudos was a central figure in the development of what Fritscher calls "the leather mural movement," executing large-scale semi-public commissions for leather bar interiors alongside more focused and iconic graphics in advertisements for bars and clubs in magazines such as *Drummer*.[17] Thus, Orejudos-as-Etienne came to be a household name within a national community of leather men. Perhaps only Tom of Finland has been more influential in cementing the visual programs of gay male leather social worlds. And for his part, Tom of Finland, whose detailed homoerotic drawings have only recently been exhibited and accepted within contemporary artistic discourse (which does not otherwise value art whose express purpose is arousal), praised Orejudos in letters to him, wondering how the younger artist could "do things more exciting than any photo ever does or any other artist."[18]

In terms of his choreography, Orejudos was a more conservative creator—finding consistent aesthetic inspiration in nineteenth- and early twentieth-century Russian and American ballet. Such interests aligned well with the economic demands and tastes of municipal ballet companies and audiences across the United States during the Cold War period—when tensions between the U.S. and the U.S.S.R. threw a

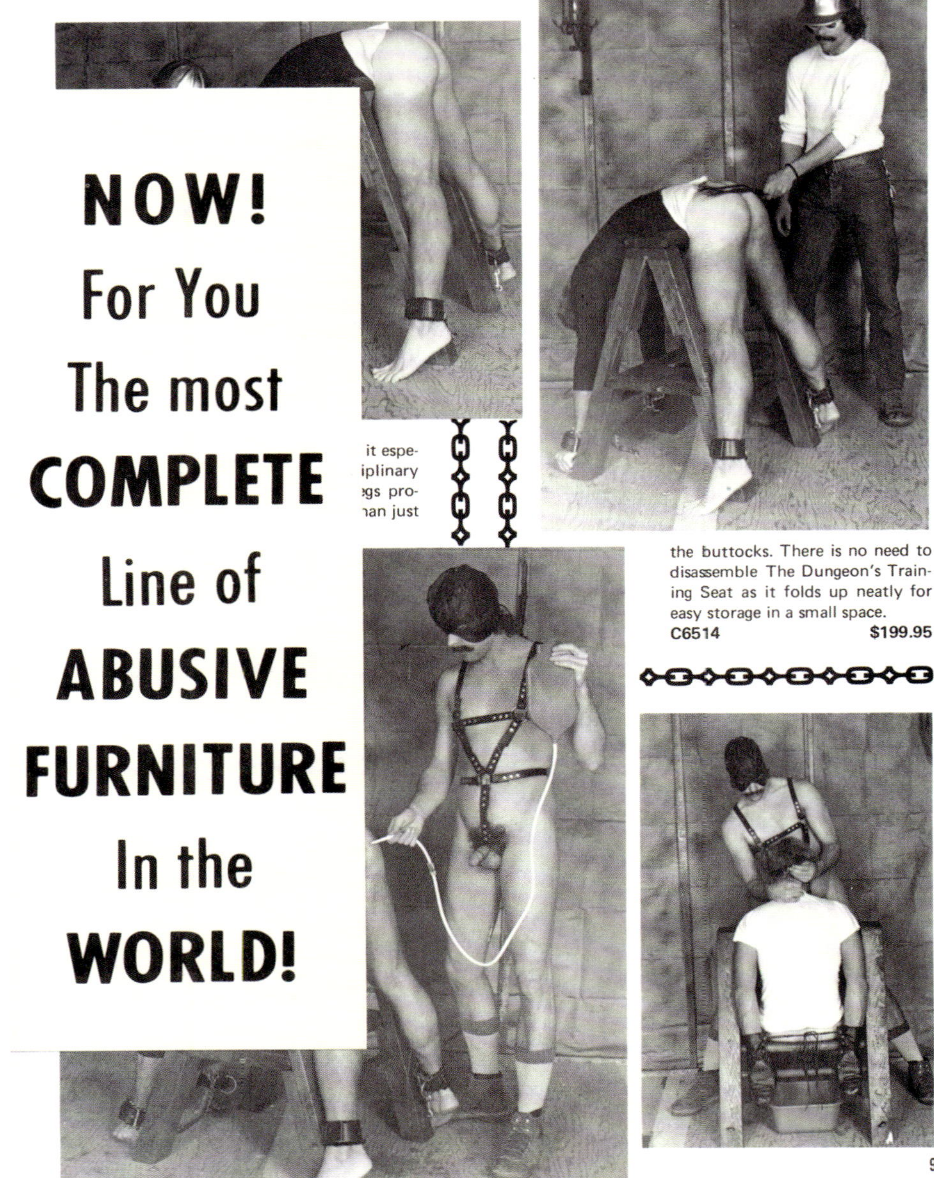

Figure 3: *S&M Dungeon Devices Catalog* (1976), from the Mariposa Foundation Collection at the Leather Archives & Museum, Chicago, Image courtesy of the Leather Archives & Museum

dramatic spotlight on two of the art form's putative centers (Moscow and New York). Orejudos was fêted for his work in dance, winning an Emmy in 1968 for his ballet, *The Charioteer*, which was staged for the first color broadcast of the Chicago-area public television station, WTTW.[19]

As a final tribute to Orejudos, and as a way of fundraising for the nascent Leather Archives & Museum, Renslow commissioned Curtis Londo and Peggy Powell, the latter of whom who had danced with Orejudos at the Illinois Ballet for many years, to perform the pas de deux from *The Charioteer* during a key moment in the 1992 International Mr. Leather competition—the first iteration without Orejudos as "head judge." There is something moving about the scene: two highly trained classical dancers, male and female, performing for a room of leathermen. Were it not a memorial performance to the departed Orejudos, it might be impossible to imagine in the context of an IML event, but in the distorted VHS footage that still exists, one sees a leather-harnessed

Londo lifting Powell into the air to the responsive and rapturous applause of the gay leathermen in attendance.[20]

Though Orejudos's choreographic and artistic work is quite different from Fernandes's, these two artists share deep affinities (as well as a geographical meeting point). In some ways, perhaps this essay is nothing more than a simple attempt to introduce them more formally to each other. What commands—of writing or otherwise—can do such suturing work? As I write, I imagine Fernandes's archival encounter with Orejudos—both in terms of finding the VHS anthology and, in a much broader sense, with the institution of the LA&M itself. I imagine the ghost of Orejudos haunting the halls of the Graham Foundation, watching *The Master and Form* with bemused approval. I imagine each teaching the other their choreography—in a dance studio and in a bar. I imagine looks and laughing. In my mind, theirs is already a duet, performed in a queer time signature shuttling between past, present, and future.

1 André Lepecki, *Exhausting Dance: Performance and the Politics of Movement* (New York and London: Routledge, 2006), 6.

2 For more on these terms and their genesis, see Andy Campbell, *Bound Together: Leather, Sex, Archives, and Contemporary Art* (Manchester: Manchester University Press, 2019).

3 In addition to ballet, Fernandes also pressurizes histories of Modernist dance (most notably the technique and choreography of Martha Graham). Another expansive text on Fernandes could integrate and compare his critique and embrace of ballet, Modernist, and avant-garde dance.

4 The author in discussion with Brendan Fernandes on January 15, 2021.

5 Brendan Fernandes, "Ballet Kink," http://www.brendanfernandes.ca/ballet-kink, accessed January 15, 2021.

6 Claire Bishop, "Delegated Performance: Outsourcing Authenticity," *October* 140 (Spring 2012): 91.

7 For example, while some ballet dancers are handsomely paid, most struggle to earn a living wage. Also, some contemporary kink communities give the impression that to be a competent player one must purchase specialized and often expensive gear, potentially creating class boundaries as to who can be a legible participant in community spaces.

8 Bishop, "Delegated Performance," 108.

9 Ibid., 111–12.

10 The Leather Archives & Museum, "About the LA&M," https://leatherarchives.org/about/about-the-la-m, accessed January 15, 2021.

11 At the time of his passing, Orejudos was living with his other long-term lover Robert Yuhnke in Boulder, Colorado.

12 Etienne is only one of the pseudonyms Orejudos used in his career, but it was the most enduring. Etienne is the francophone version of Stephen (one of Orejudos's given names) and was also a character in Frank Yerby's *The Foxes of Harrow* (1946), a dynastic novel set in pre-Civil War New Orleans that Orejudos was reading when he devised the name. New Orleans was also a place where Orejudos would later find work with the Delta Festival Ballet.

13 I would point any reader wishing to learn more about Orejudos to one of the best summations of his life and career, Dwight Skeates's essay, "Foundations: Dom Orejudos, the Artist Etienne," in Jakob VanLammeren and José Santiago Pérez, eds., *Leather Archives & Museum: 25 Years* (Chicago: Leather Archives & Museum, 2016), 35–39.

14 For more on the history of IML see Joseph Bean, *International Mr. Leather: 25 Years of Champions* (Nazca Plains Corporation, 2004).

15 Jack Fritscher, *Gay San Francisco: Eyewitness Drummer*, ed. Mark Hemry (San Francisco: Palm Drive Publishing, 2008), 437.

16 Kenan Heise, "Dom Orejudos, 58, Ballet Dancer and Artist Known as 'Etienne,'" *Chicago Tribune*, October 2, 1991.

17 Fritscher, *Gay San Francisco*, 455.

18 Tom of Finland, Letter to Dom Orejudos, September 30, 1979, Twitter/@Artist_Etienne, May 6, 2016, https://twitter.com/Artist_Etienne/status/728732668607668225/photo/1, accessed January 15, 2021.

19 This was part of a larger, ongoing effort by National Educational Television (a precursor to the Public Broadcasting Service) to record modern and classical dance for public television audiences. Orejudos choreographed many such programs for NET.

20 The Leather Archives & Museum, "The Charioteer Performed at IML 1992," Vimeo, https://vimeo.com/151318786, accessed January 15, 2021.

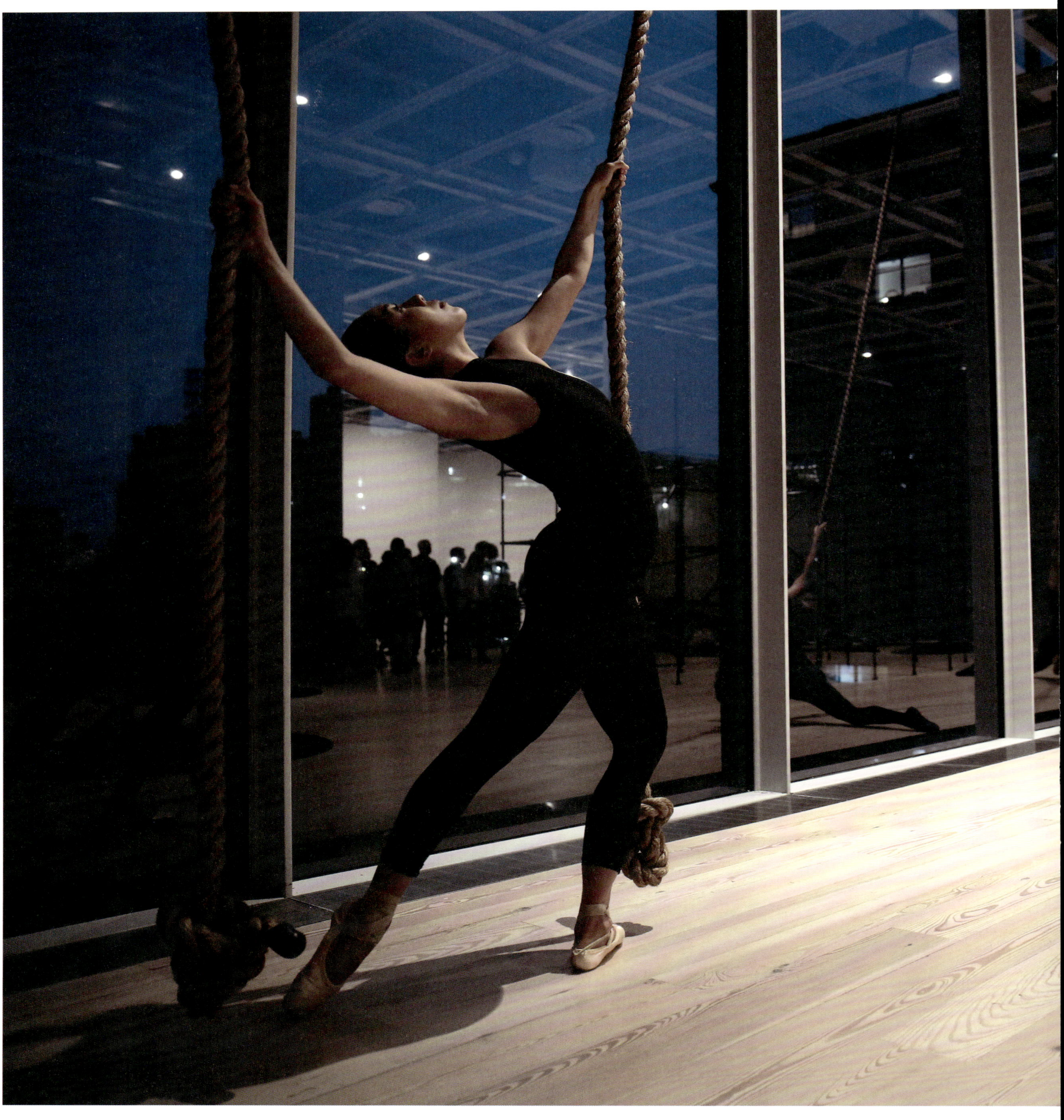

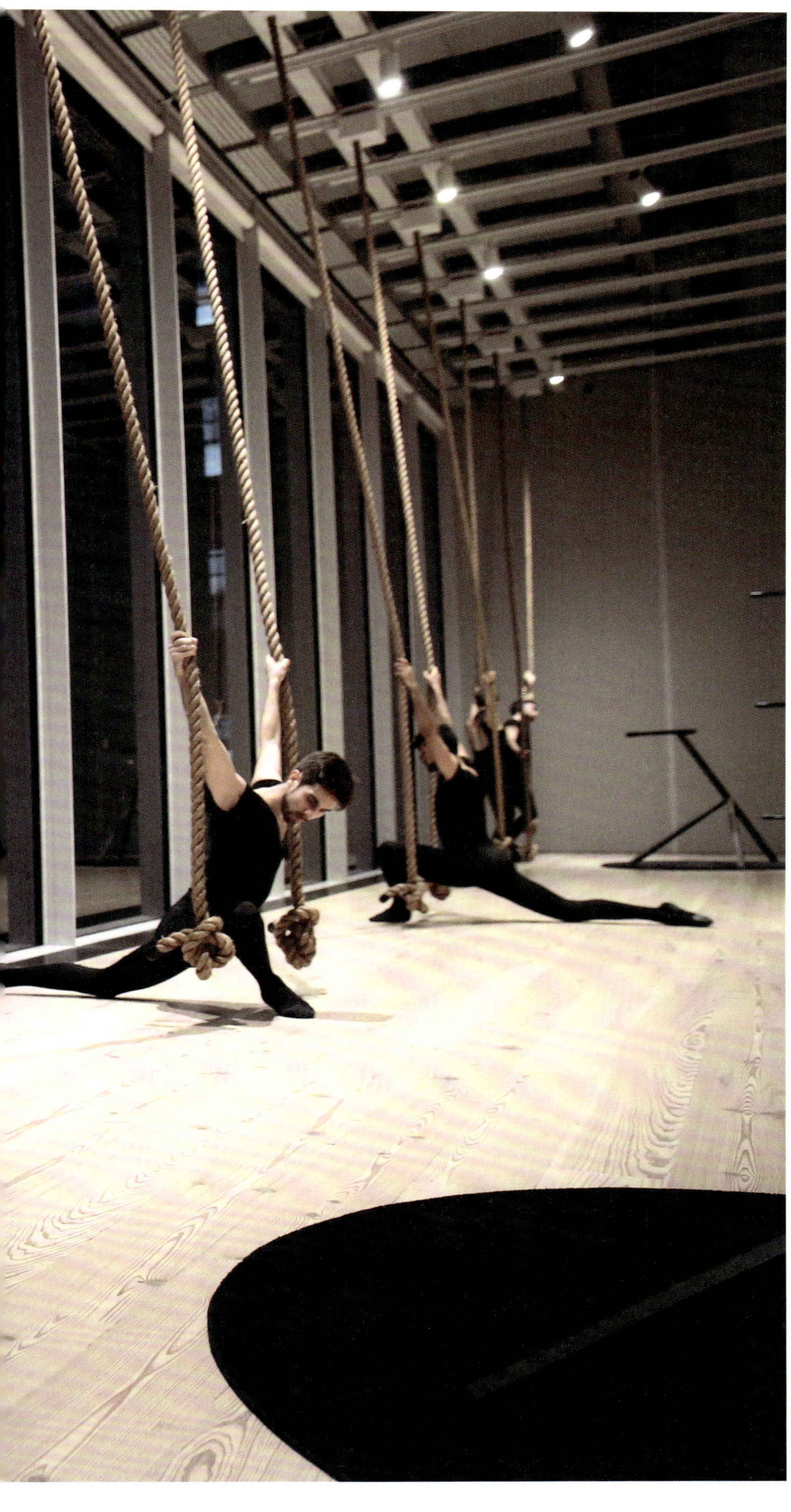

Surface Movements

Hendrik Folkerts

The role of sculpture in performance is not reducible to bodies as living sculpture in a certain scenography or sculpture as mere prop in performance, but rather it is a question that needs to be addressed through the inherent materiality and relationality of the two mediums. Whether by way of the body vis-à-vis sculpture, or vice versa, it requires a discussion about agency and how performative gestures are enacted through sculptural forms. To that end, I remember Brendan Fernandes sharing a story about his education as an artist. While a student at York University in Toronto, he moved—or, I should say, danced—across the hallway from his dance class to his sculpture course, from the leotard to the mold and back again, uniting his classical training in ballet with a burgeoning interest in sculpture.[1] The anecdote conjures a powerful image and can easily be regarded as the premise for Fernandes's practice, reconciling the body and the object through the intertwining paths of dance and sculpture. For Fernandes, the two forms have always existed in relation to each other, albeit more subtle or pronounced at times, and his approach points to the many intricacies of how dance and sculpture co-exist in the expanded field of performance today. For instance, how does the relationship between the two reverberate in space? Can sculpture mirror the body and reflect from its surface back onto the flesh? What happens if the agency of a living body is transposed onto wood, iron, or steel? To address these queries, I will explore the evolving relationship between performance and sculpture in Fernandes's practice, introducing a number of terms that speak to how Fernandes configures this relationship, and then extrapolating it through the notions of support structure and the agency of sculptural objects.

Fernandes's sculptural practice of the last decade includes various approaches that each suggest different relationships between the object and the body, as well as diverging attitudes towards the art object itself as a site of representation, value, and signification, and as a "thing" that is void of its previous functionality—a Heideggerian *dérive*. In *Standing Leg* (2014) and *Still Move* (2014), Fernandes introduces objects as *prosthetic devices* or extensions of the body [Reference Images p. 128]. Evoking Fernandes's own experience and labor as a dancer and probing the body politics of classical ballet, the solo performance *Standing Leg* comprises a meticulous choreography with a foot stretcher, a wooden device typically used by ballet dancers to manipulate their feet to attain an "ideal" arched shape. The video *Still Move* shows an undefined space, in which a rubber massage ball that is typically used to relieve stress and tension in the muscles is rubbed against a body, shot in extreme close-up. Manifesting as both discrete object and as part of the anatomy of the undisclosed body, the rubber ball is simultaneously an extension of and integral to that body, proposing an important counterpoint to *Standing Leg* in emphasizing release and care over constraint and oppression.

A second category, of sculpture as *relational object*, is apparent in the performance and photography series *The Working Move* (2012) [Reference Images p. 128]. Centered around endurance and repetition, the live performance was staged as a long-form rehearsal for seven dancers, directed by a figure reminiscent of a ballet instructor who stops and restarts the sequences based on her evaluation of the dancers' performance. As part of the choreography, the dancers interact with a number of white museum plinths of various sizes and heights, which also form a scenography. As the performers push and pull these heavy bases or use them as support for choreographed movement, they become mobile and modular apparatuses that point to the long and problematic history of the display of othered objects in the museum context, whether it be ethnographic artifacts or living bodies presented as objects of study. This is further amplified in the photographs of the performance, which capture, alternatingly, the dancers clad in ballet costumes displayed on the plinths or moving with the plinths. The specific relationship between the moving body and the plinth not only anticipates Fernandes's later work about the systems of value that commodify and institutionalize the body in dance and visual art, but also proposes an interdependent dynamic between performance and sculpture, blurring categories of performer/prop and body/object.[2]

The sculptures in *Inverted Pyramid* (2014) and *Stand Tall* (2017) serve as *choreographic mimesis*, mirroring the positions and movements of the live dancers that perform alongside them—or, arguably, vice versa [Reference Images p. 128]. The sculptural choreography of *Inverted Pyramid* is loosely based on a famous scene in the Orientalist ballet *La Bayadère* (1877), in which the deceased *bayadère* (a female Hindu dancer) appears to the warrior Solor in an opium-induced dream by having the entire *corps de ballet* enter the stage one by one to perform an extended sequence of arabesques, also referred to as "inverted pyramids." In *Inverted Pyramid*, one ballet dancer performs the series of arabesques, competing against static, abstracted cut-outs of her own body until she can endure no longer, moving the sculptures to initiate the next sequence of the choreography. Eliciting similar notions of labor, endurance, and power relations, and de facto uniting the arguments of *The Working Move* and *Inverted Pyramid*, Fernandes's performance and installation *Stand Tall*, which debuted at Cravens World collection in the University of Buffalo Art Galleries, saw an ensemble of six dancers perform alongside a series of four wire sculptures. The sculptures are evocative of the armatures used for the display of African masks in the adjacent galleries and served as buoyant companions to the dancers who wore white replicas of those masks and, in powerful though only partial ways, restituted some of the objects in the Cravens World collection by bringing them back into a relational and performative atmosphere.[3]

Fernandes synthesizes these categories of prosthetic device, relational object, and choreographic mimesis in two recent projects, *The Master and Form* and *Contract and Release*, advancing a more comprehensive approach to the entanglement of performance and sculpture in his practice. Both works are part of the artist's ongoing investigation of dance traditions and movement vocabularies, anchored in Fernandes's own history and practice as a dancer and choreographer. *The Master and Form*, developed in collaboration with the architecture and design collective Norman Kelley, debuted at the Graham Foundation in Chicago in 2018 and was subsequently featured in the 2019 Whitney Biennial in New York. The work consists of a durational performance of four hours in conjunction with an installation of numerous sculptures, referred to by Fernandes as devices, which take the form of five structures produced in dark wood, a steel cage-like armature, and thick ropes hanging from the ceiling of the gallery. In his use of such evocative materials, Fernandes draws on numerous references and resources, including fetish objects from the Leather Archives & Museum in Chicago, technical training objects that connote the arguably problematic notions of mastery and discipline in classical ballet, as well as anthropomorphic architecture. With *The Master and Form*, Fernandes enacts a significant shift in his practice: the sculptures are embedded in the live performances *and* presented as autonomous objects. In this double role, the sculptures are part of an installation that remains on view even when there is no performance taking place. In other words, their presence is not legitimized by liveness per se.

Similarly, *Contract and Release*, which premiered at the Noguchi Museum in Long Island City, New York, in 2019, introduces a series of sculptural devices that exist in relation to and separate from the body. These sculptures, most notably a series of six abstract rocking chairs titled *Still Release I–VI* (2019), were presented alongside a selection of Noguchi's works from the museum's collection that emblematized the artist's playful and corporeal approach to object-making as it pertains to the body. Taking its title from a famous technique by the American dancer, choreographer, and frequent Noguchi collaborator Martha Graham, *Contract and Release* challenges the fetishization of the body through such and other dance techniques. The procession of the dancers marks the beginning of the performance, as they enter the gallery executing a series of "Graham" walks and move towards Fernandes's sculptures. Fashioned after a series of rocking chairs by Noguchi that were designed *not* to rock, these devices are made functional, with the caveat that the dancers are not supposed to move the chairs. As a result, the dancers sit on the sculptures, their muscles constantly contracting and releasing as they keep the rocking chairs still. The position is, obviously, untenable and extremely exerting. As the dancers inevitably fall out of position, they perform another set of movements that are freer and more improvisational.[4] With *Contract and Release*, Fernandes transposes sheer physicality into the sculptural form of the rocking chair, which is not only suggestive of motion in and of itself, but also amplifies the dancers' minute muscle movements and physical exhaustion as they hold their position during the live performance—the hard wood and soft tissue becoming a spectacular microcosm of uncanny and eerie motility. This tension is heightened by the installation overall, which highlights Fernandes's and Noguchi's shared affinity for treating the museum as a non-neutral and politically-charged space in which both bodies and objects are subject to fetishizing impulses, yet also as a space that carries the potential to displace violent and hegemonic narratives.[5]

The relationship between sculptures and living bodies in *The Master and Form* and *Contract and Release* offer an important point of departure to meditate on the meaning of a support structure. Although physical and conceptual manifestations of such structures are ubiquitous in cultural production and spatial practices, the discourse around them is still largely absent. Writer and architect Céline Condorelli argues that "[t]here can be no discourse on support, only discourse in support."[6] In other words, the notion of the support structure cannot be approached through an analytical model that presupposes an objective, external position from its object of study, but rather needs to be embedded within support itself, understanding its operations as part of the very same structural modality. Condorelli identifies four key coordinates that articulate an actionable definition of support structure: support always occurs in proximity to something; given its subsidiary position, support "sits right against the object" and, as a consequence, exists in contrast and antagonism; support is supplementary, both external and inherent to the object it holds; and lastly, it is temporary, existing within a logic of disappearance once the object of concern can be independent.[7] This insightful definition resonates with Fernandes's scrutiny of the historical and institutional systems that shape and condition the body in the world of dance, whether it be physically or metaphorically. Akin to the foot stretcher that molded Fernandes's feet into the "perfect" arch in *Standing Leg* or the white plinths that regulate the choreography of bodies in *The Working Move*, the sculptures in *The Master and Form* and *Contract and Release* support the bodies that use these objects to hold their position, although it should be added that this is also their most torturous employment. As the dancers move from object to object, exerting their bodies in positions and sequences that are strenuous to say the least, the visual pleasure of observing their poses soon merges with the discomfort of bearing witness to the violence that is inflicted upon their bodies by the objects. Fernandes deftly positions the sculpture as a support structure that is simultaneously hostile and accommodating, offering pleasure and relief as well as pain and exhaustion—the resonant body politics in ballet and other forms of classical dance. In these pieces, bodies and objects exist simultaneously and within a narrative of interdependence, echoing Condorelli's definition of support as proximity, antagonism, supplement, and temporality.

Fernandes advances his ongoing exploration of sculpture by installing the objects in *The Master and Form* and *Contract and Release* so as to populate the space independently from live bodies, effectively destabilizing the persistent interpretation of performance as "activation." Generally speaking, it has been the unfortunate fate of spaces, situations, and objects in works that also encompass a live element to be "activated" by performance rather than approached through their own materiality and relationality. Moving beyond activation, and thus beyond seeing the sculptures as a mere extension, stand-in, or substitute for the human body, allows Fernandes to embrace and experiment with form, pose, motion, and agency in the non-human, inanimate objects that are part of these works. The artist does this, in part, by acknowledging these objects' presence through an intentional *absence* of the body. In this way, Fernandes's recent deployment of sculpture sits in alignment with certain aspects of the discourse on new materialism. Departing from the mind-body dialectic, new materialism embraces posthuman theory and aspects of feminist philosophy that champion Marxist, phenomenological, and embodied materialism to center matter, both human and non-human, as a critical lens through which we might understand the connections between embodiment, material agency, and subject formation within the global context of late capitalism. Rather than proposing a uniform school of thought, new materialism is fundamentally interdisciplinary and seeks to move beyond the body-mind or nature-culture binaries of humanist thought that has pervaded Western philosophy for centuries. In a recent interview, feminist theorist Karen Barad summarily encapsulates the scope of new materialism, pointing to "the entanglement of matter and meaning [that] calls into question this set of dualisms that places nature on one side and culture on the other [a]nd which separates off matters of fact from matters of concern … and matters of care."[8]

In particular, new materialism's equal approach to human and non-human agents is crucial for the purpose of this essay, as are Barad's notes on agency and the neologism "intra-action." Agency is commonly described as something that is given to or to be had by someone—or rarer still, given to or had by *something*. However, Barad suggests that agency actually unfolds dialogically, through what she terms "intra-action": "[A]gency is a matter of intra-acting; it is an enactment, not something that someone or something has. Agency is doing/being in its intra-activity."[9] This "intra-activity" is closely tied to how Barad describes the interdependent, almost symbiotic, relationship between an object and its measuring agencies. She argues: "[T]he object and the measuring agencies emerge from, rather than precede, the intra-action that produces them."[10] In typical 2020-fashion, a year shrouded by the COVID-19 pandemic, one might explain this as a body cell coming into contact with a hostile agent: it responds, they become entangled, and both of their resulting behavior is based on this interaction/intra-action. Not entirely dissimilar to how Condorelli sees a theory on support structures as being embedded within a support structure, Barad argues that we can never place ourselves outside of (the interaction with) our object of study: "Practices of knowing and being are not isolable; they are mutually implicated. We don't obtain knowledge by standing outside the world; we know because we are *of* the world."[11]

This was on my mind when I visited the Graham Foundation on a rainy Saturday to see Fernandes's sculptures in *The Master and Form* outside of the staged performances of the work. I entered their space as much as they did mine. The geometric shapes of these objects aligned with the lines of the bodies that had previously used them as a support structure. Their presence was framed by the surrounding architecture of the Prairie-style mansion that is the Graham Foundation's Madlener House. The absence of sound emphasized the physical properties of the rooms that housed the objects and in turn made the objects seem suspended in time and space. This dialog reverberated across two floors and throughout the body of work. I remember my physical engagement with the sculptures; a manifest desire to touch them and simultaneously feeling repelled by their harshness as disciplinary devices. I could sense their resonances with other works by Fernandes, *Contract and Release*, *Standing Leg*, *The Working Move*, *Still Move*, *Stand Tall*, *Inverted Pyramid*, and so on. At that moment in time, these objects were the inhabitants of the house, following in the footsteps of the Madlener family. The materiality of Fernandes's sculptural agents—wood, leather, iron, steel—was tactile, smooth, seductive, and repugnant in equal measure next to my human skin, flesh, and bones. We met again, a couple of months later, at the Whitney Museum of American Art. My intimate encounters at the mansion in Chicago had made way for a grandiose space, with New York's Meat Packing district as an illustrious background. The sculptures danced more in this room, captured in mid-flight, though I missed sitting down with them. Here, they commanded the space, reciprocating the attention of whomever came to see them, waiting for the *Still Release* chairs to join them in the action a few months later, on the other side of the city.

Fernandes is part of a generation of artists who continuously traverse and intersect histories of dance, performance, and visual art in their practice, along with the gallery and theater spaces these histories are traditionally anchored in.[12] The terms of such histories are complicated by artists such as Fernandes, who reconfigure the spatial and temporal coordinates of performance, constantly moving between performance as event, as duration, and as installation and exhibition. Necessarily, this is paired with radical new approaches and, in this essay, I have outlined a handful of typologies that emerge from Fernandes's practice: sculpture as prosthetic device vis-à-vis the body, sculpture as a relational object situated in the time and space of a performance, and sculpture as choreographic mimesis, aimed at mirroring and anticipating the positions and movements of live dancers. Fernandes's works *The Master and Form* and *Contract and Release* invite an understanding of sculptures as support structures and as objects whose agency as non-human actors is determined through and entangled with the experience of other phenomena including the bodies that interact with them and the spaces they inhabit. Their material, spatial and performative qualities coalesce in movements that happen on and against their hard surfaces. In the end, it is not only Fernandes, but also us, moving across the hall from the sculpture workshop to the ballet class and back again.

1 Conversation between Brendan Fernandes and Maite Borjabad López-Pastor, November 16, 2019, Monique Meloche Gallery, Chicago.

2 For a more in-depth discussion about the relationship between performer and prop, as well as the term "sculptural prop," see Kristen Poor, "Handling Judson's Objects," in Ana Janevski and Thomas J. Lax, eds., *Judson Dance Theater: The Work Is Never Done* (New York: The Museum of Modern Art, 2018), 76–81.

3 For a more exhaustive discussion of Fernandes's early work, including *The Working Move*, *Standing Leg*, and *Still Move*, see Crystal Mowry, ed., *Still Move: Brendan Fernandes* (London: Black Dog Publishing, 2016).

4 Fernandes sustained his own injury while doing Graham-technique contractions, which brought his career as a professional dancer to an untimely end. In an interesting anticipation of events, one of the first sculptures that Fernandes made as a student was a curvy piece created to embody the idea of contraction.

5 Dakin Hart, "Brendan Fernandes: Contract and Release," exhibition brochure of *Brendan Fernandes: Contract and Release*, The Noguchi Museum, September 11, 2019 – March 8, 2020.

6 Céline Condorelli, "Directions for Use," in Céline Condorelli, ed., *Support Structures* (Berlin: Sternberg Press, 2009), 13.

7 Condorelli, "Directions for Use", 14–22.

8 "Interview with Karen Barad," in Rick Dolfijn and Iris van der Tuin, eds., *New Materialism* (London: Open Humanities Press, 2012), 50.

9 Karen Barad, *Meeting the Universe Halfway: Quantum Physics and the Entanglement of Matter and Meaning* (Durham: Duke University Press, 2007), 235.

10 Barad, *Meeting the Universe Halfway*, 128.

11 Ibid., 185.

12 Regarding the staging of dance and performance in museums, see Claire Bishop, "Black Box, White Cube, Gray Zone: Dance Exhibitions and Audience Attention," *TDR: The Drama Review* 62, no. 2 (Summer, 2018), 22–42.

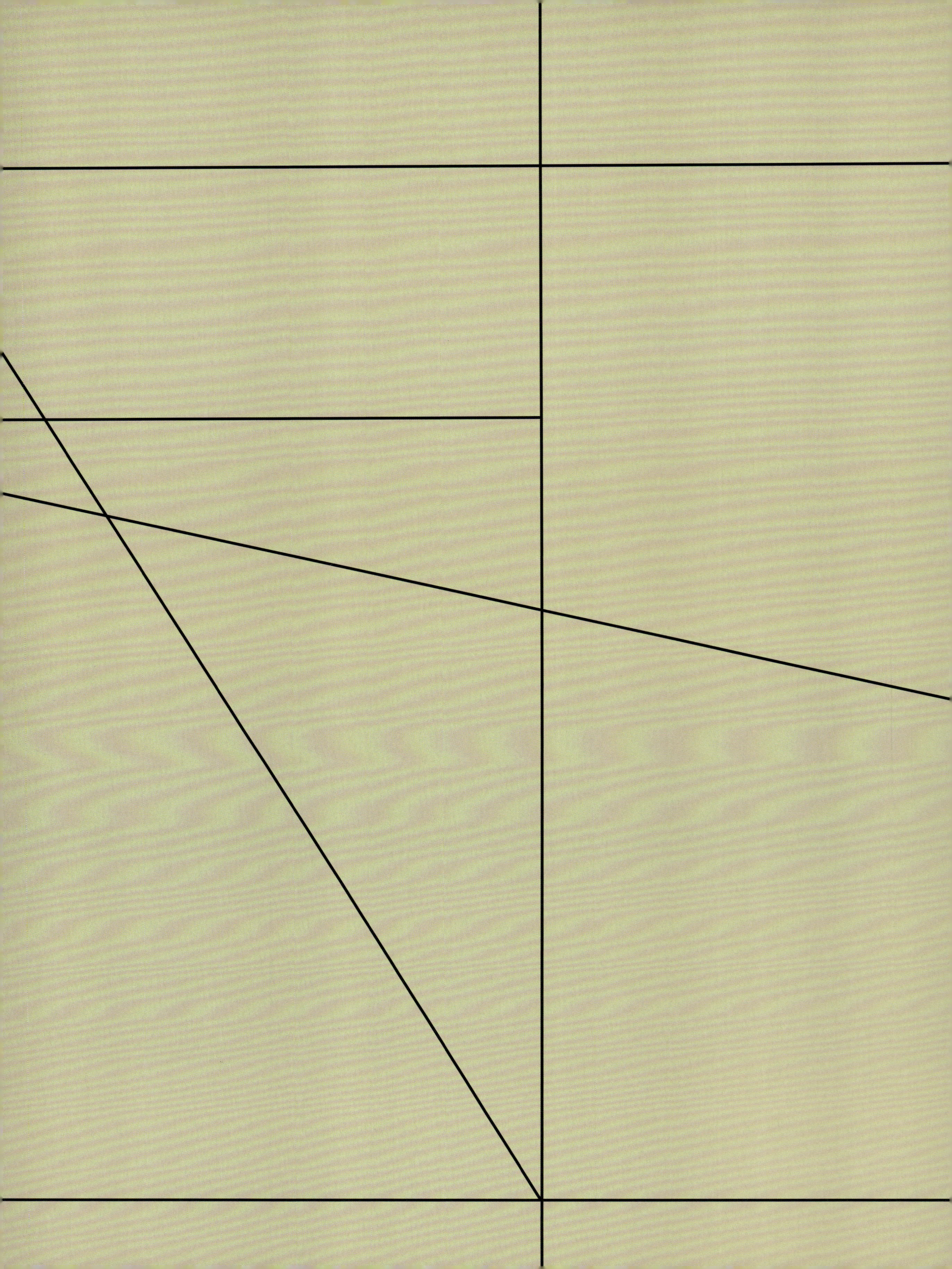

Contract and Release

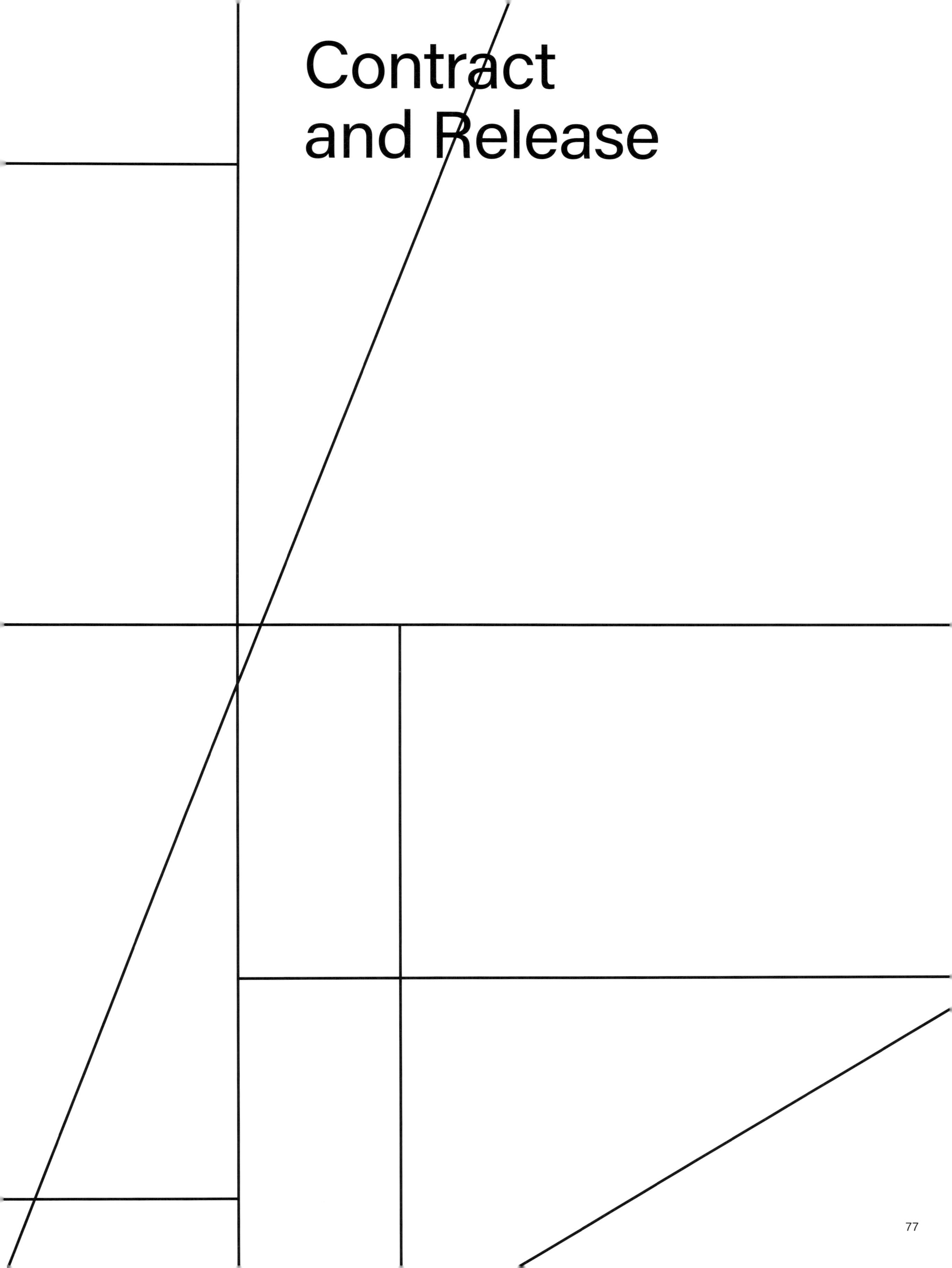

Score

Walks

1
2
3 Turn Transition 1
2
3 Break

Chairs

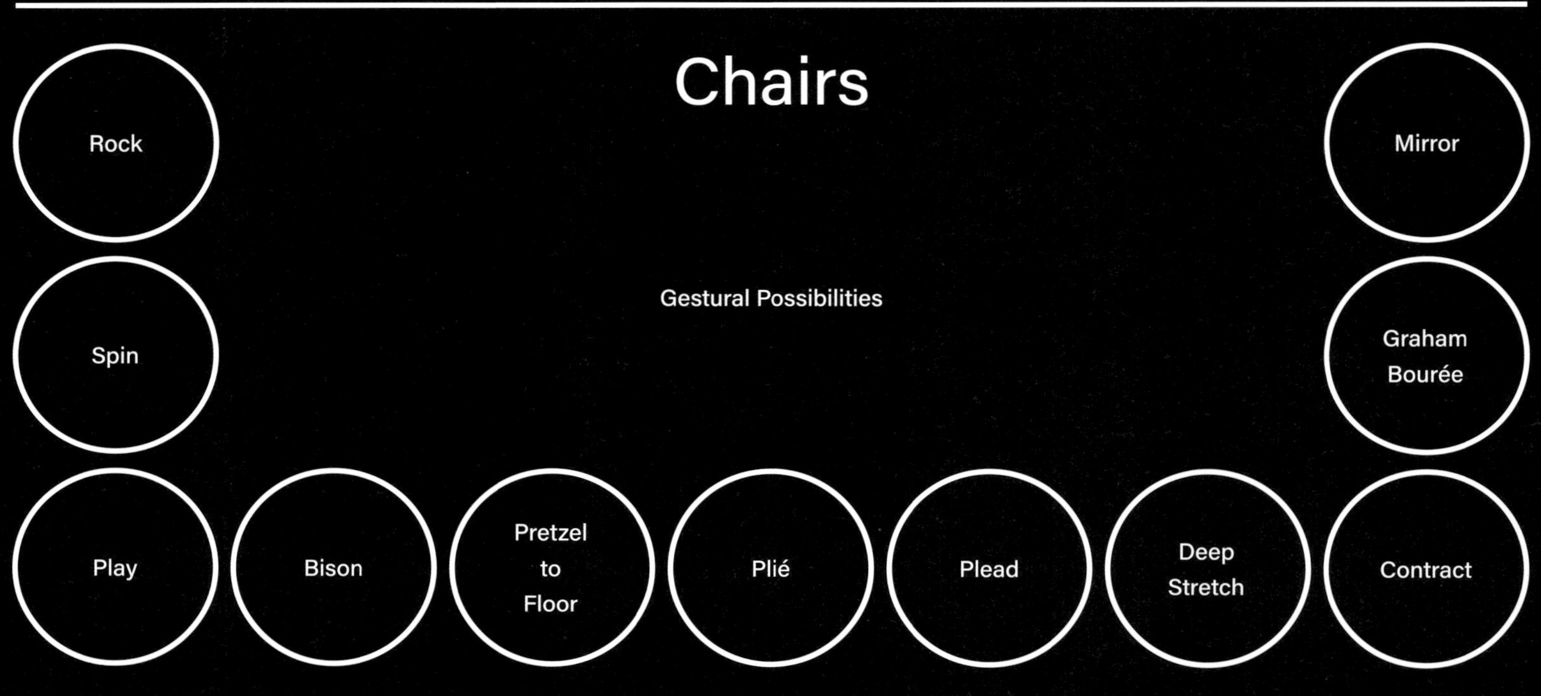

Walks

1
2
3 Turn Transition 1
2
3 Break

Assembly

Build One Sculpture at a Time

Nurture	Motifs	Show Generosity
Grieve	Care	New Noguchi

Pause and Leave Space

Walks

1
2
3 Turn

Transition

1
2
3 Break

Chairs

Rock

Spin

Play

Gestural Possibilities

Mirror

Graham Bourée

Contract

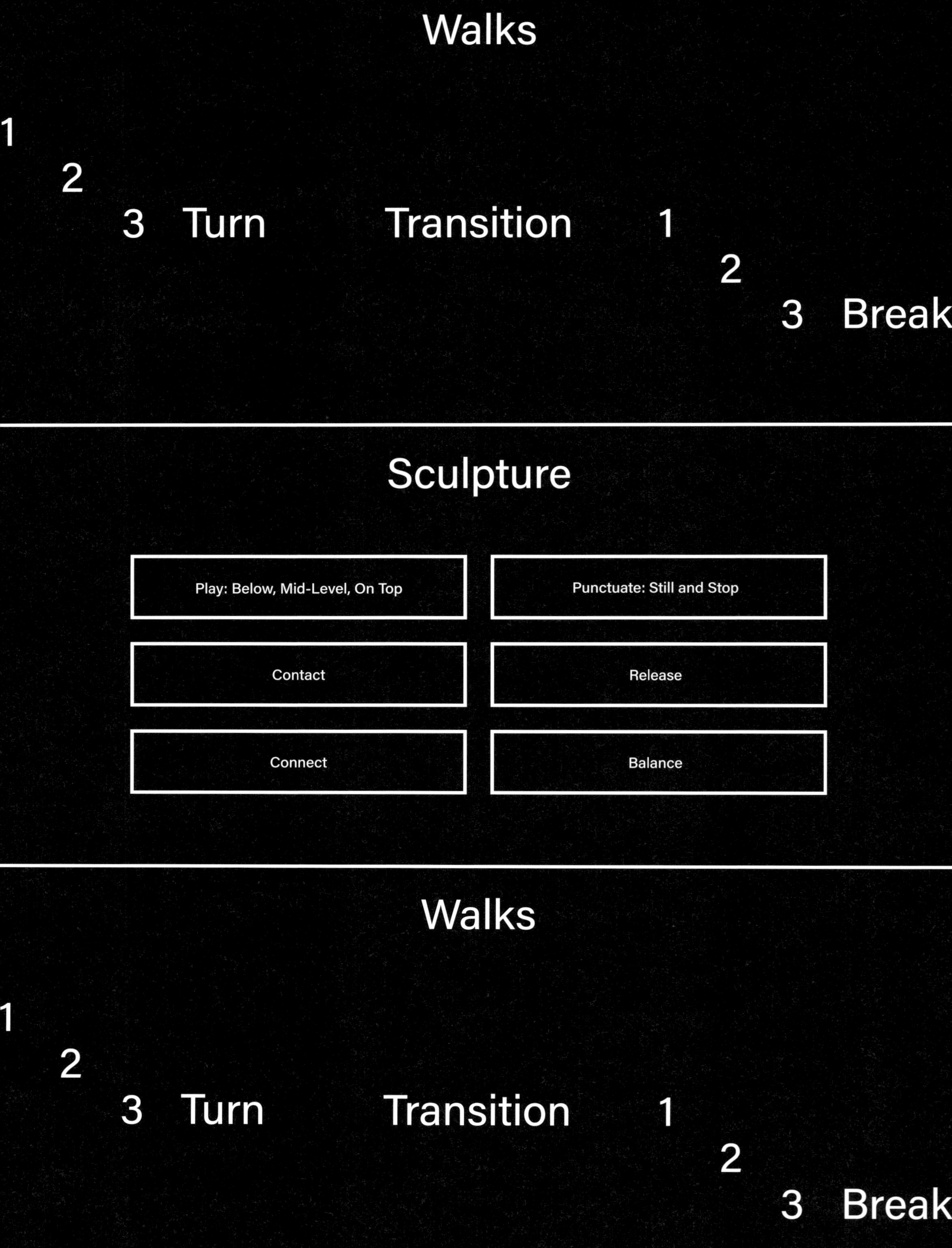
Walks
1
2
3 Turn
Transition
1
2
3 Break
Sculpture
Play: Below, Mid-Level, On Top
Punctuate: Still and Stop
Contact
Release
Connect
Balance
Walks
1
2
3 Turn
Transition
1
2
3 Break

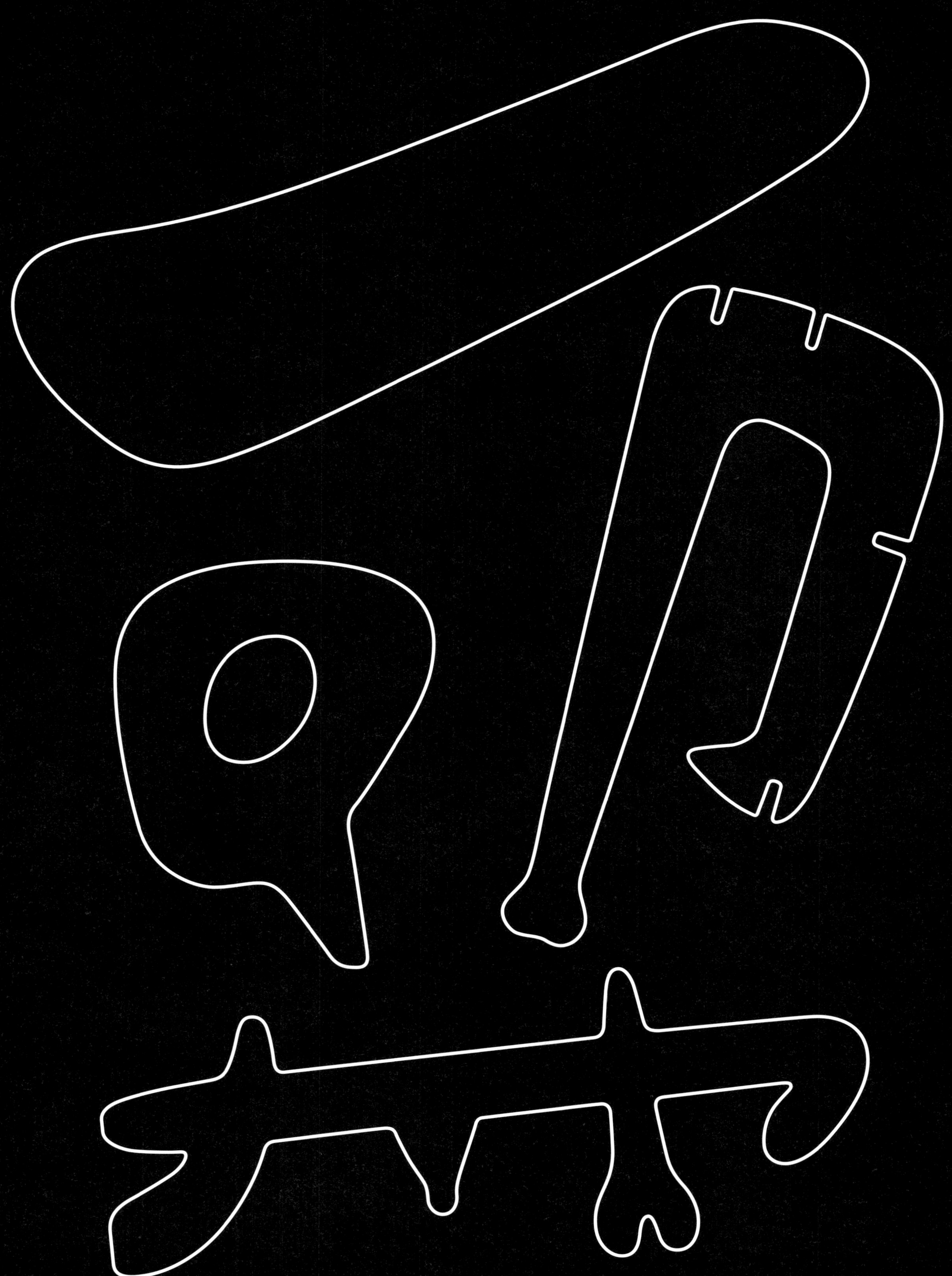

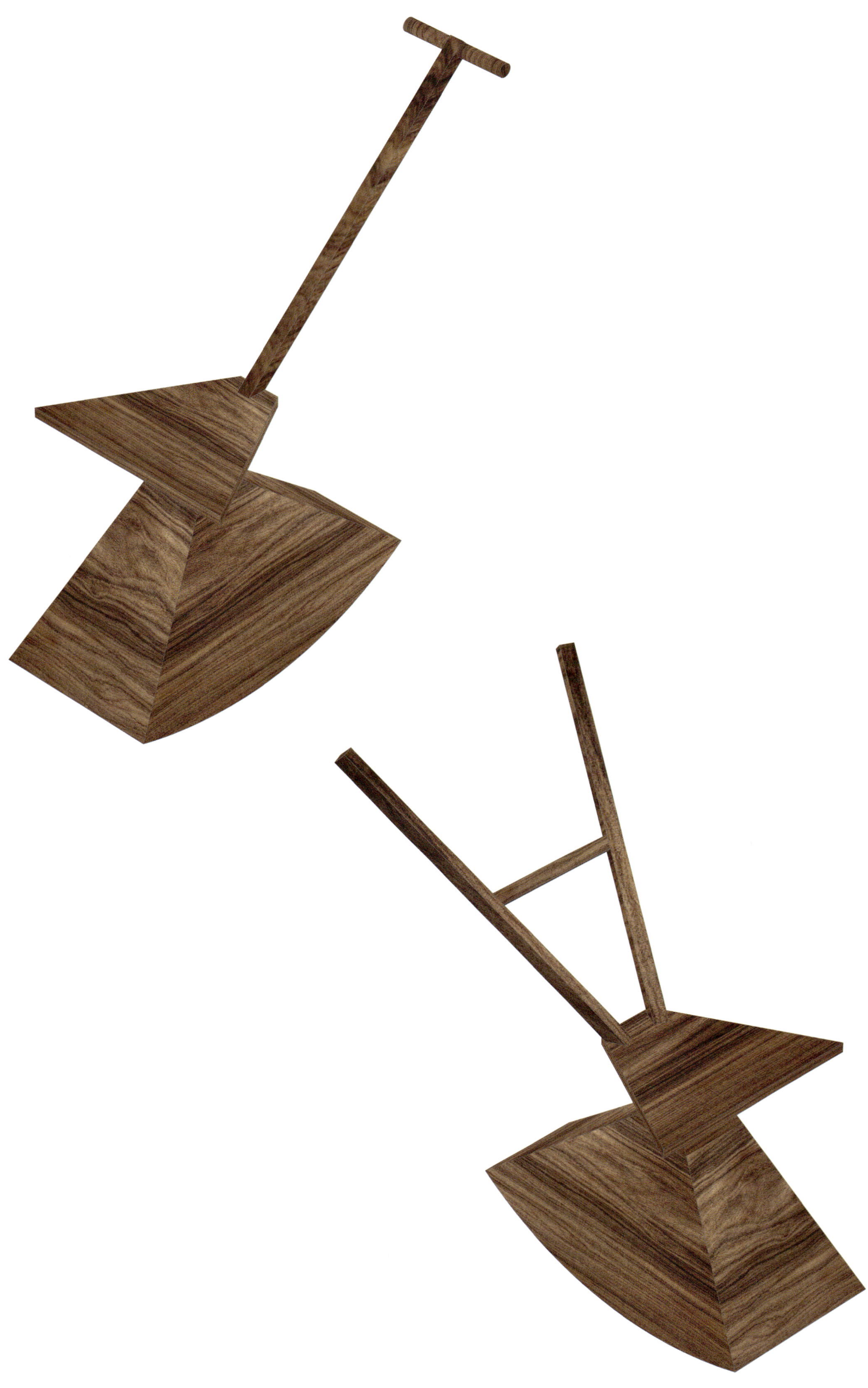

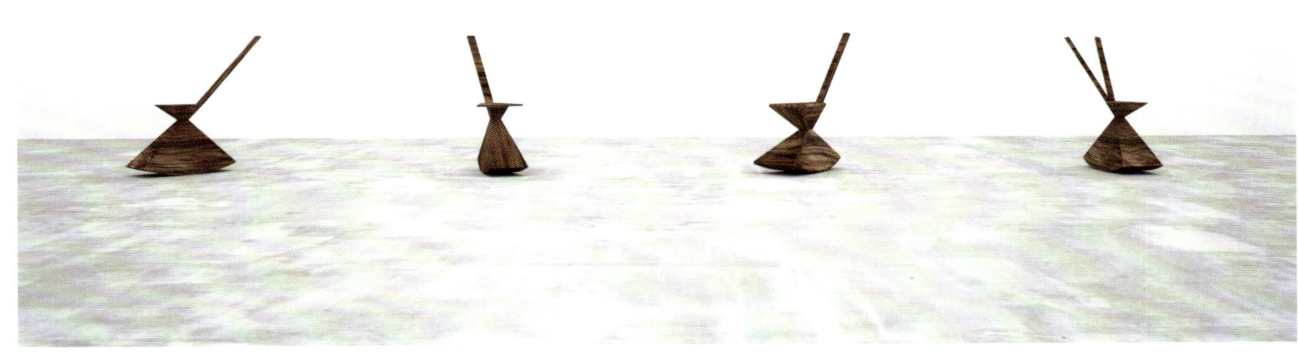

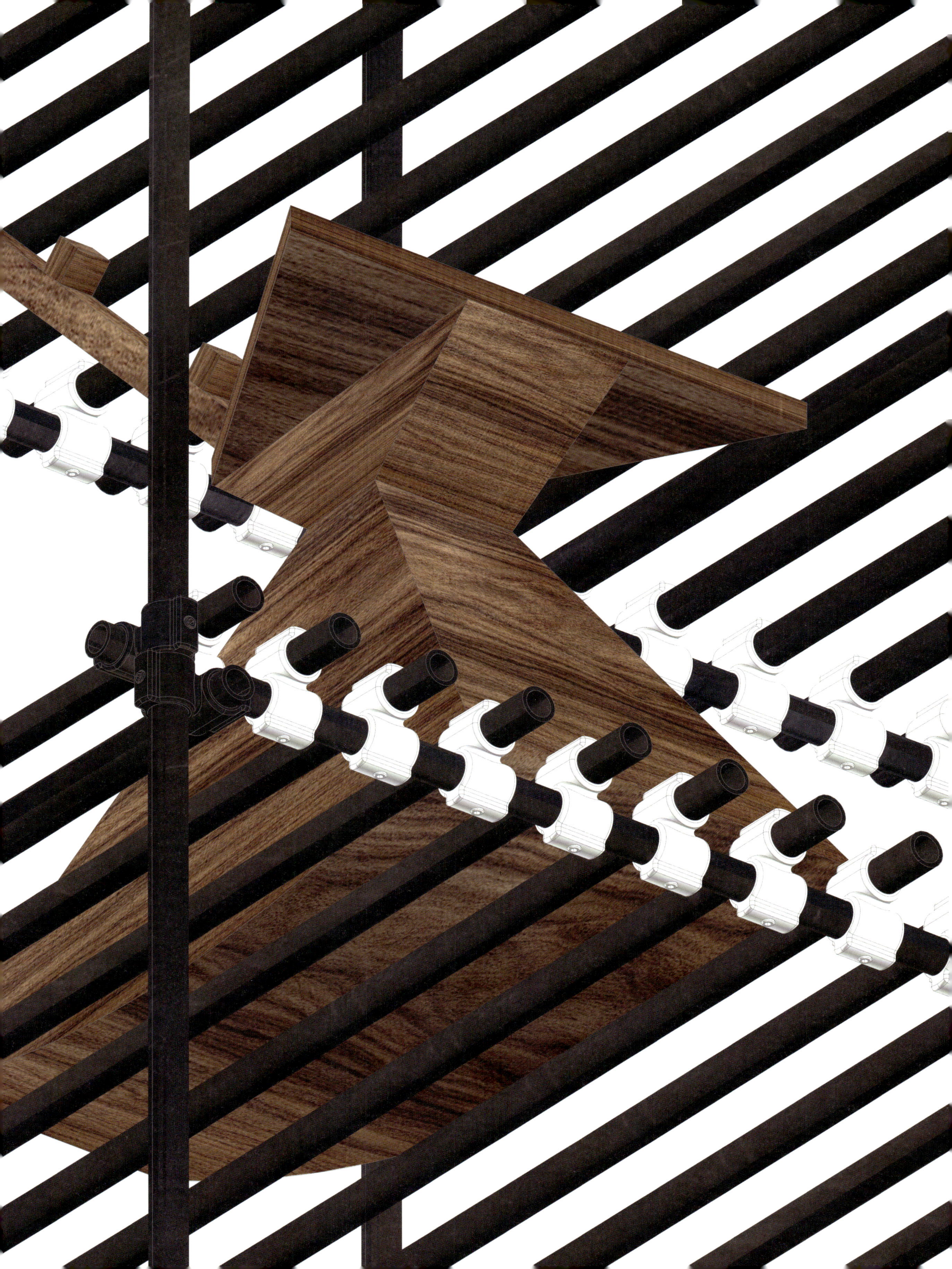

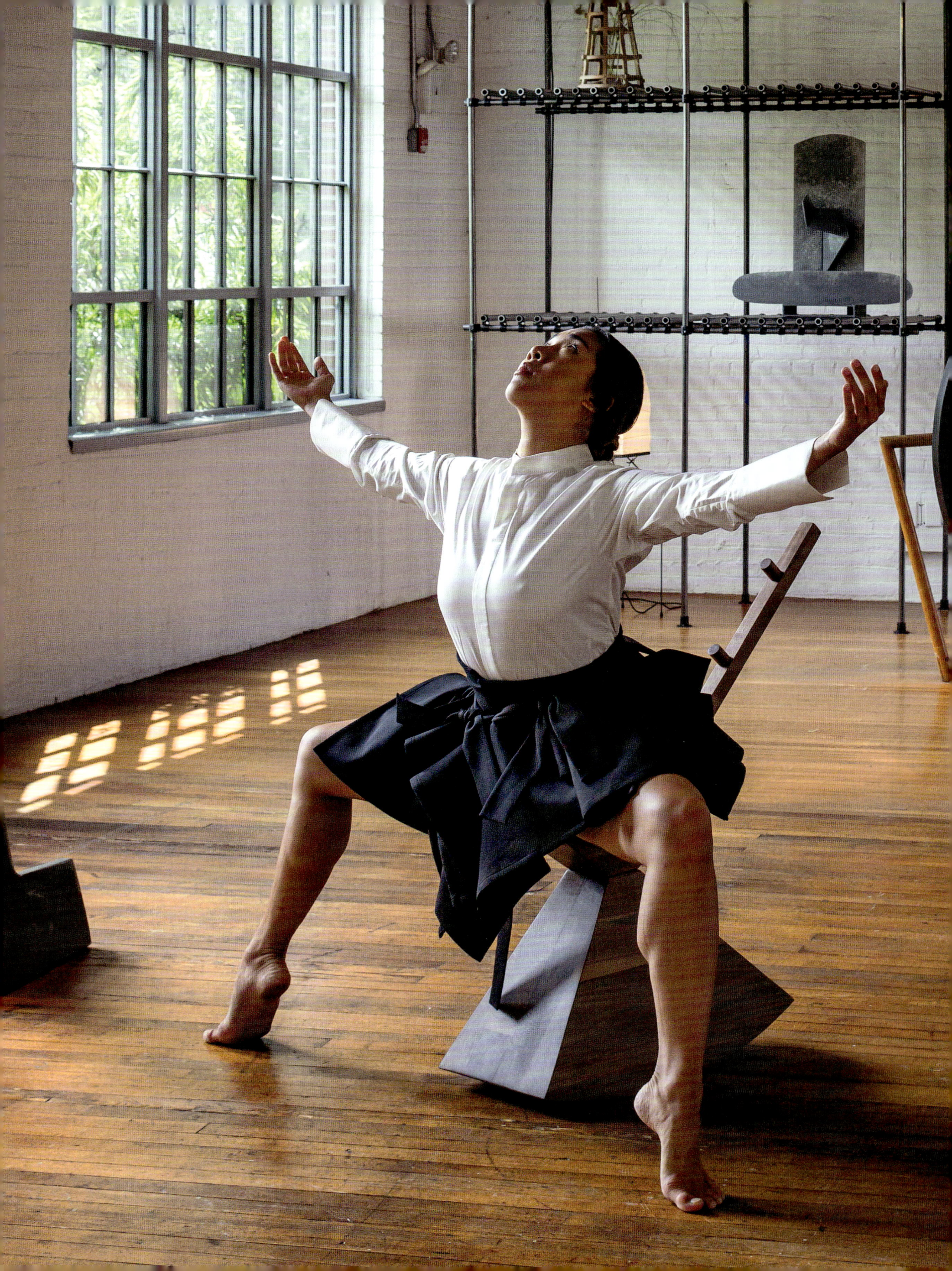

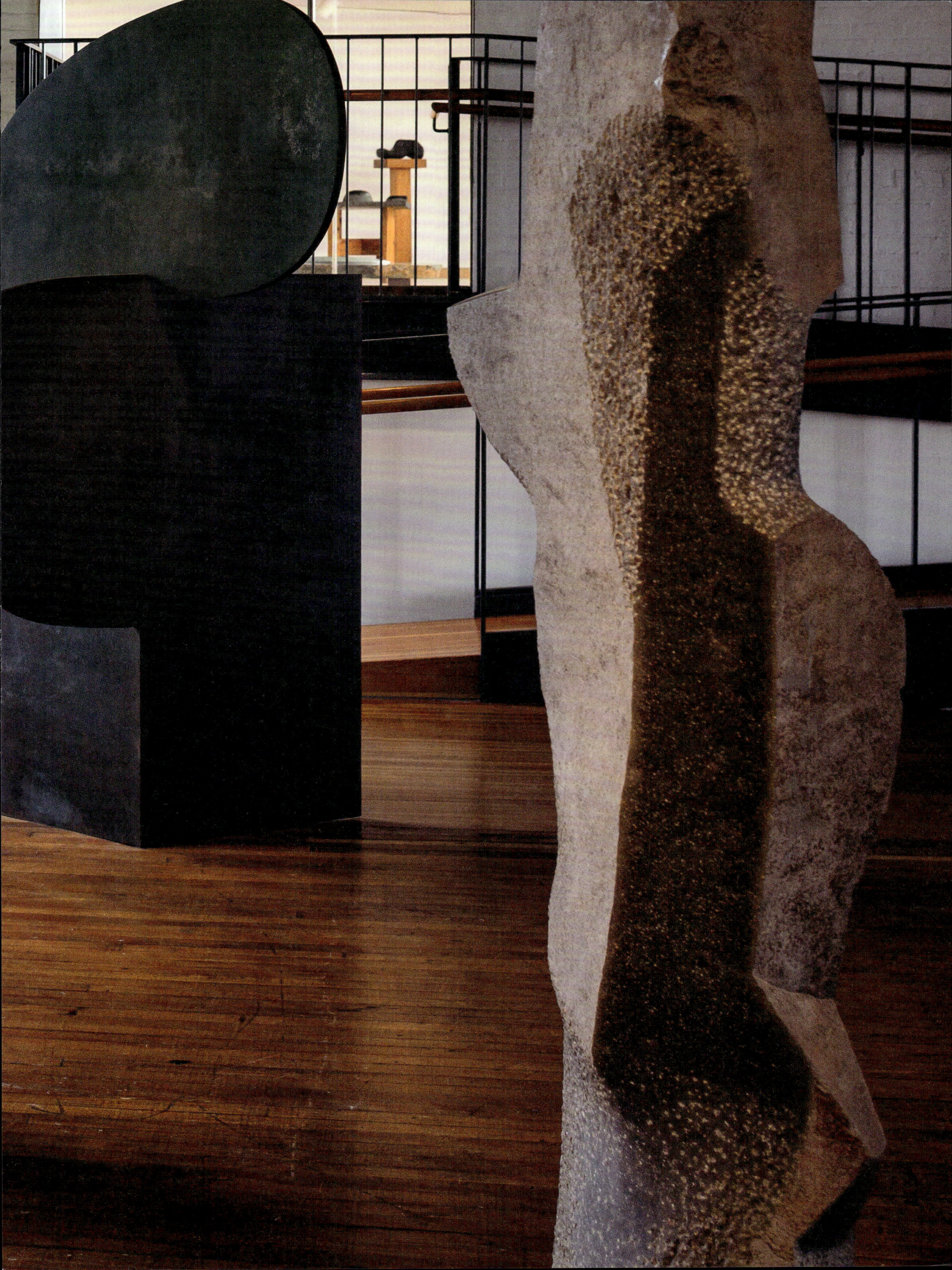

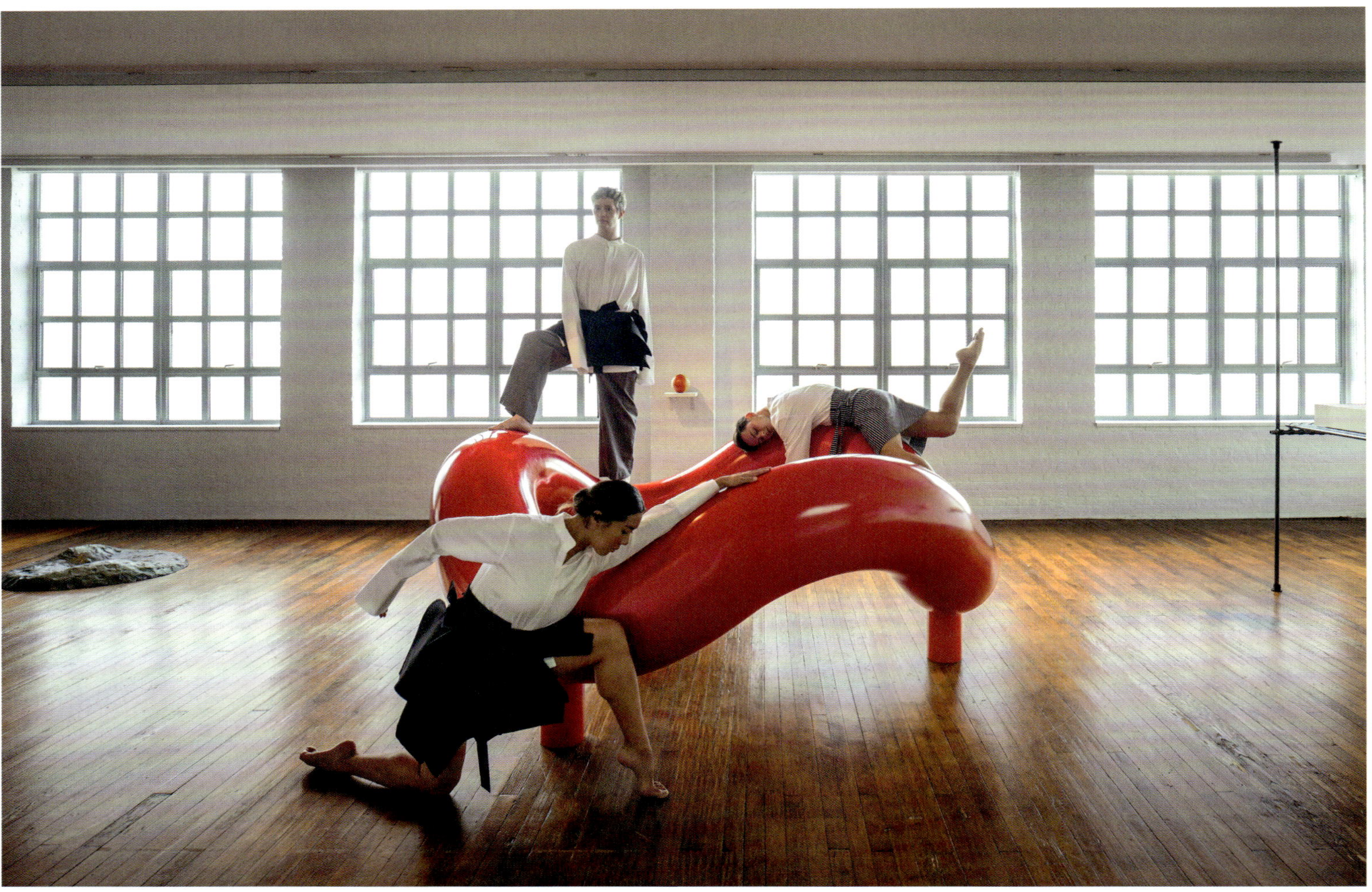

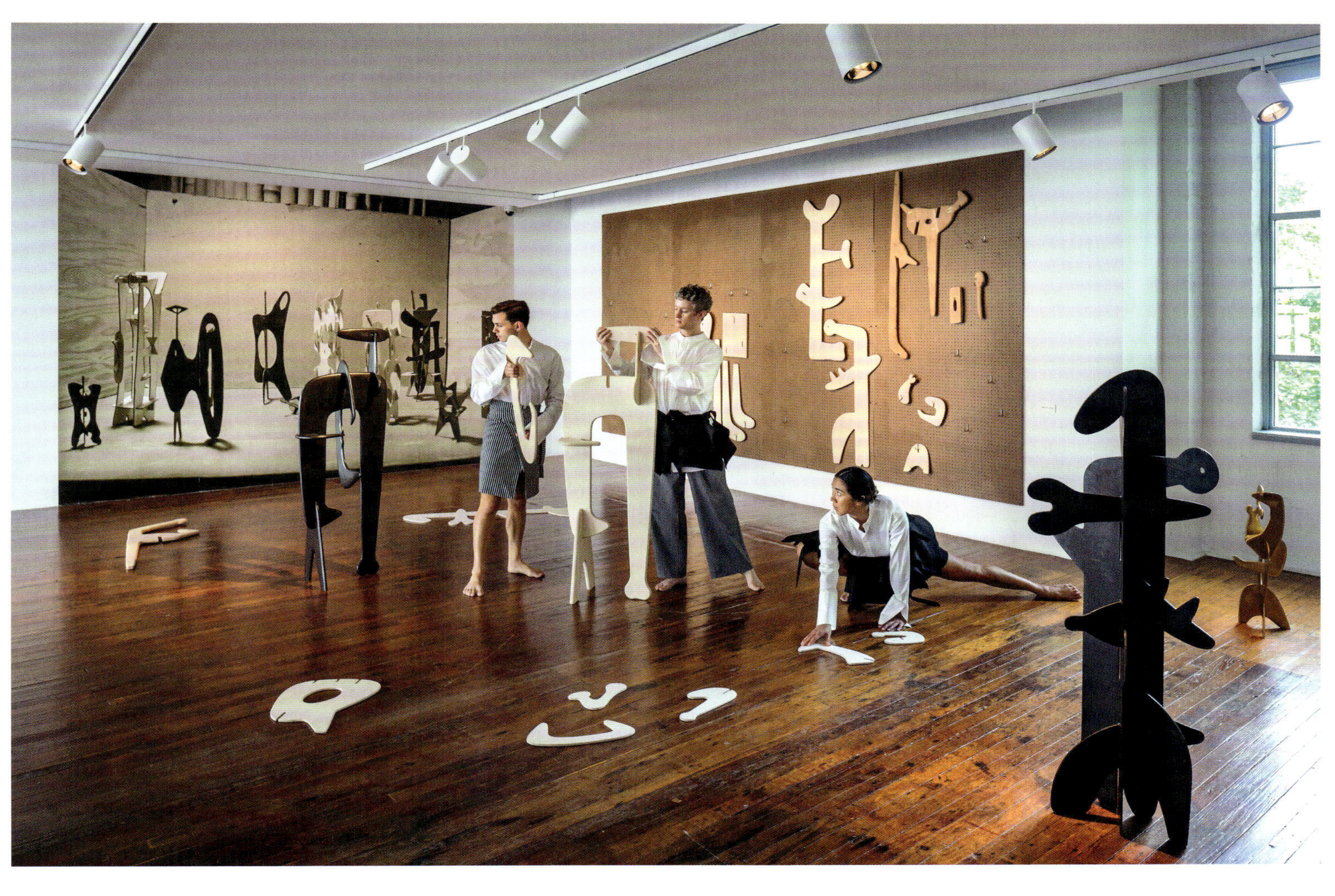

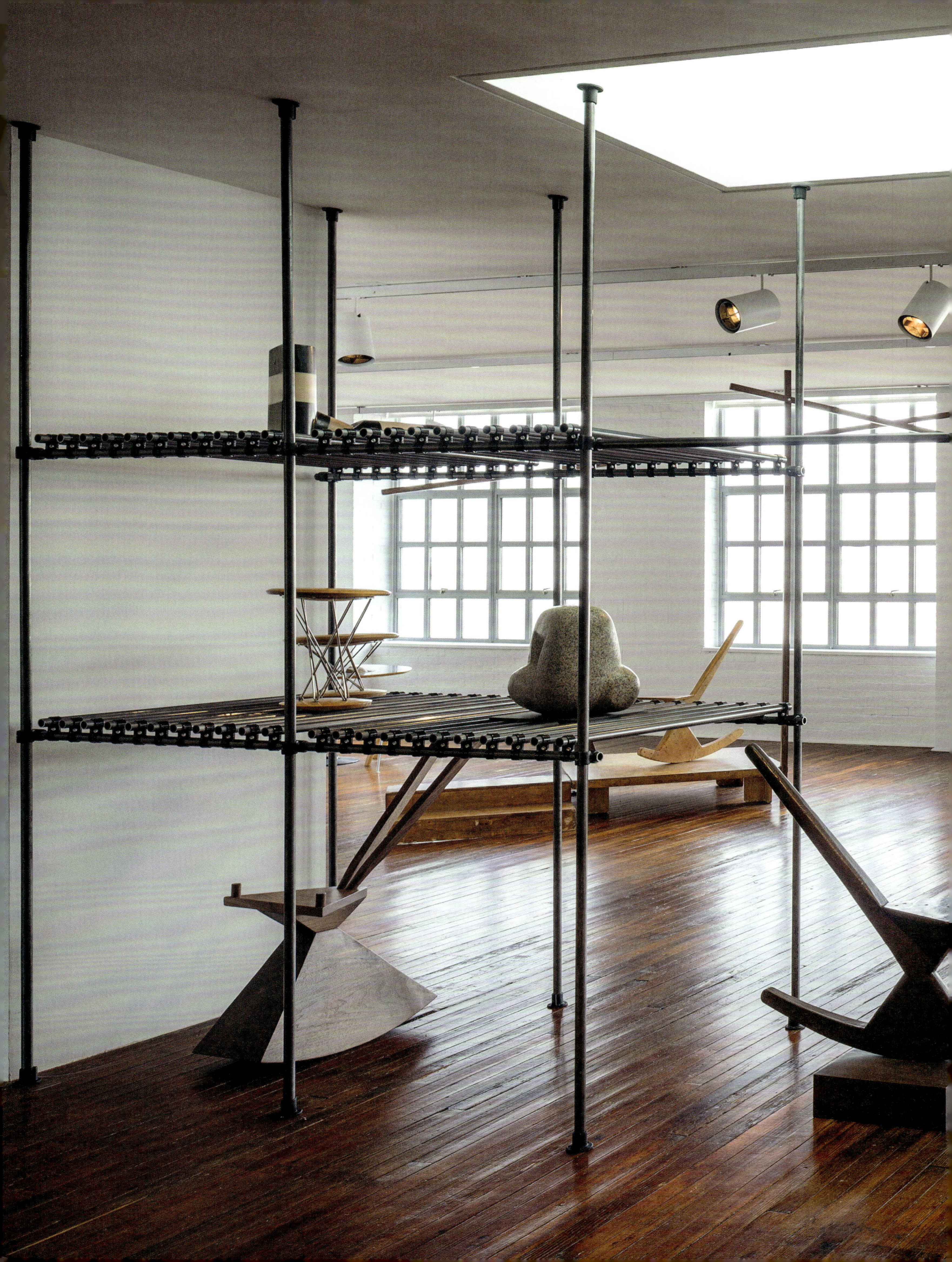

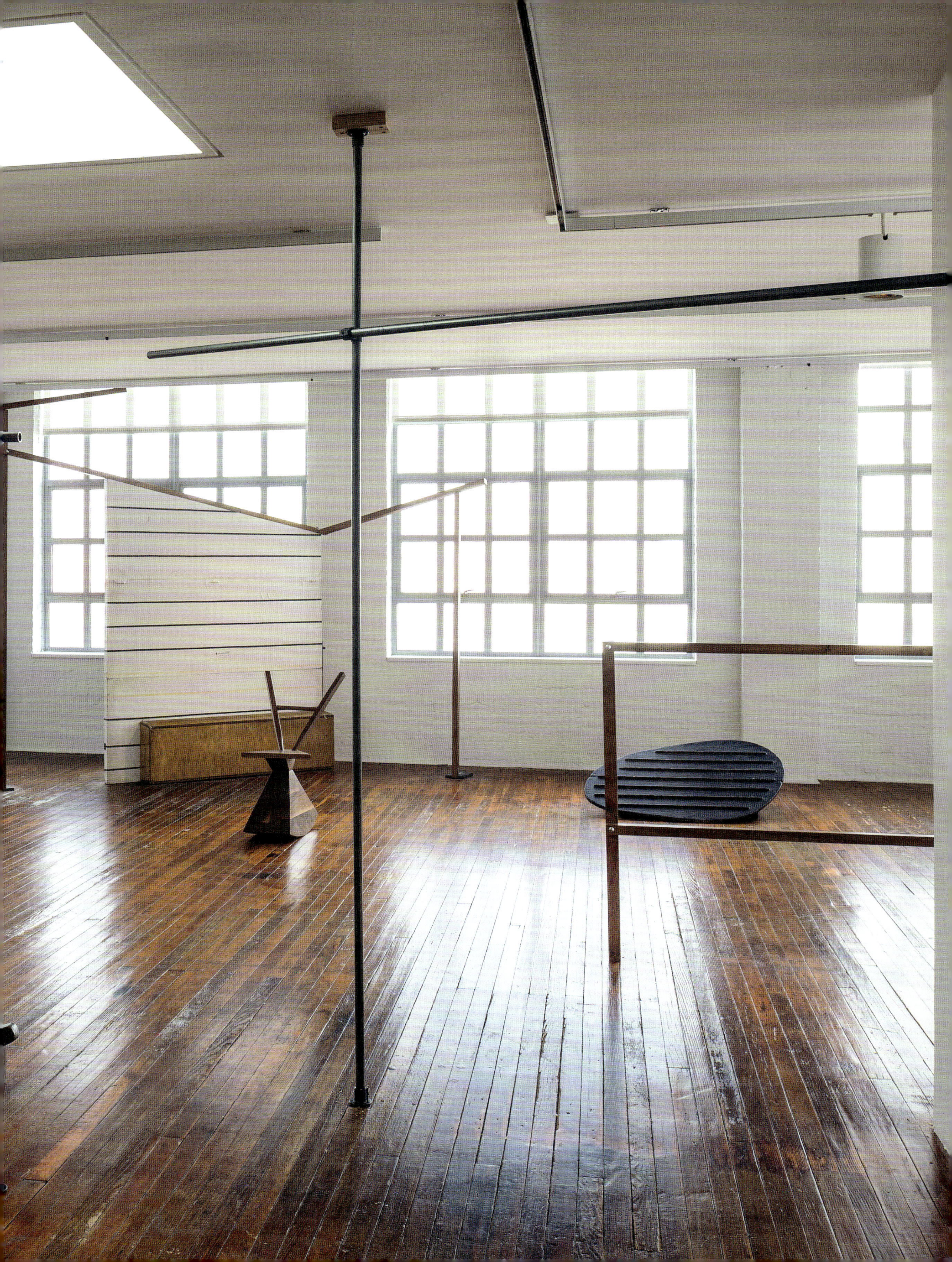

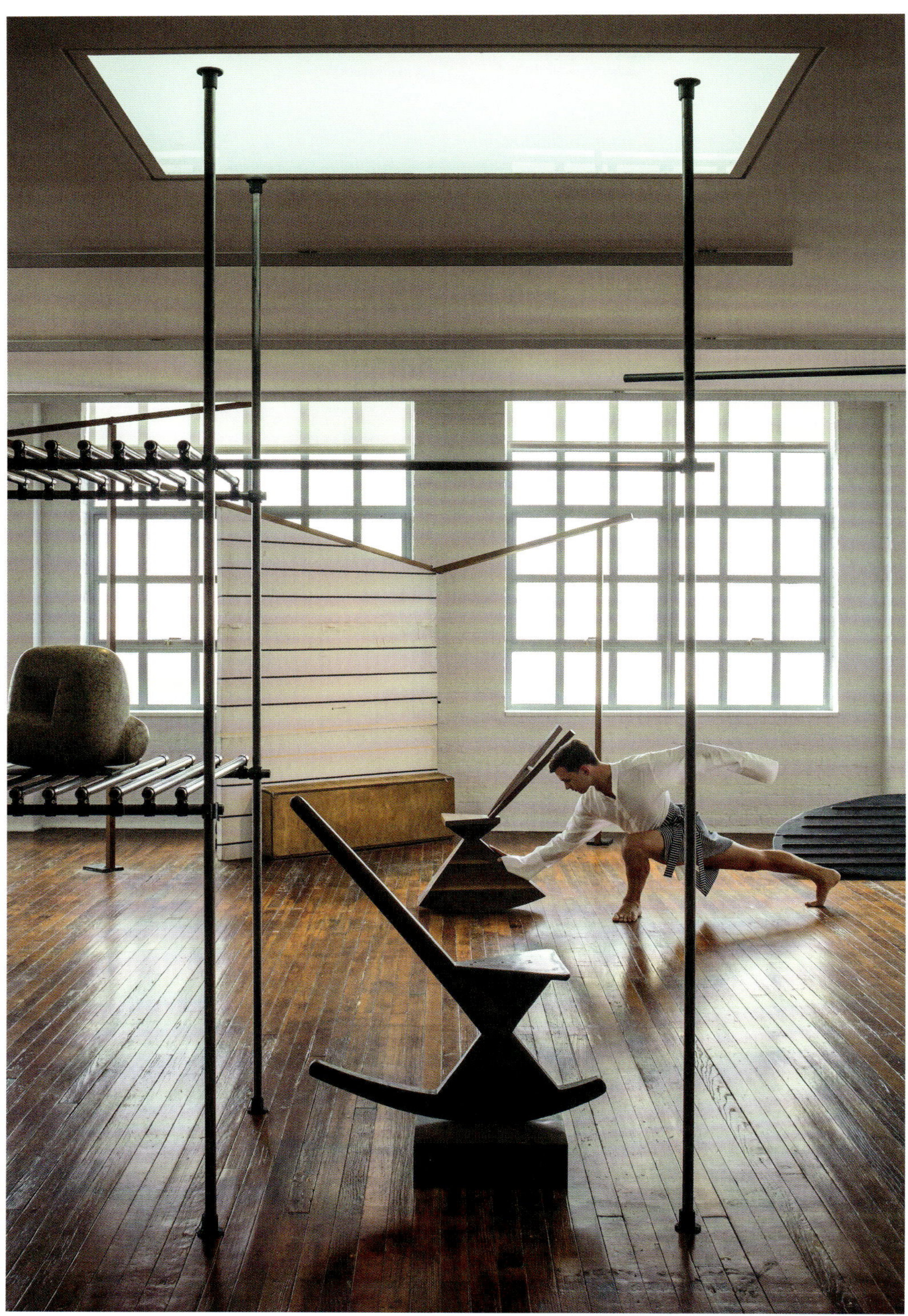

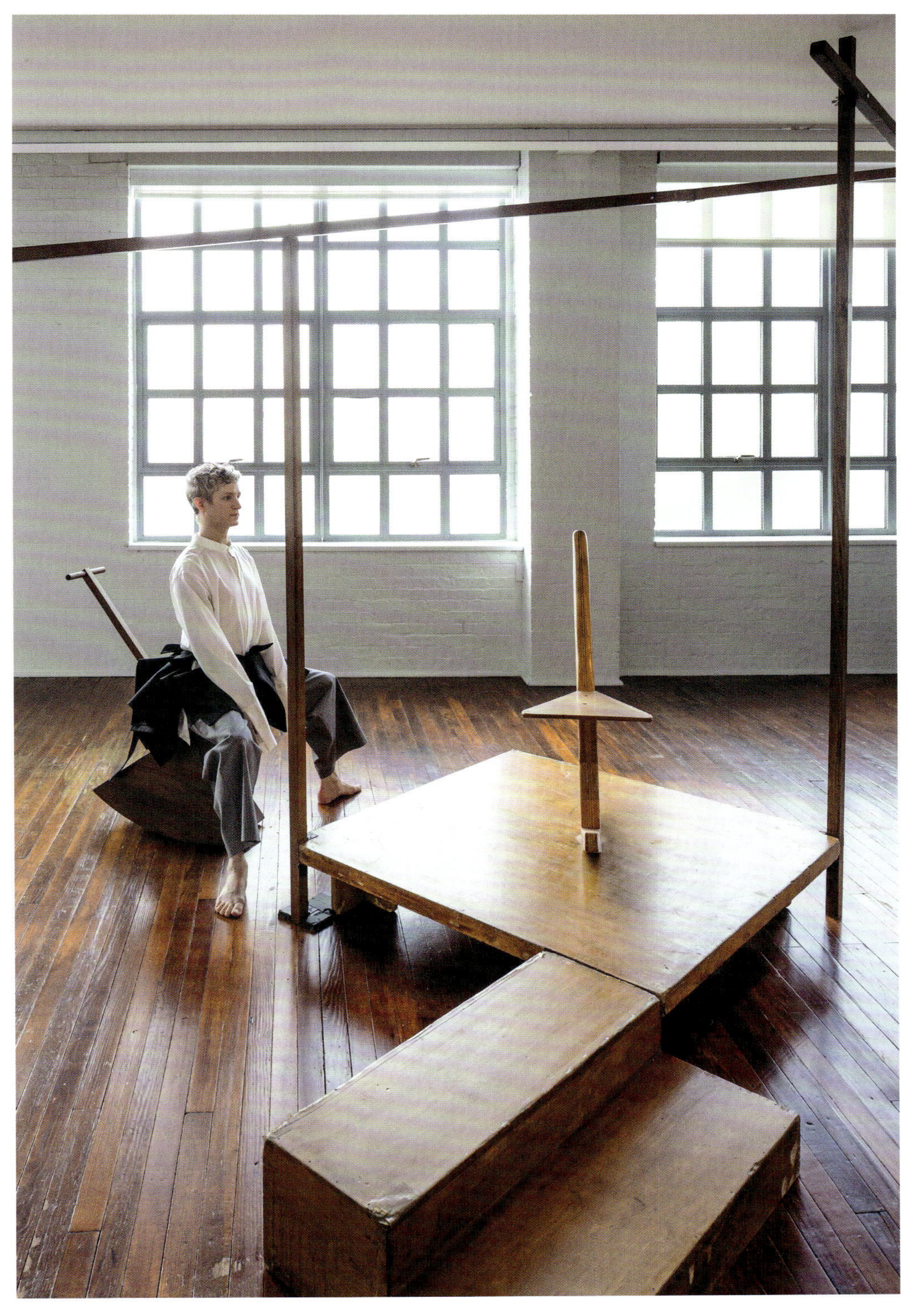

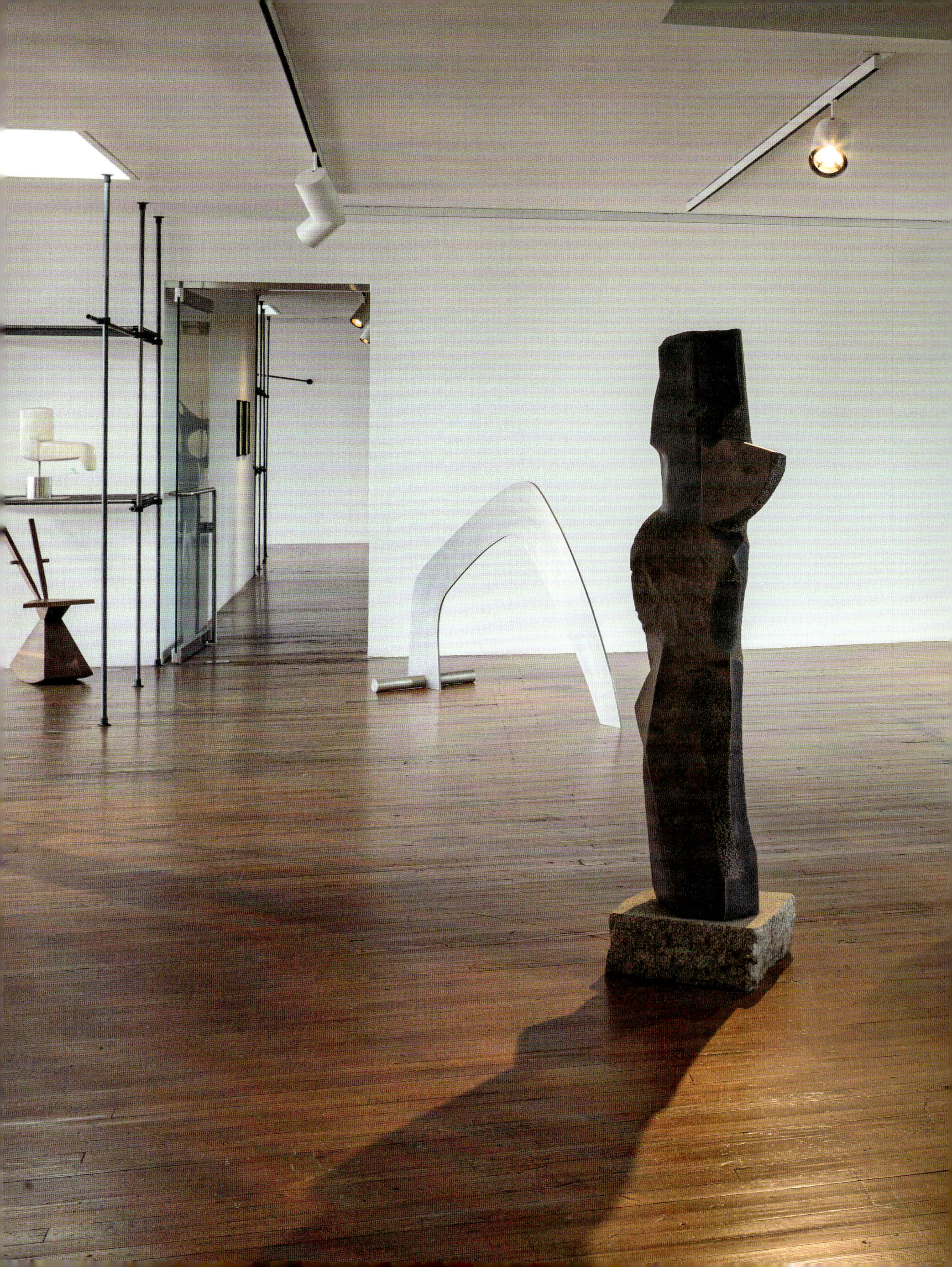

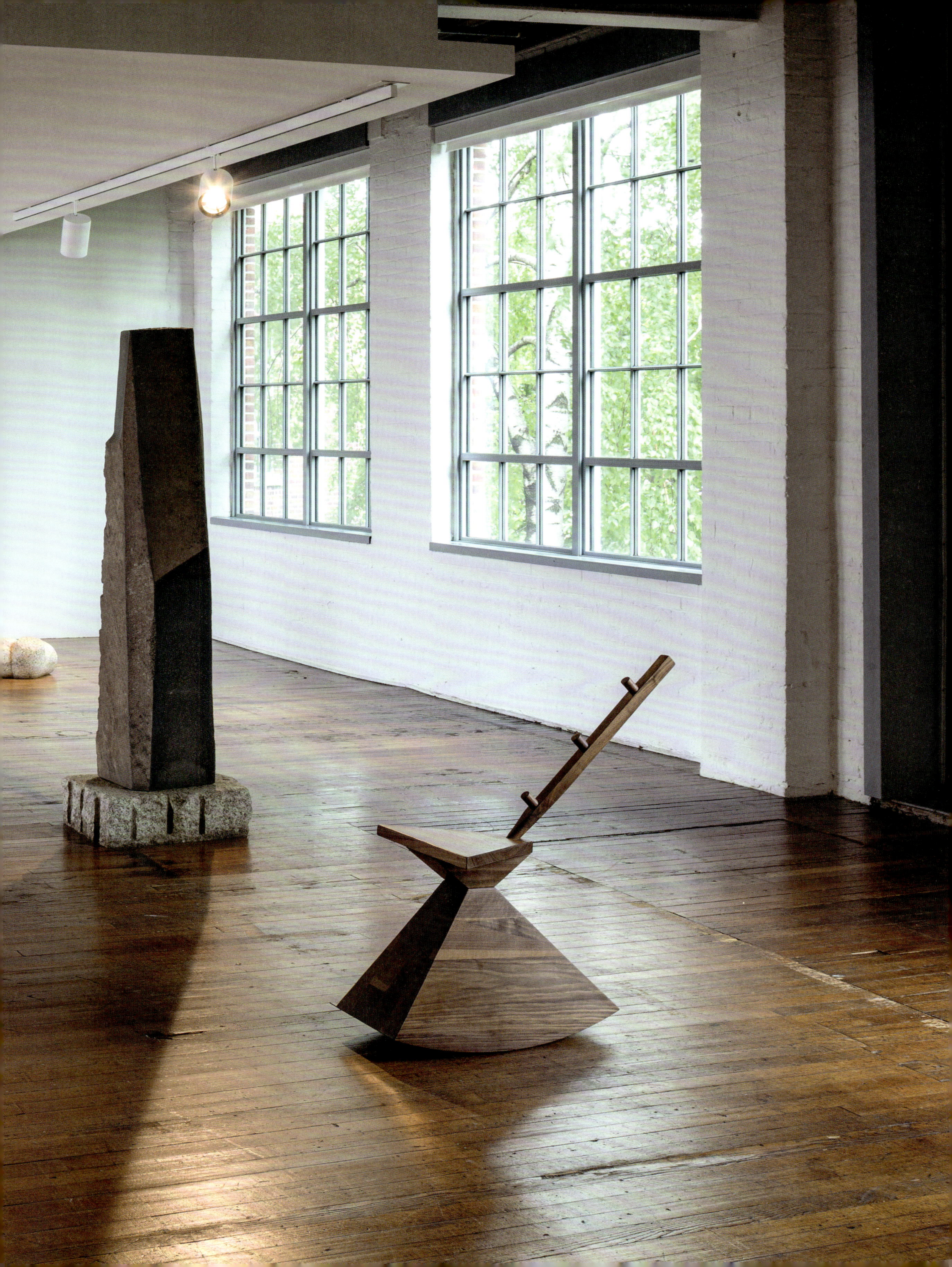

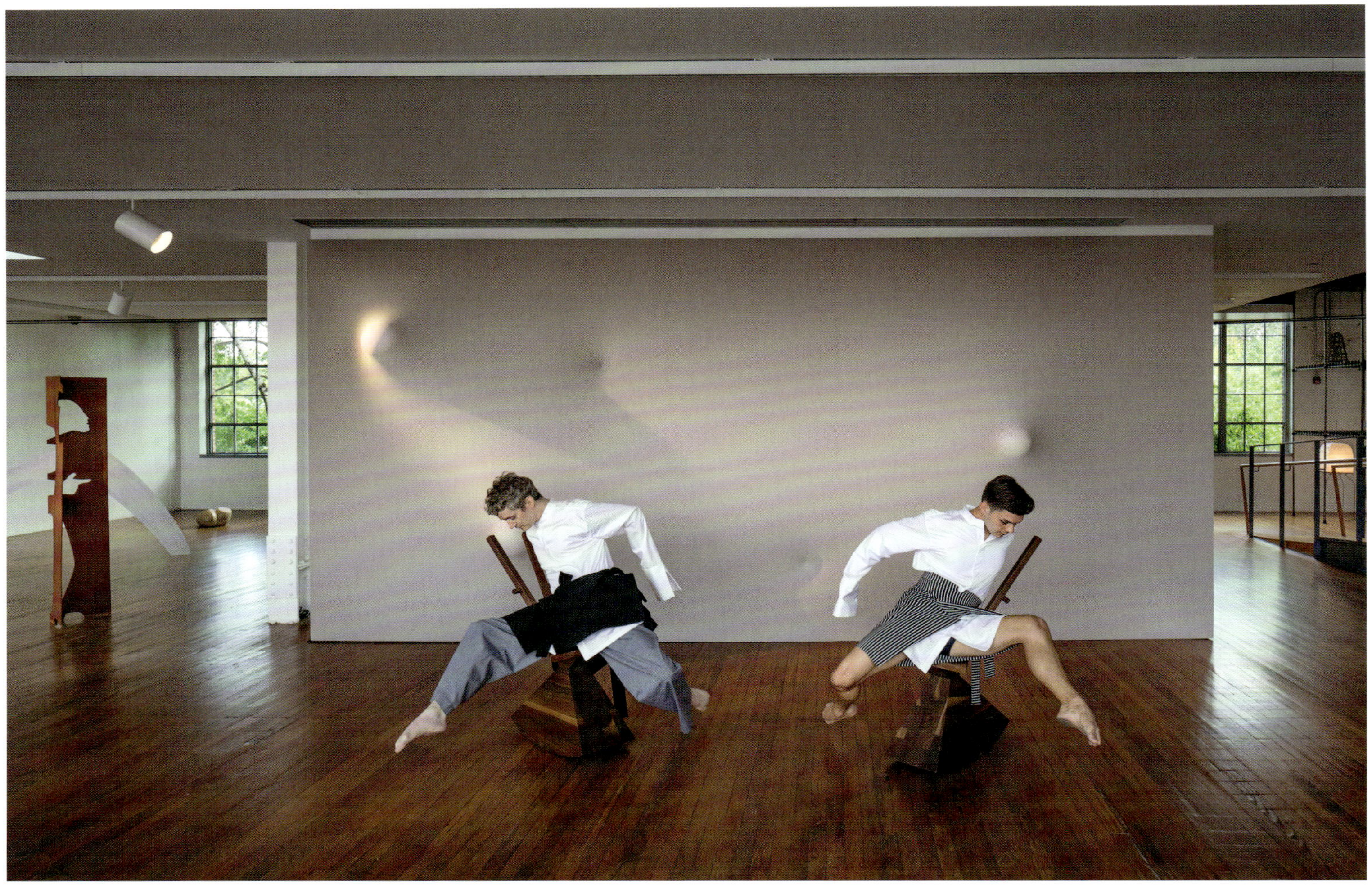

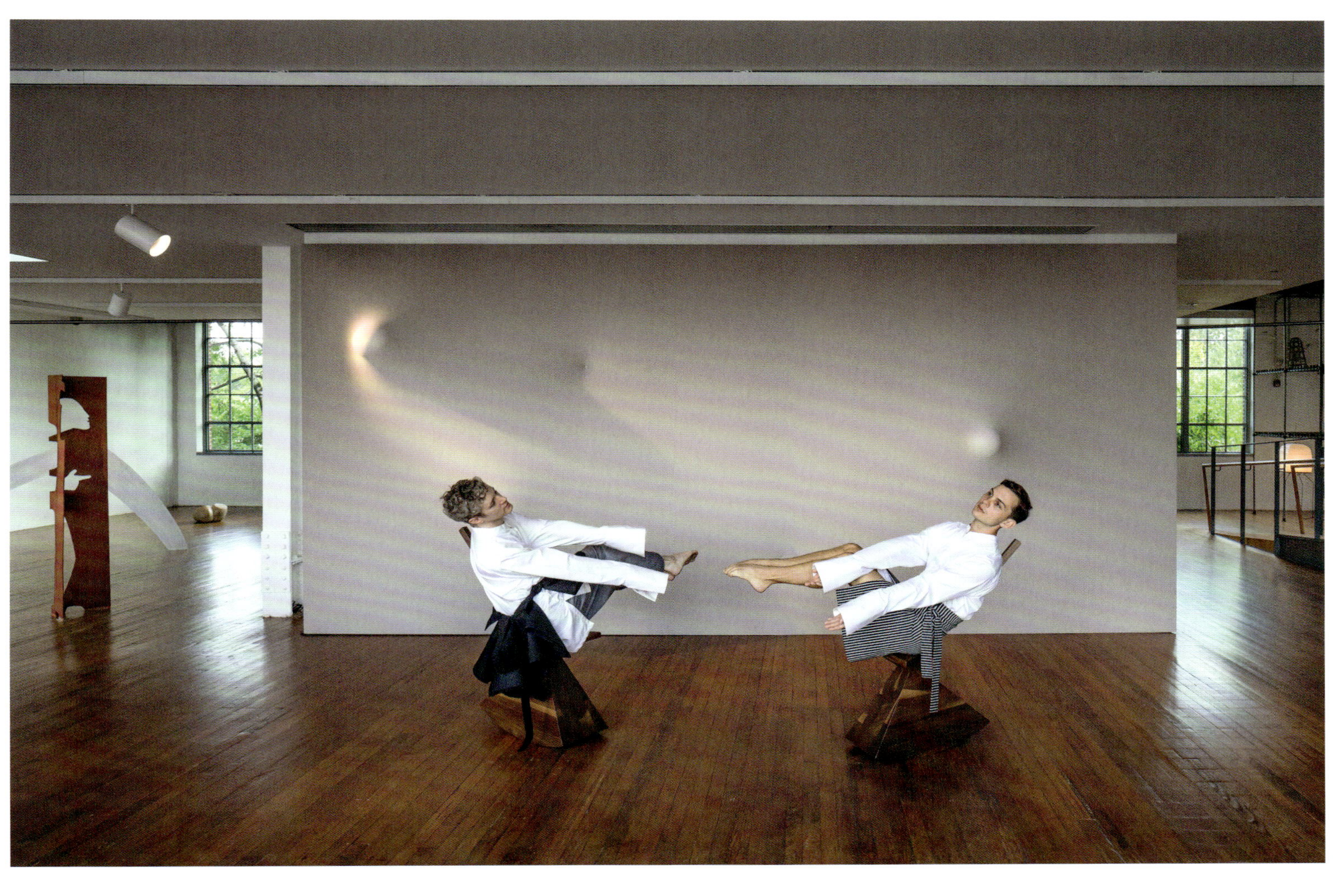

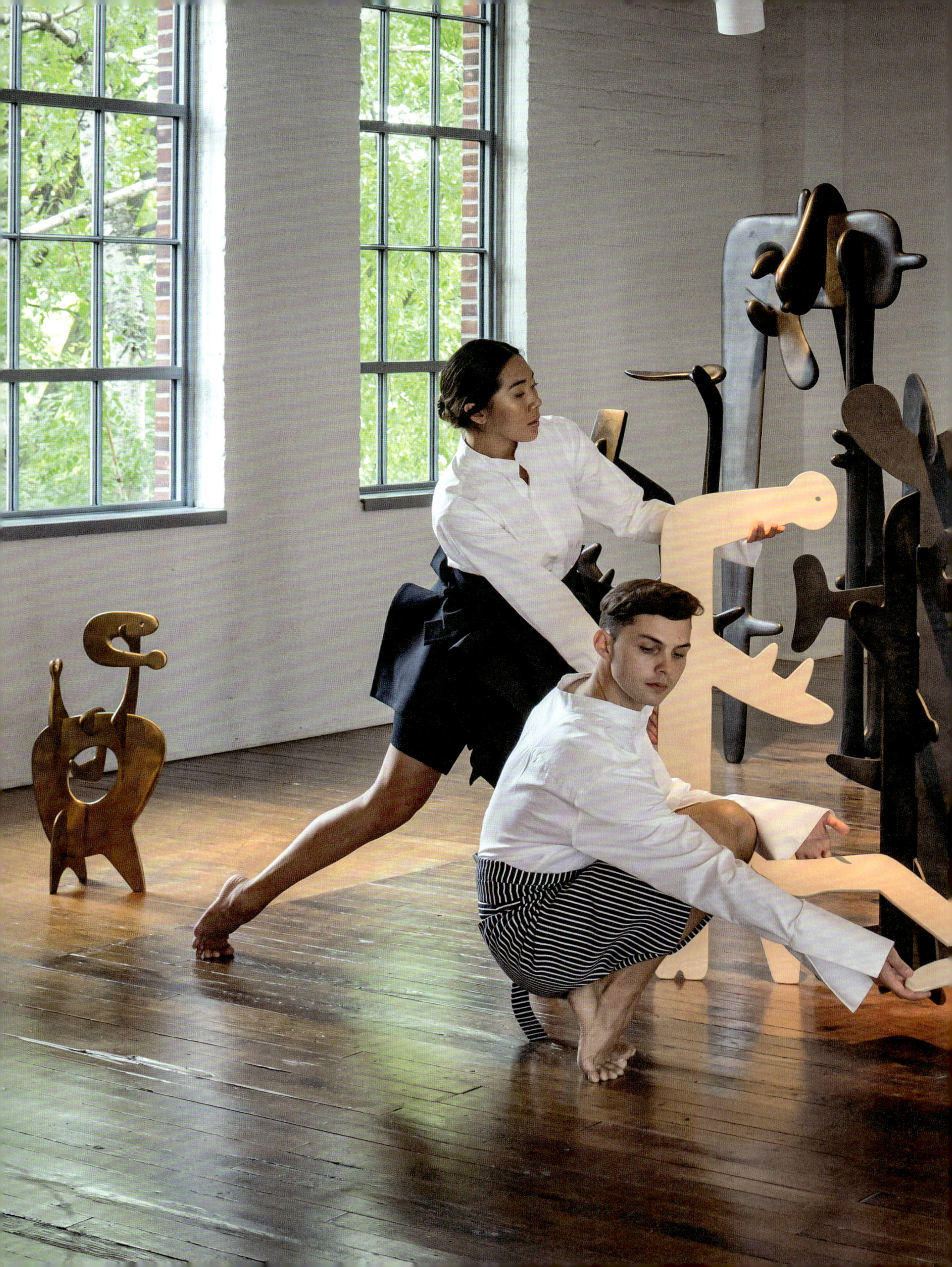

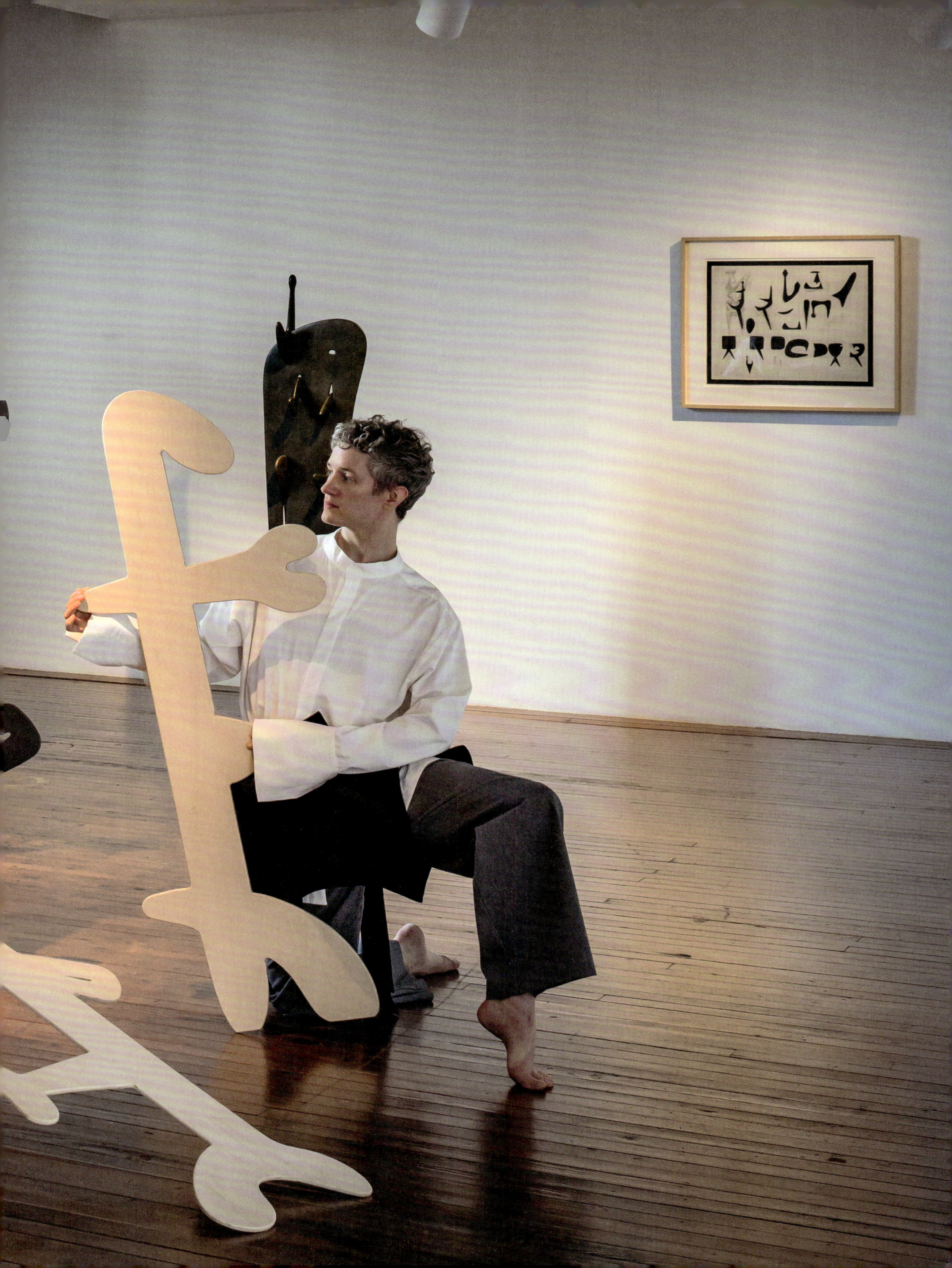

Extended Agency: Compulsive Empathy in the Work of Isamu Noguchi and Brendan Fernandes

Dakin Hart

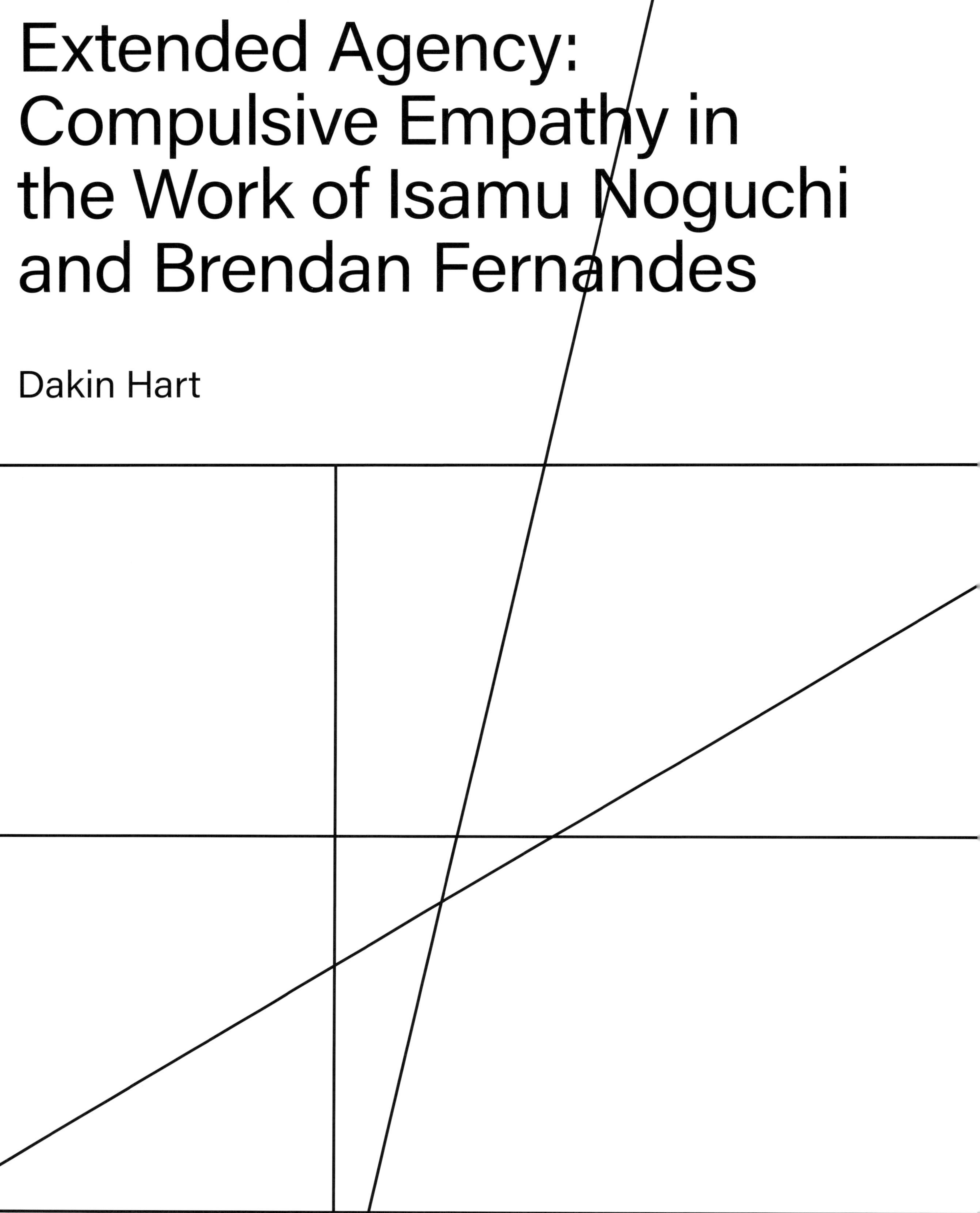

The sculptor-choreographer Brendan Fernandes is no stranger to museums. Actually, he's in the early stages of building one of the more generous and meaningful critiques of the institution since the epochal series of installations Fred Wilson made in the 1990s, in which he re-presented museums to themselves by reorganizing their collections to reveal explicit and implicit racial prejudices.[1] Wilson's efforts to provide diversity, equity, and inclusion training to museums in the form of exhibitions crafted from within their institutional souls (aka their permanent collections) didn't end a culture of systemic racism. But the impact of his "minings"—equally notable for their incisiveness and altruistic spirit—on the generations of museum employees who are now in leadership positions cannot be overstated.[2] Fernandes's collaborations with museums have followed Wilson's fundamental strategy of working from within to generate empathy by way of encouraging institutional change. Fernandes's body of work in this area is rapidly expanding. Early examples included pieces such as *In Touch* (2015) and *As One* (2015) for the Seattle Art Museum that made innate discrepancies in the relationships between object, institution, and visitor visible, and others such as *The Working Move* (2014) and *Closing Line* (2014) that engaged museums' procedures, routines, and systems in processes of self-awareness and self-reflection [Reference Images p. 128].[3] The difference between what Wilson achieved and what Fernandes is attempting has most to do with a significant shift in context. Fernandes is working in what has become a far more expansive and transdisciplinary field of sculpture, which now includes performance.

Both Wilson and Fernandes have (consciously) orbited in conceptual spaces also frequented, and in some cases pioneered, by the Japanese American sculptor Isamu Noguchi a generation or two earlier. Noguchi's commitment to empirically-charged forms of social improvement formulated around the margins of the Western painting-sculpture-architecture canon has proved a surprisingly generative source for other artists—especially as consensus seems finally to have been achieved that the narrow center cannot and should not hold. Leaving aside the art world's surrender to celebrity, money, and other toxic distractions—which by the late 1980s made Noguchi want to renounce the title artist entirely—no one would be more proud of the kaleidoscopic profession it has become when attending to the better angels of its nature than he.[4] And there, at the flowering end of one of the more improbably productive branches (choreographic collaboration) of the far-reaching root system Noguchi's point of view has come to represent, is Fernandes, in motion. Deploying the disciplined body, in the form of teams of local, usually young, highly trained dancers, Fernandes transforms the museums he collaborates with into something new. Noguchi, who wanted "sculptures equal to myself walking,"[5] would have heartily approved.

The effect of inserting a diverse, organized array of living bodies into the museum system—as interactive interlocutors—is to transform the tacitly balkanizing regime of display by shifting the operation of empathy in the viewer from the conscious to the subconscious, from intellectual "appreciation" to autonomic response. Dance is the software layer, the spatializing GUI (general user interface), that sculpture (and art) never knew it needed. Except of course that it has known and did know.

Beginning in 1935 and continuing through the 1960s, Noguchi sculpturally supercharged more than twenty ballets for Martha Graham exploring, in particular, fundamental archetypes of human behavior. Many artists have worked with choreographers since then, and several notable artists have brought dance into museums, but not since Noguchi has anyone synthesized sculpture, dance, and institutional critique with social purpose in quite the way that Fernandes is doing. And for his part, Noguchi never put all of those efforts together outside of the totality of his life's work.

In response to a question about why making dance sets interested him, Nochuchi once wrote, "We breathe in, we breathe out, inward turning, alone, or outgoing, working with others, for an experience that is cumulative through collaboration. The theater is the latter.[6] Though his imaginary landscapes for Graham are at the heart of his redefinition of sculpture, they are also, in a sense, the least important part of the story that matters most: his commitment to social progress. Would Noguchi have traded his relationship with Martha Graham for the ability to shape a world in which Japanese Americans were not imprisoned en masse in their own country for no reason but their ethnicity and no human being would design, develop, or deploy an atomic weapon? Certainly. But what he did was to recast sculpture as a social tool, embed it in the broadest possible matrix of civic life, and use it to reshape our relationship with the world by making work designed to generate holistic forms of empathy. It took him decades, assembling his perspective one piece at a time, to understand that this was what he was after. When he had it, the task basically boiled down to one thing: sculpture, in every and any form, should seek to nurture society—to be, in its day and context, as important as the churches, temples, and mosques around which life once turned nearly everywhere.

Taking its title from a foundational Martha Graham technique, the exhibition *Brendan Fernandes: Contract and Release* was organized to build on and complement a thematic collection installation at The Noguchi Museum, *Noguchi: Body-Space Devices* (May 15, 2019 – May 2, 2021). The core premise of that collection exhibition was that empathy is a physical discipline that can be modeled, taught, and learned through the body, below the level of conscious thought. Both exhibitions were born out of conversations with Fernandes about Noguchi's sets and props for Graham and—following Noguchi's talent for engaging the whole person through sculpture—what it takes and means for an object to motivate and mediate movement: literal and metaphorical. And building on that, what it might mean to consider any and all of Noguchi's sculptures as props—which is to say as devices for affecting the way our bodies engage with space and with narratives of living (FIGURE 1). This was all part of The Isamu Noguchi Foundation and Garden Museum's ongoing efforts to understand the radiant implications of Noguchi's often rhetorically elusive conceptualism. Although in this case, he was quite clear about what he had in mind.

> I never subscribed to the idea that sculptures are just sculptures and not something that is a tool. These are symbolic or gestural tools she [Graham] was using. They were an extension of her body. It's my own approach to sculpture as being part of living, not just part of art. I don't look at art as something separate and sacrosanct. It's part of usefulness. It's probably why I was able to do those things. Also, if you look at what I was doing outside the theater at that particular time, it often relates to what I did in the theater. Especially with *Herodiade* it was very similar. I used an interest that I already had elsewhere—the skeleton of the body.[7]

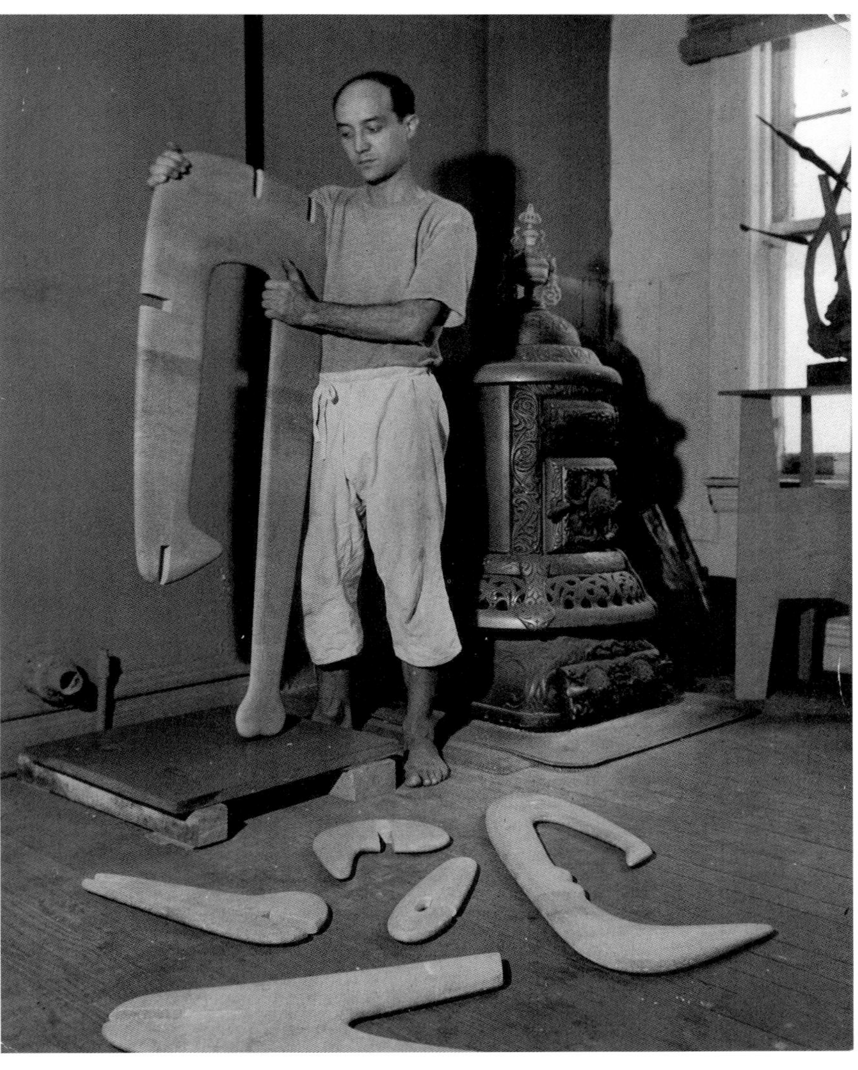

Figure 1: Isamu Noguchi in his studio with *Figure*, © The Isamu Noguchi Foundation and Garden Museum, New York / The Estate of Rudolph Burckhardt / ARS, Photo by Rudolph Burckhardt

Reflecting on that same idea, of sculpture as an armature for life, he told the filmmaker Michael Blackwood that in *Cave of the Heart* (1946), "The props become an integral part of the anatomy."[8] Elaborating on this idea, Thomas Hess, the editor of ARTnews wrote that Noguchi "carried his exile inside him like his skeleton." And as Noguchi wrote of Graham, "the wonder of [her] magic with props," was that she used "them as extensions of her own anatomy."[9]

For his part, as he freely admitted, Noguchi long underestimated the nature of his work with Graham. For the first two decades of their collaboration he considered it a somewhat unrelated, extra-sculptural sideline. "Still, I considered myself a sculptor, so that I tended to think that what I did in the theater was peripheral to my activities as an artist. A correspondence, perhaps, an application or performance but with a doubt as to their reality."[10] He eventually came to realize how generative it had been in providing the theoretical framework he needed to rethink sculpture's place and purpose in society. Specifically, making the sets and props that were responsible for constituting and defining the natural laws and culture of entire imaginary universes gave him the opportunity to learn how to make devices: active objects capable of training humanity to live in synchrony with the world.

Theatrical space can be a safe space for the point of view in motion—that is, for a perspective that is capable of change. Understand the production of that space as an inherently pluralistic, polyphonic, or many-bodied enterprise, and seek to move that openness to the world, and to call that sculpture, and you understand Noguchi. "Call it sculpture when it moves you so."[11] That is the final line of Noguchi's museum catalog, a fittingly open-ended index to his point of view. But moves us how? Noguchi's version of collaboration is one in which we're all implicated, and what it amounts to is a recognition of both our interdependence and of our need to be moved. This is the unique legacy to which Fernandes is so extraordinarily well attuned.

It is Noguchi's position as a purposeful exile that gave him the perspective he needed to seek universal sculpture solutions capable of achieving his insanely ambitious goal. He had many ways of describing his at first inescapable, but ultimately self-imposed, subject position of in-betweenness: the perpetual state of not belonging precisely anywhere so choosing to make himself at home everywhere. But they all amount to the same sense of mission: being connective and interstitial, in himself and in his work. The means to that end was otherness as a form of agency trained on generating the most basic forms of rapport and affinity. Not strangeness as an artistic conceit—as the surrealists employed it—but what we might call embodied alternative perspectives.

Noguchi could simply have accepted rootlessness. He could have succumbed to the alienation and despair that generally go with being, or feeling, shut out. But Noguchi was the exploding outward sort. From the disparate threads of his inheritance and his experiences, he fashioned multiple matrices of connectedness: whipstitching the past into the future, harmonizing natural and human systems, craft and technology, hybridizing cultural perspectives drawn from all over and whenever. In short, working between categories and wherever he saw gaps in conventional wisdom, using his concept of sculpture to shape meaningful environments and experiences of awareness.

Noguchi's statement "To be hybrid anticipates the future"[12] was aspirational, a prophecy. For the dominant culture he dealt with for much of his life, his hybridity was a kind of science-fiction. Several generations on, harnessing an analogously multifaceted heritage, Fernandes has chosen a parallel course as an ambassadorial empath. A queer Canadian of Indian heritage with family roots in Kenya, teaching in the United States and making work around the world, Fernandes is determined to express the full complexity of theoretical paths through the world that his own hybridity enables. He is an archetype and a glorious fulfilment of Noguchi's vision because his work—like Noguchi's—is, in its powerhouse marginality, primarily oriented towards altering perspectives, in order to expand the space of our mutual comprehension.

Noguchi was a social activist, before social activism became an accepted subdiscipline, or an integral part, of art making, and before the terminology and theory to explain what that might mean had been developed. As a result, most of his efforts to shape society were indirect and abstract—which was his natural inclination. His consideration of how children play—the multiple attempts he made to build nature-inspired playgrounds and nondirective, but physically pedagogic play equipment—is an example of this. The plaything (to use Noguchi's term) called *Play Sculpture* was on view and available for play in the collection exhibition and was integral to Fernandes's project. Offering 540 degrees of curve to cover 360 degrees worth of ground, it is a physical philosophy lesson: in prioritizing the journey over the destination; in seeing the body in motion as inherently meaningful; and in understanding circularity as a paradigm of progress every bit as valid as a vector. In the context of socially active art making, Noguchi's work is a product of its time that virtually everyone—particularly those in the creative and technical professions—intuits as profoundly ahead of its time.

Synthesizing dance performance and sculpture, Fernandes is working at a time when we are in the process of becoming finely attuned to the social content of art and increasingly conversant with the language and concepts to explain it. While maintaining the basic, universalizing, poetic, and elliptical qualities that have given Noguchi's work such great staying power, Fernandes's social content is more explicit and more specific. Of his recent work, Fernandes has written:

> I am returning to my past life as a dancer. I aim to highlight the various meanings that the body can encapsulate: it is both a kind of object, endowed with cultural meaning, viewed by others and labored on by ourselves. It is also our expressive

access-point to the world, constitutive of our subjectivity and selfhood. I investigate how movement techniques are recalled in the body via muscle memory and explore this phenomenon through cultural dance, ballet, and the languages that prescribe directions for dancers to move … I look at movement through queer and laboring bodies as it relates to the construction of gender roles and physicality. As such, this work continues to engage with the transitional nature of identity, while exploring how this is enacted and experienced on the level of embodiment.[13]

Noguchi understood that museums are not neutral spaces for bodies or objects. Fortunate at the end of his career to be in a position to exercise an unusual degree of control over how his identity, work, and values would be framed, Noguchi chose to make his own. Fernandes, who is at an earlier stage of his career, has developed strategies—rooted in institutional critique—for engaging with museums through dance-based encounters between active viewers and charged objects. The sophisticated but accessible conversations about authority, subject and object position, otherness, and appropriation that he initiates, while emphasizing the importance of agency and self-determination, constitute a powerful new discipline.

We often refer to Noguchi as a permanent voluntary exile from the dominant culture of his time. Given the complexity of the interactions Fernandes creates in institutional contexts by confronting, and in service to, "transitional and transnational identities"[14]—which often requires operating in semi-hostile territory produced by prejudice and structural injustice—we hope that his extended and ongoing collaboration with Noguchi's legacy has provided him with something like a homecoming. Because Fernandes, like Noguchi, undaunted by the divisiveness of nationalistic notions of belonging, seeks a meaningful universal personhood for all of us.

1 Lisa G. Corrin, ed., *Mining the Museum: An Installation by Fred Wilson* (New York: The New Press, 1994). Published in conjunction with the exhibition *Mining the Museum*, organized by The Contemporary, Baltimore and the Maryland Historical Society and displayed at the Maryland Historical Society, April 4, 1992 - February 28, 1993.

2 I was incredibly fortunate to work on one of these exhibitions with Wilson at the de Young Museum in San Francisco in 1999, *Fred Wilson: Speaking in Tongues: A Look at the Language of Display*.

3 All of these are included in the following monograph: Crystal Mowry, ed., *Still Move: Brendan Fernandes* (London: Black Dog Publishing, 2016).

4 For Noguchi's views on the art world and his place in it in the late 1980s see Noguchi, Isamu and Rhony Alhalel, "Conversations with Isamu Noguchi," *Kyoto Journal* (Spring 1989): 32–37.

5 Isamu Noguchi, "[Untitled Artist Statement]," c. 1959, unpublished, Stable Gallery records, 1916–99, bulk 1953–70, Archives of American Art, Smithsonian Institution.

6 Isamu Noguchi, *Isamu Noguchi: A Sculptor's World* (New York: Harper & Row, 1968), 123.

7 Robert Tracy, "Noguchi: Collaborating with Graham," *Ballet Review* 13, no. 4 (Winter 1986): 10.

8 *Isamu Noguchi*, directed by Michael Blackwood (USA: Michael Blackwood Films, 1972).

9 Noguchi, *A Sculptor's World*, 123.

10 Isamu Noguchi, "My Sculpture," *Sculptures By Isamu Noguchi*, exhibition catalogue (Tokyo: Minami Gallery, in association with Asahi Shinbun, 1973).

11 Isamu Noguchi, *The Isamu Noguchi Garden Museum* (New York: Harry N. Abrams, 1987), 286.

12 Typescript draft of "I Become a Nisei," Isamu Noguchi's unpublished essay for Reader's Digest on the internment of Japanese Americans during World War II, The Noguchi Museum Archives, MS_WRI_005_001.

13 Brendan Fernandes, "Artist Statement," http://www.brendanfernandes.ca/new-page, accessed August 2, 2019.

14 Fernandes, "Artist Statement."

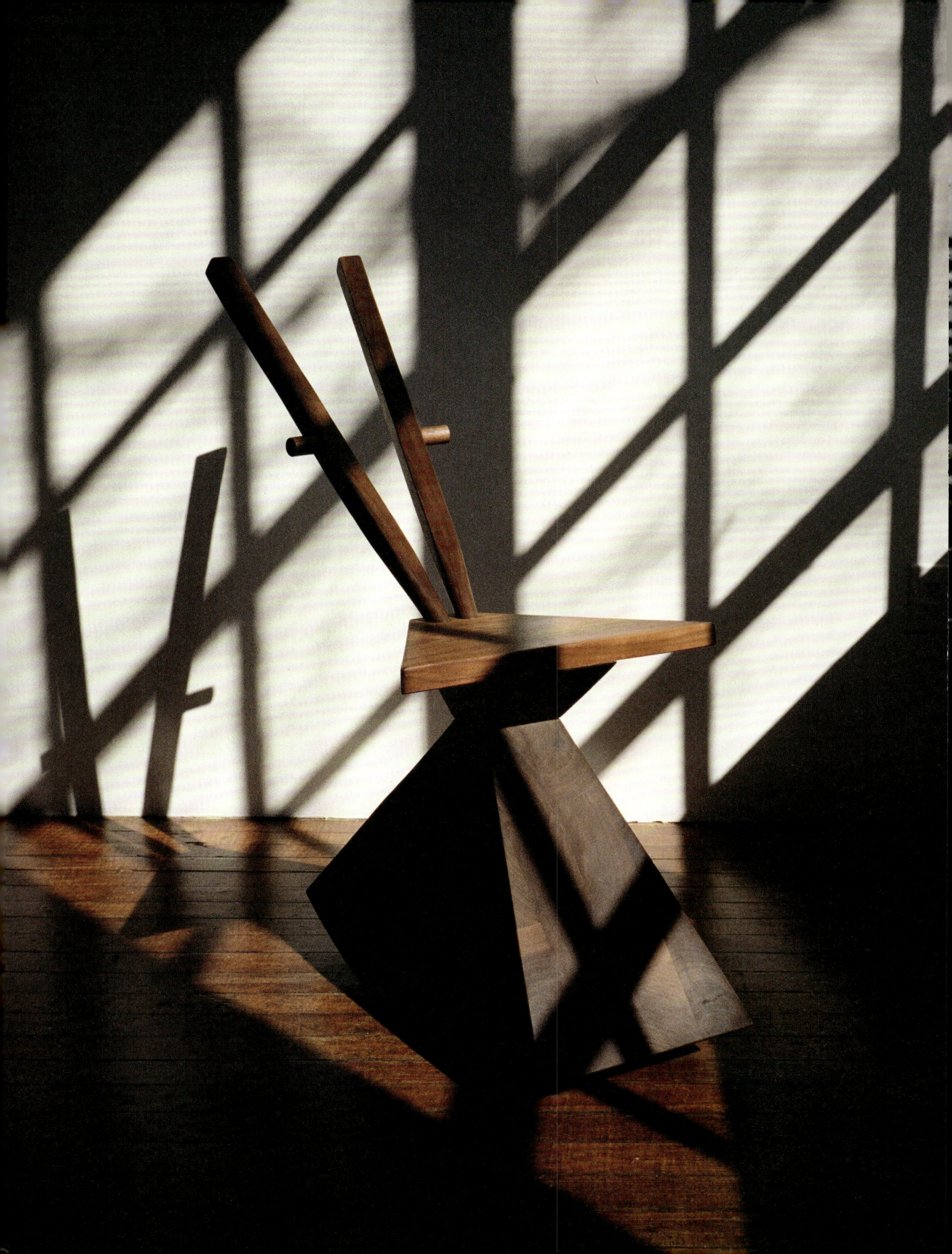

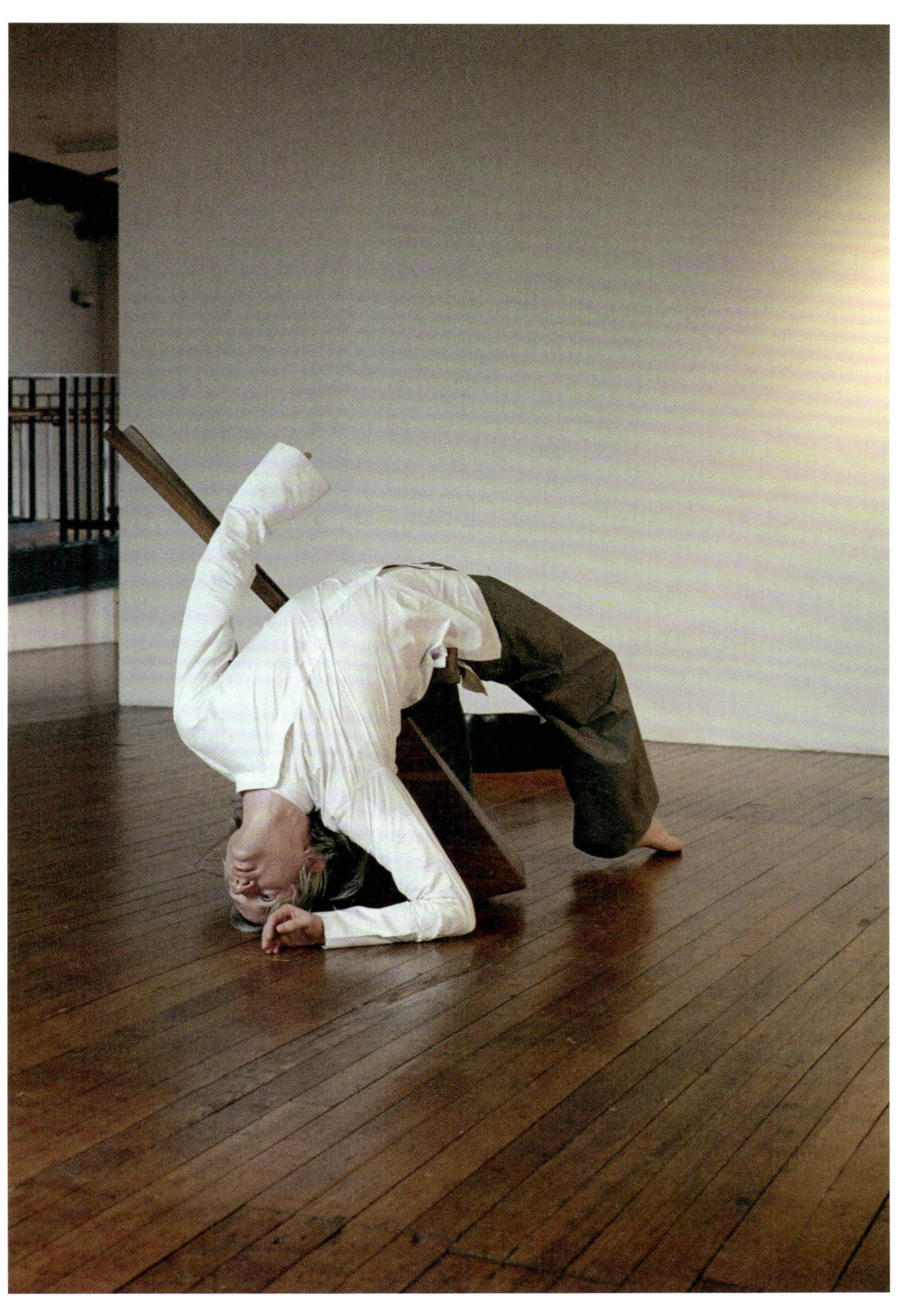

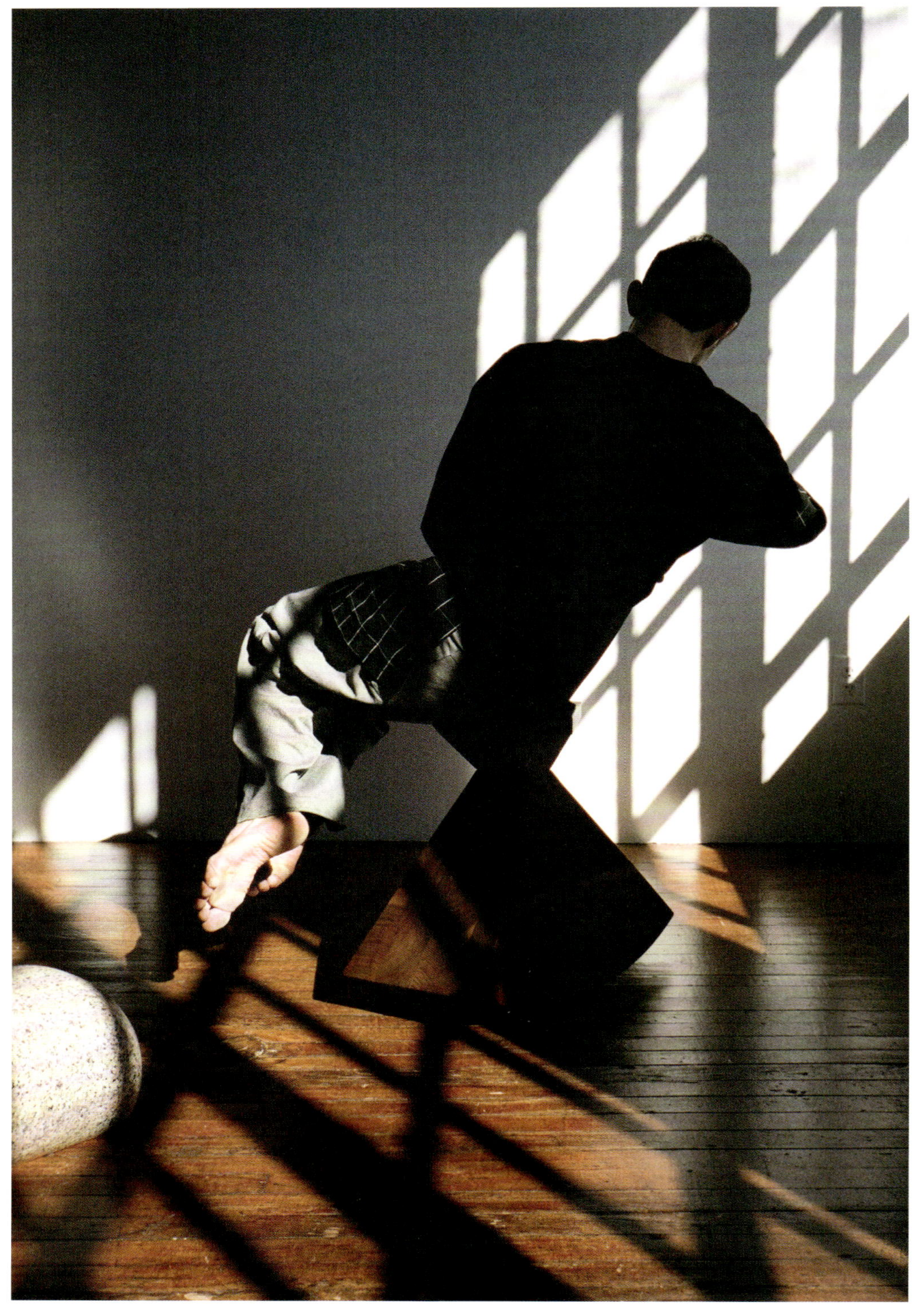

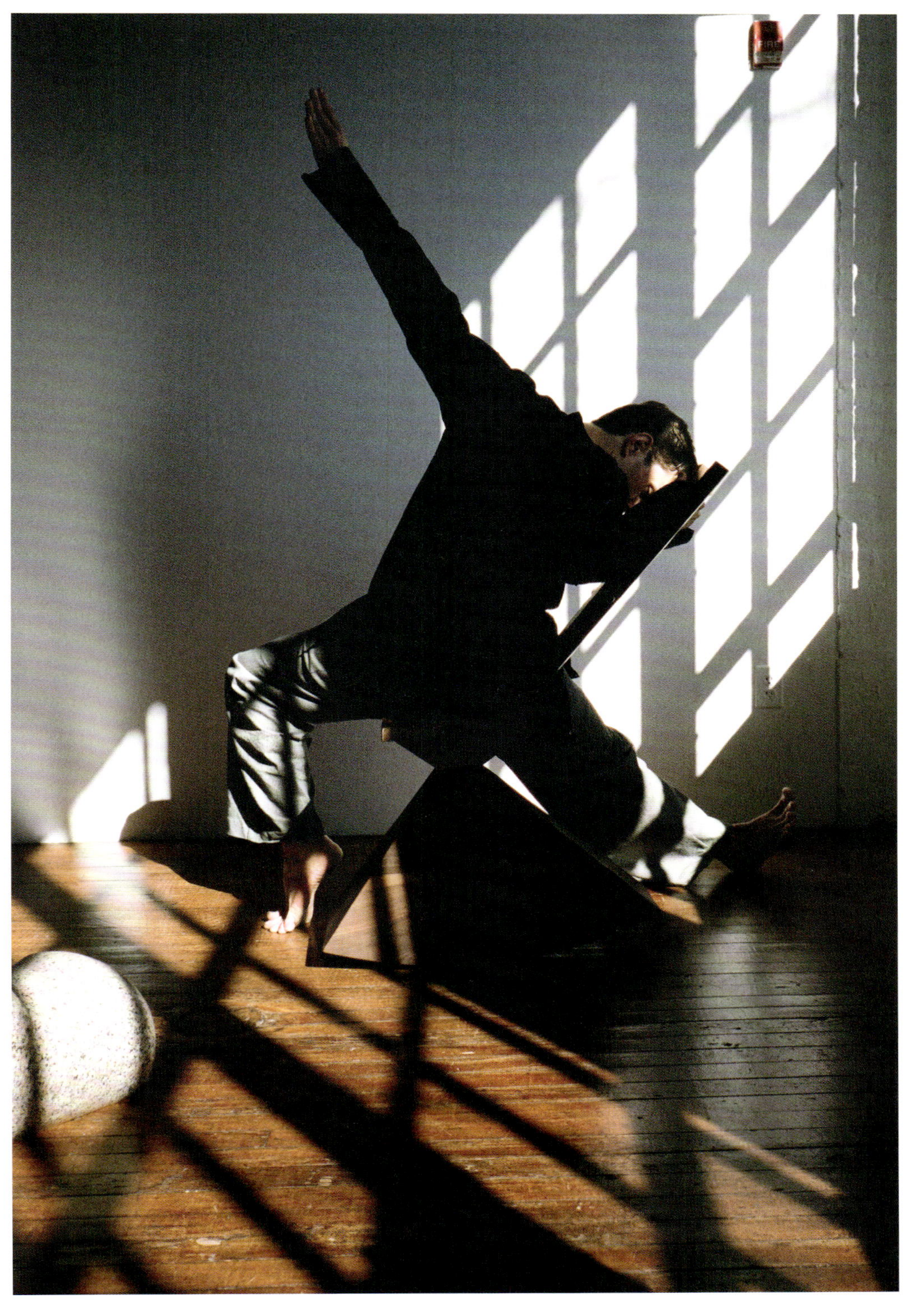

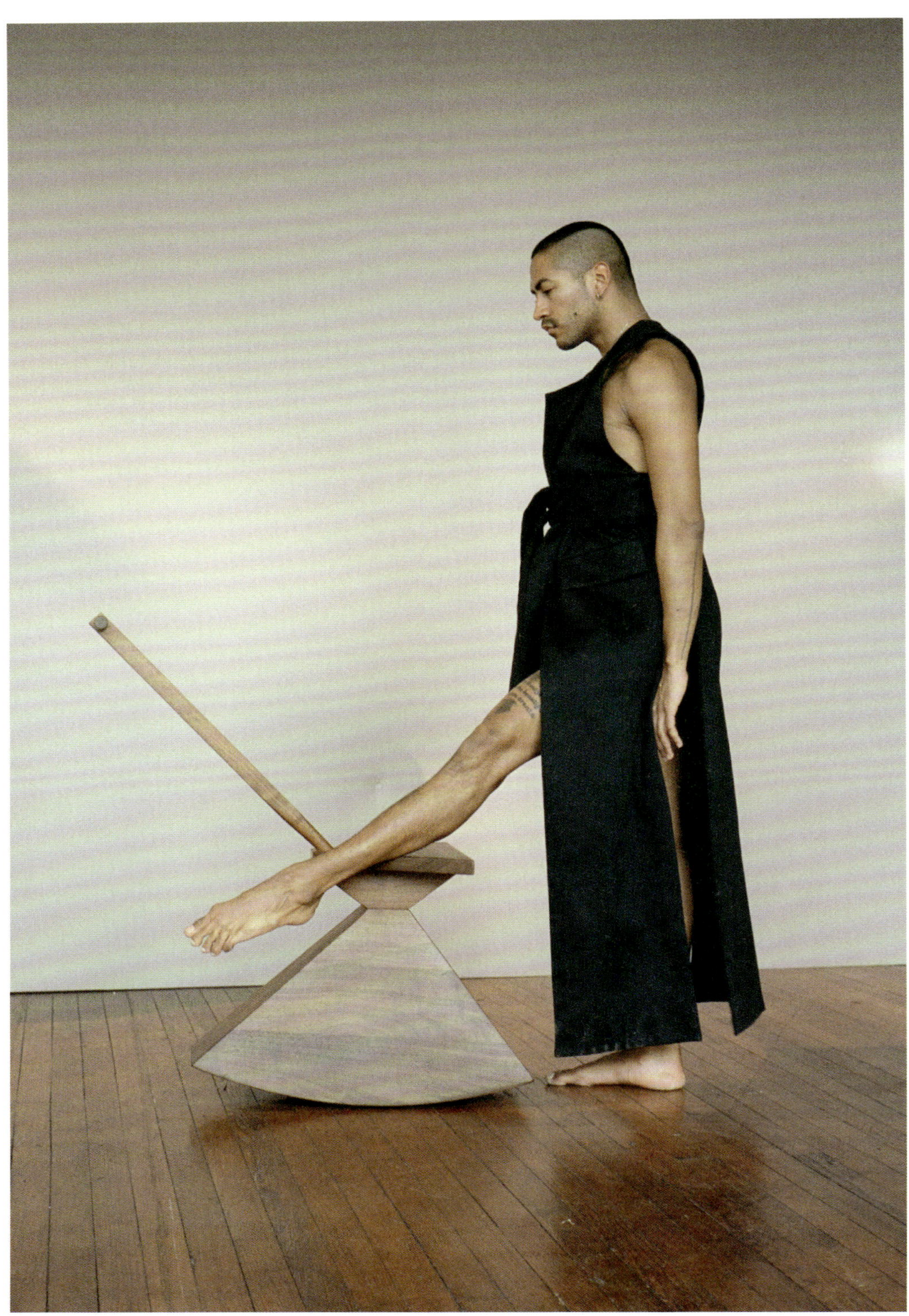

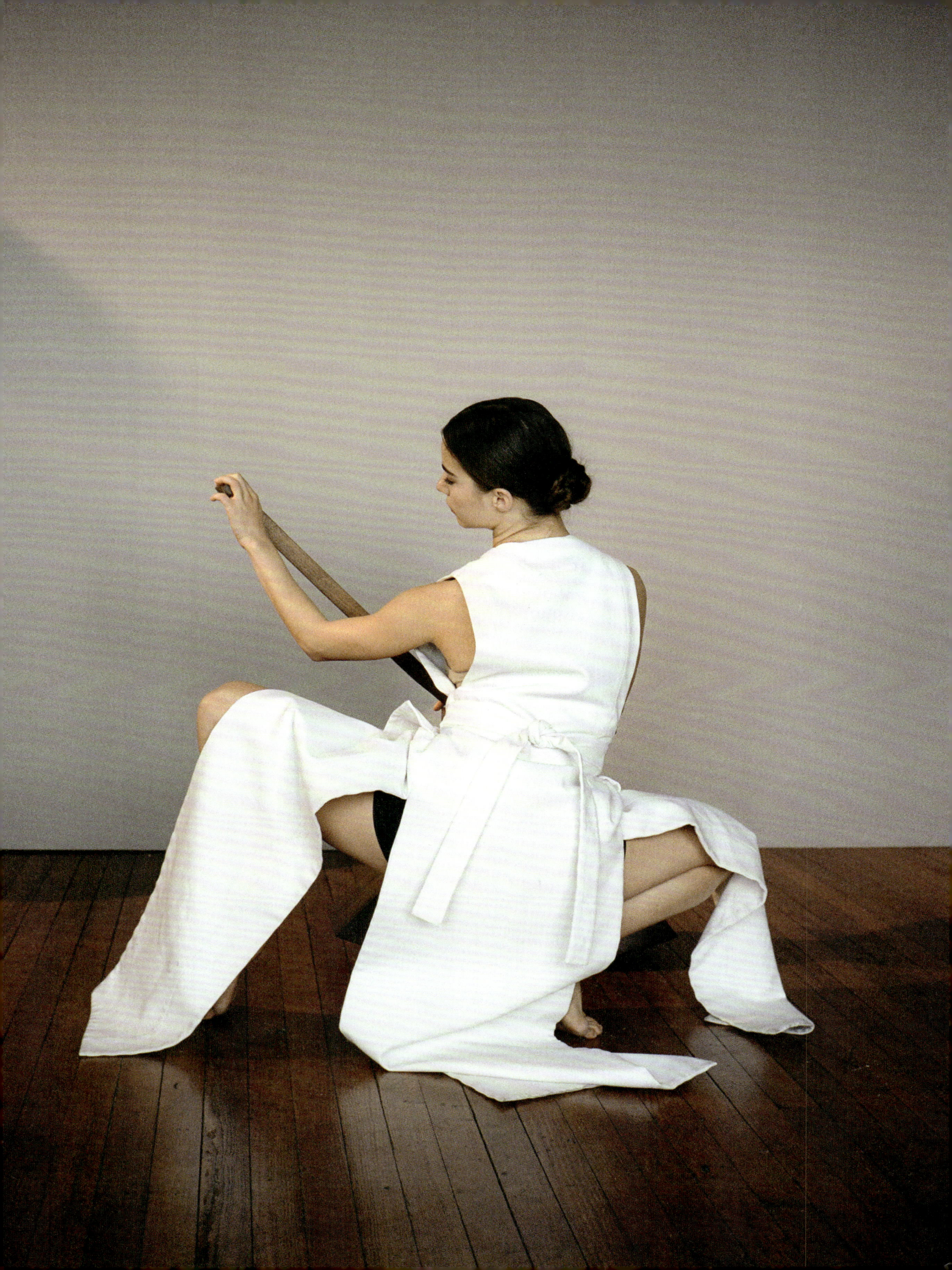

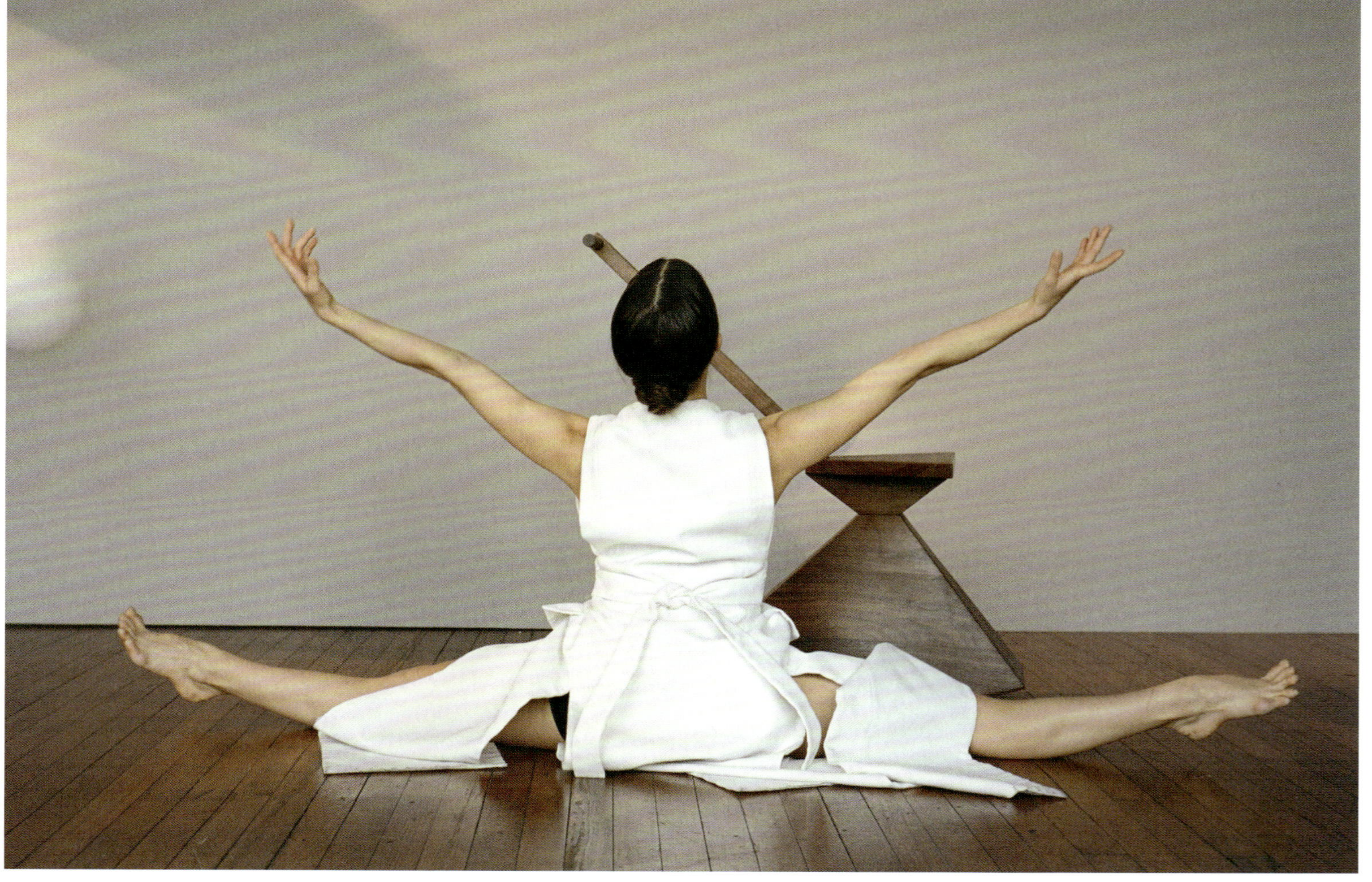

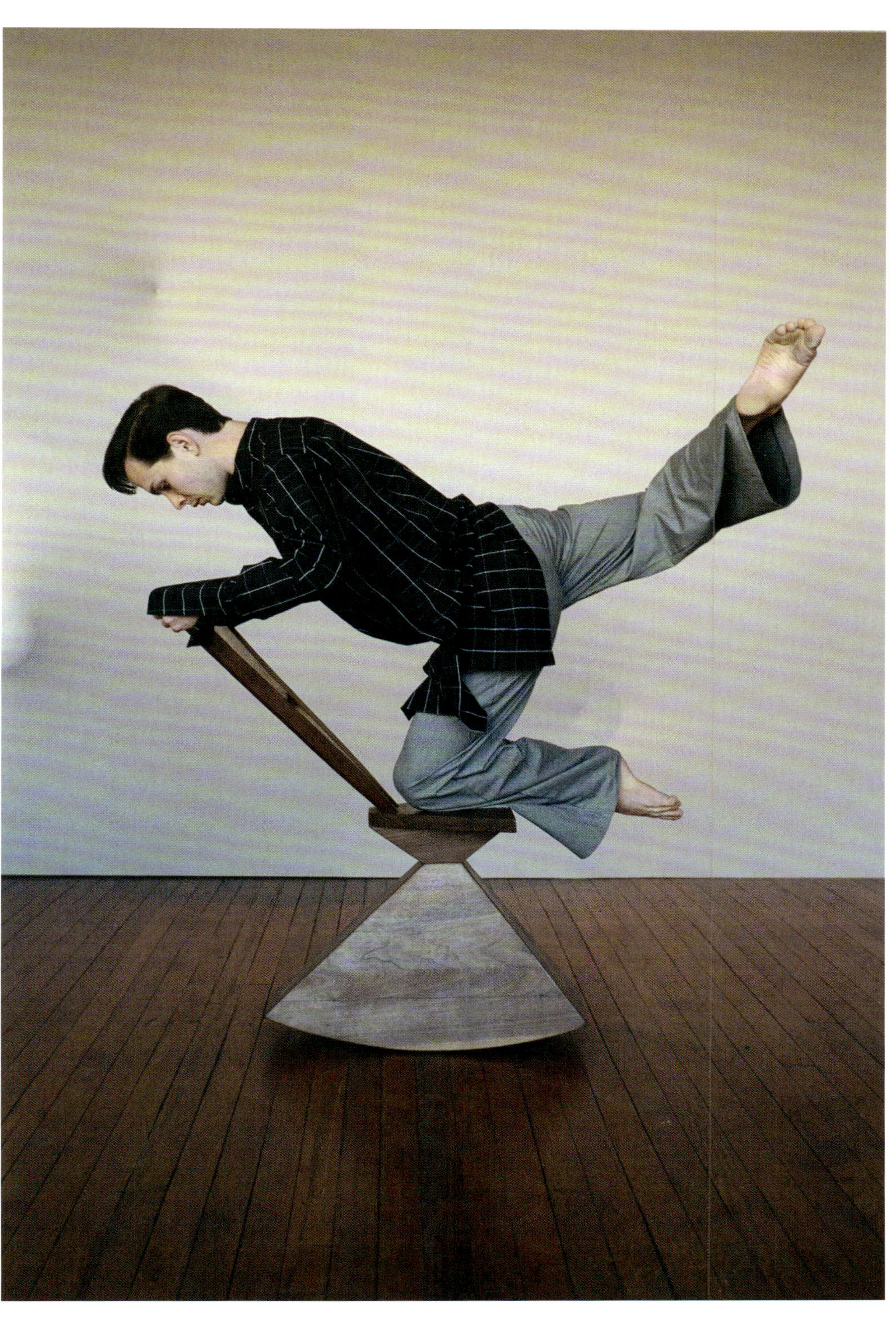

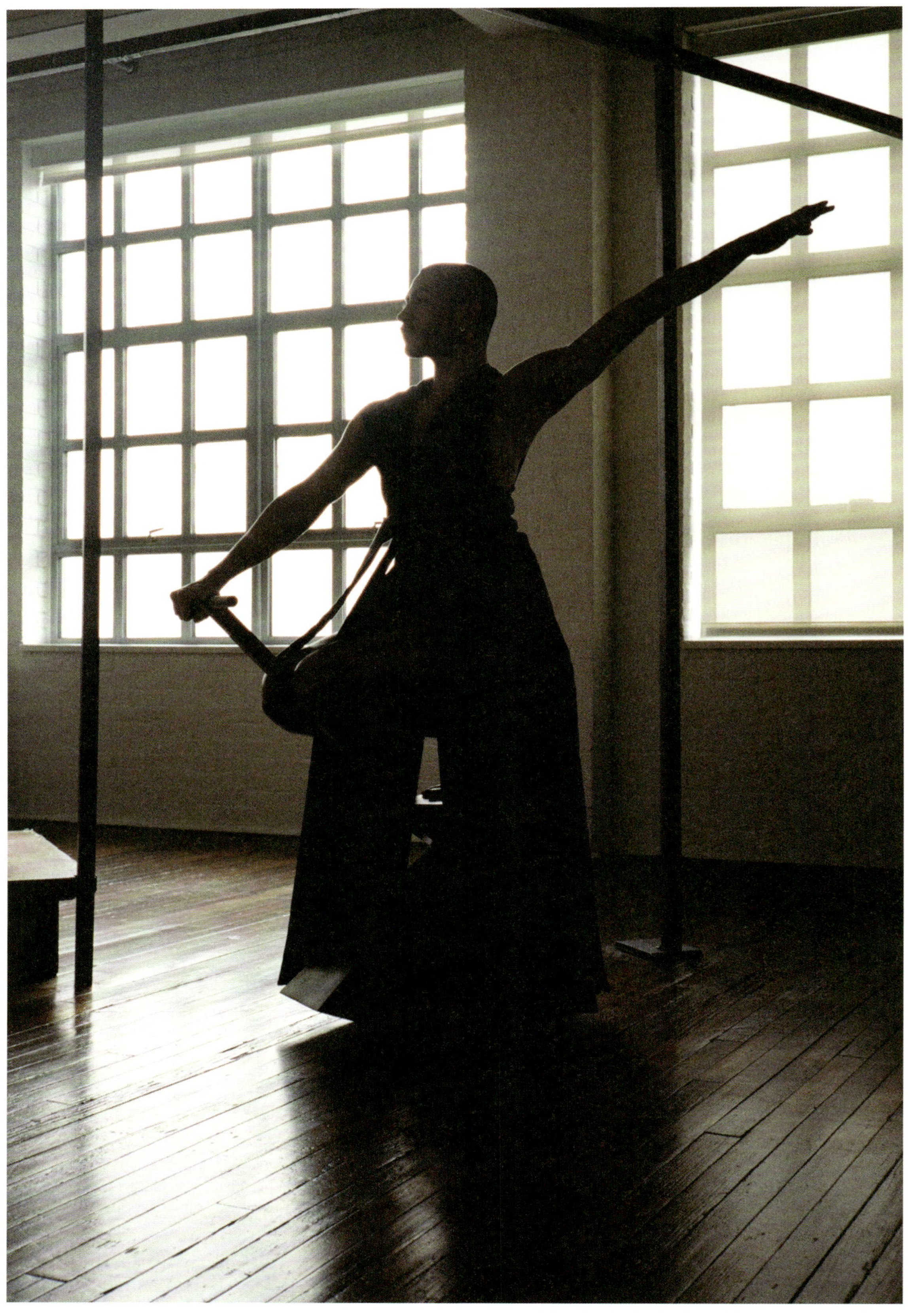

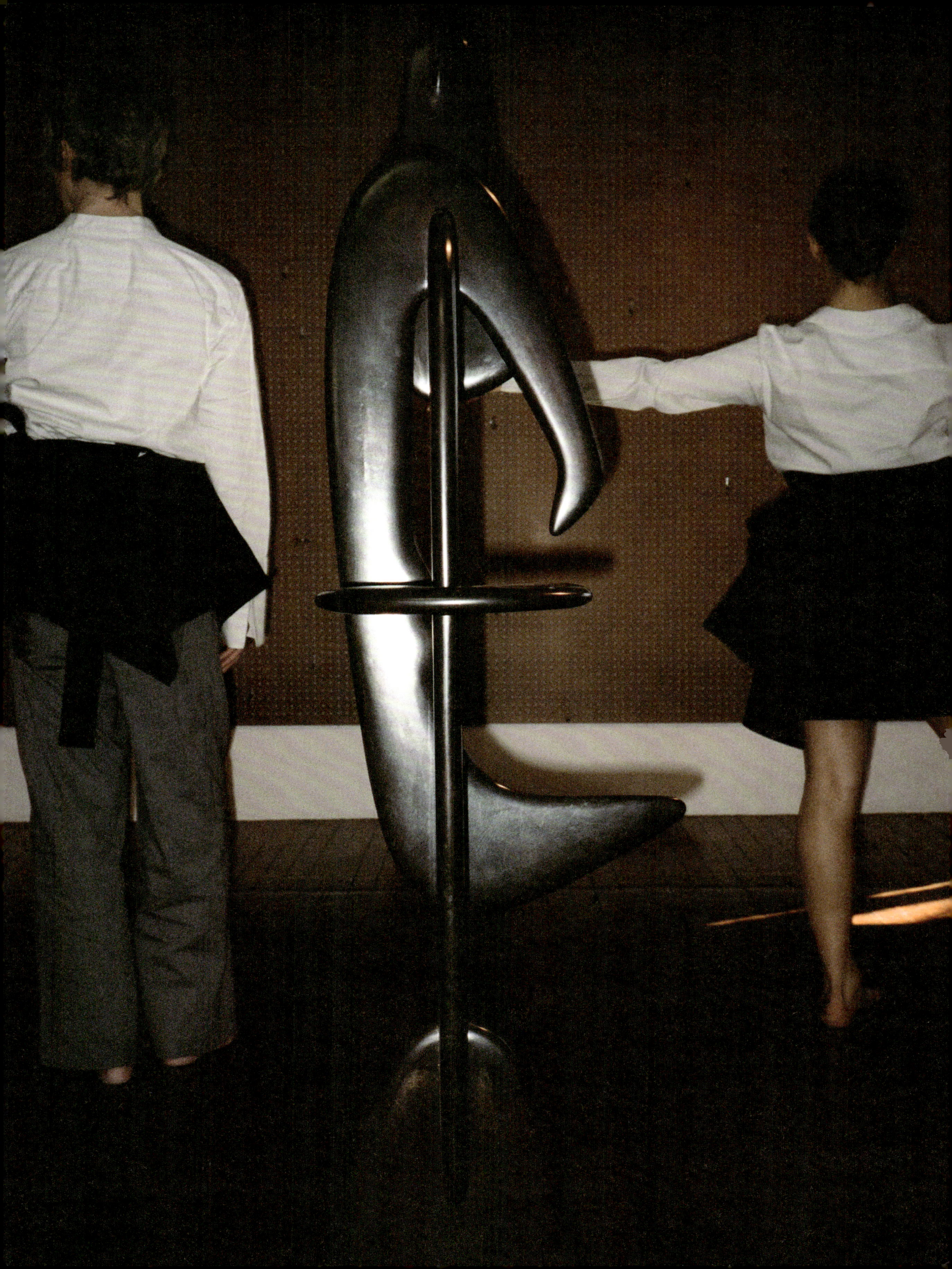

A Conversation with Brendan Fernandes, Sarah Herda, and Thomas Kelley

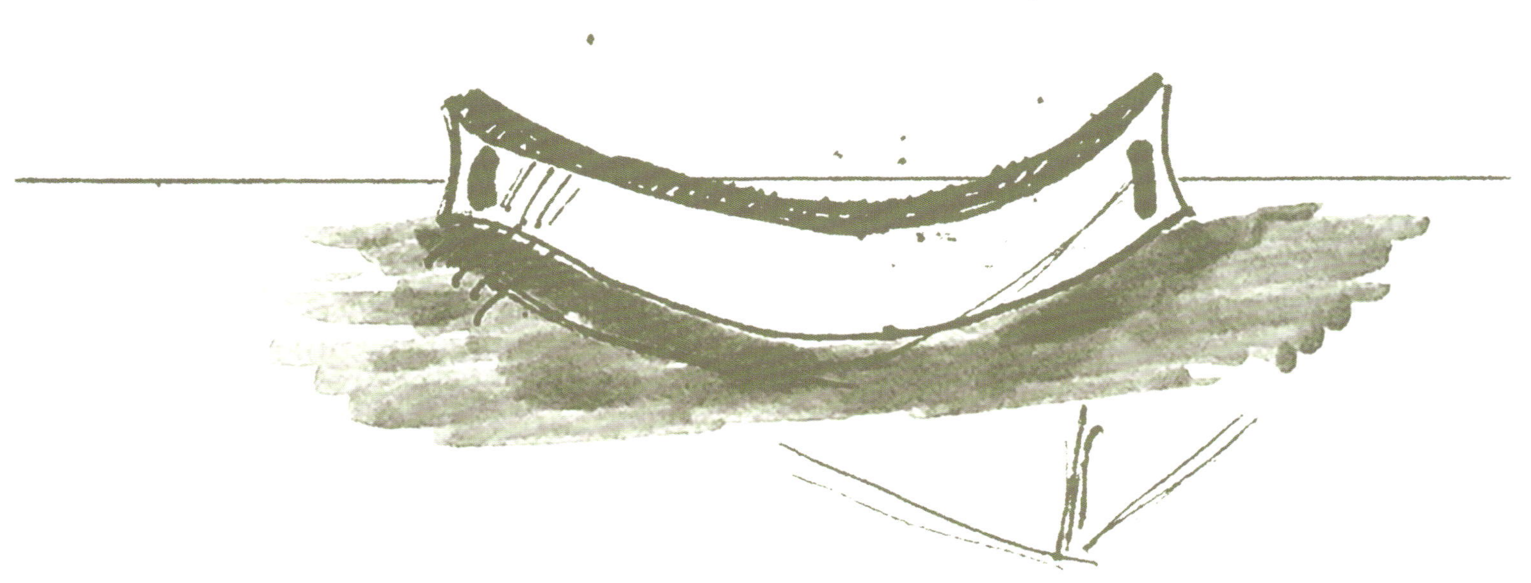

This conversation with Brendan Fernandes, Sarah Herda, and Thomas Kelley took place on November 12, 2020.

Sarah Herda: Brendan, you first came to the Graham Foundation for the *Kjell Theøry* performance by the collective ATOMr in 2017.

Brendan Fernandes: Yeah. And I was still new to Chicago.

SH: It was working with ATOMr that helped the Graham establish a performance residency and it started with space—a need for space. We had a ballroom and they needed space to work. But the experience of working with them also helped us expand our thinking about the intersection of performance and architecture and how to support it. It reminds me of something Roselee Goldberg (Founding Director and Chief Curator of Performa) wrote in her introduction to *Bodybuilding*.[1] She calls architecture a platform for action and suggests performance as a radical tool to rethink architecture. And that is an apt way to think about working with you—exploring that platform of action.

Shortly after we met, the Graham hosted a program to launch your publications *Lost Bodies*[2] and *Still Move*[3], which quickly led to your performance residency and Graham Foundation Fellowship. We did not start out by thinking about making an exhibition together, though it almost immediately became that.

BF: Yes, our collaboration started organically—it began with the book launch, and then the residency, which we originally thought would culminate in a one-time performance in the ballroom. As I spent more time at the Graham's Madlener House, I felt like an inhabitant. These interesting feelings emerged, feelings of intimacy within the house. And our conversations contributed to that also.

When we expanded the residency to include an exhibition, I remember saying, "I want this." I wanted to change the scope and scale of my work and the Graham Foundation Fellowship offered support for that growth. I often think about how the body is supported or burdened by structures. These considerations prompted Sarah to introduce me to Thomas, and the design practice he started with Carrie Norman—Norman Kelley.

SH: Elements of your work were already architectural, like *Future (. . . . - - - - . . .) Perfect* from 2008 [Reference Images p. 128]. This project took on the scale of architecture and looked specifically at the architect Moshe Safdie's Habitat 67.

BF: Totally. And the summer before my residency, I presented *Steady Pulse* (2017) at Recess in New York, which explored the relationship between dancers and the resistance of the dance floor [Reference Images p. 128].

SH: That's when I really started to understand this project as an installation and how the work could manifest as an exhibition, as opposed to a performance. It was the perversion of the floor that immediately made me think of Norman Kelley. Specifically, their *Wrong Chairs* (2014) project that played with the classic Windsor chair construction. It felt like you shared a similar sensibility or way of approaching an archetypal object or form. Of course, you were doing this within a different field or discipline—ballet.

BF: That was our first conversation, Thomas. This idea of the discipline—the mastery or masochism of ballet—and how I wanted to make these structures that were seemingly torture devices. These kinds of wicked, austere, medieval tools that support and then change the body. I initially drew some really weird things, but Thomas took the vision into his world and produced these amazing renderings that elevated my sketches into something that could be realized as functional sculpture. In the end, the devices are very beautiful.

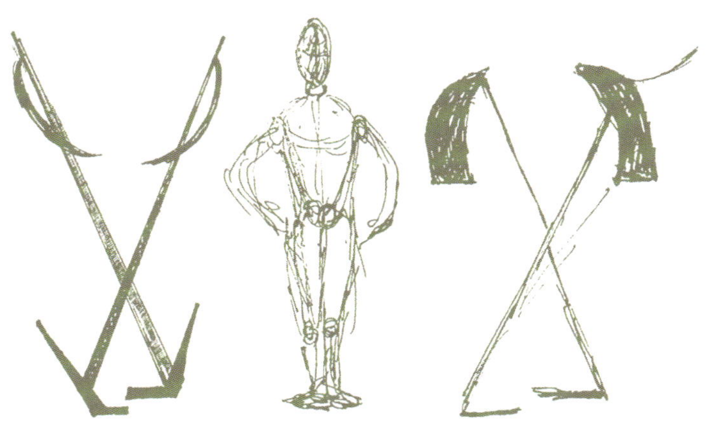

Thomas Kelley: When Sarah called, asking if I had heard of Brendan Fernandes and if Norman Kelley would be interested in having a conversation with you about this project, I turned onto an unfamiliar road. And Brendan then introduced us to the world of S&M and the resources of the Leather Archives & Museum. The key to our collaboration, ultimately, was our ability not to transform, but instead transpose, the instruments that you see in ballet training—like the barre becoming a cage. I think it manifests beautifully as an exercise in collaboration—translating a variety of elements into a choreographed sequence. Hopefully, if you look closely, you don't even see the objects. You just see the dancers.

BF: That was another thing I loved: the objects. We created something that seemingly felt like it was part of the Madlener House. It wasn't an interruption. It was like a seamless intervention. There are these two moments: one when you're in the space, looking at these devices as sculptures, as architectural stand-ins for where a body would be. Then there is another, when a performer's body enters the device, making it into a different kind of platform. In those moments, the audience would watch the dancers instead of exploring the space. This kind of tension is great. We brought together architecture, ballet, visual arts, theater, and the subcultures of Leather and BDSM—coalescing and challenging ballet norms.

I got a lot of questions like: "Are you making the connection that this is kink?" And I'm like, "Yes, but in different ways. Ballet has its own fetishized system. But it's still a dynamic of power, like BDSM..." I was conflating them. When we went to the Leather Archives, we were looking at images, but also thinking about how the archive was started by a ballet dancer. It is so interesting that there is that kind of connection.

SH: Another collaboration touchpoint we looked at early on was the iconic work of Isamu Noguchi and Martha Graham, and their major collaboration between visual arts, sculpture, and dance. They designed sets for performance that included objects that also stood on their own as sculptures. Like what you and Thomas did together—it became something else.

BF: We were creating a set. When Thomas and I were there, we'd walk and think together. That's how I choreographed. On walkthroughs, Thomas discussed the architecture. We made space to think about how to move within it. Upstairs became a space for the dancers to rest, relax, and free themselves—a nod to the original uses of the space as bedrooms and dressing rooms for the Madlener family.

Thomas, you opened my mind to see things differently, which is so important to the collaboration. Working with you gave me new scope to think through how to expand and combine architecture and dance.

TK: Well, my education suggests that architecture is a conflation of the body, the objects that sit within the space, and the space itself. And I think your practice, Brendan, is one that is also trying to make a statement within these three elements. One of the most challenging parts of this project was the prescribed sense of how the body needed to engage both with the space and with the objects in regard to the culture and traditions of ballet.

From the outset, the project reminded me of Noguchi—including architectural references and measurement units based on the human body. The unit of a brick, for example, is meant to replicate the size of a hand. All of the devices—though maybe the cage is an exception as the most open-ended object—have to index the body. I felt it was really challenging to enhance what is already a beautiful moment in a space, seeing a ballet dancer holding a pose, and to find ways to do that with static objects.

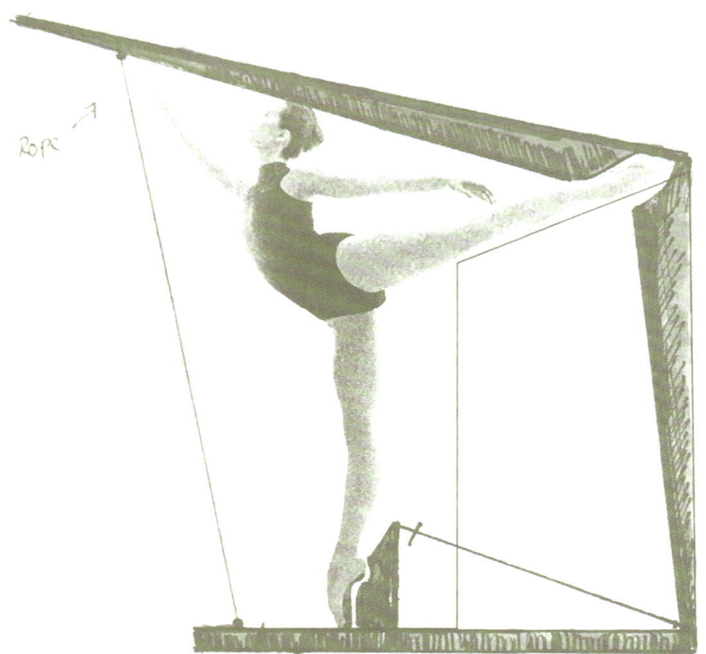

SH: I rediscovered a series of drawings done when you were together in the space and Brendan was blocking the Joffrey dancer, Leah [Upchurch]. As Leah went through positions, these really incredible drawings emerged. It's interesting to see so much of what ended up being articulated in the objects in these early drawings.

TK: That's the challenge! In no way can we ever match the complexity of the performance with an object. The best you can do is try and use the object to alter one's reading of the performance. Which is why, whether it was at the Graham or at the Whitney, it is best to see the show twice—to see it performed and then to see the installation without dancers.

BF: Definitely. People would say to me: "Oh, we missed the performance." You still get something from seeing it without bodies. But, of course, I think you need to see it twice. Each device design allowed for use over long periods of time, but the form still fatigued and labored the body. It was important to consider how dancers work with the devices to challenge themselves and also create fortitude. One of the things that unfolded during rehearsals and performances was that dancers would trade shifts on the devices, because some bodies don't move in certain ways. And, of course, the devices were designed initially for Leah's body.

TK: To that end, the objects were inflexible and not designed for multiple body types. To have used a model who—I believe in your words, Brendan—was not characteristically the ballet standard, was fascinating for many reasons.

BF: That was a super important decision, because when we started looking at the written standards of a ballet body—starting with the "standards" of arm length, body weight, etc.—we were very aware of the fact that these "standards" don't apply to most people. We began by using them in the drawings, but the devices quickly evolved into something else.

TK: Right. It's interesting to hear how dancers other than Leah respond to the devices.

BF: Dancers started to take liberties and found other ways to use the devices. I liked that they gave themselves agency.

SH: I remember this issue of agency also being a challenge in the beginning. If the objects were about control—holding over-extended positions and an idealized or exaggerated form—the cage offered a different set of conditions. You talked about the challenge of imbuing the dancers with agency when they entered in the scaffolding cage, which you talked about as the free space.

BF: 100%. Everything else in the choreographic score was counted. But the cage was unstructured: "Here, you have ten minutes of free time." Because of the discipline of ballet, the dancers responded to my prompt with a question and a request for guidance: "I need you to tell me what to do because this is a performance." And so, I said: "You can just stand there." And they were like, "Okay, but..." And they did, but they didn't see that as performing—they wanted to be jumping or turning. So even the act of stillness, resting, or breathing—which I understand as an act of dance making—is part of that piece.

At first, the Joffrey Academy dancers were very timid and shy. I encouraged: "Go up to the audience! They'll move when you get there." Once the dancers did start approaching the audience and saw that power, or the agency, they slowly played with it more. But it was hard. This was a primary difference between *The Master and Form* and *Contract and Release* [at the Noguchi Museum]. The more contemporary dancers took the liberty to experiment from the outset.

SH: I'm happy that you mentioned the audience, Brendan. We've been focusing on the dancers, the performance, and the space. But the audience is also critical. As I understand it, you envisioned this as a space in which they could confront their own bodies?

BF: Yes, and that confrontation was because of proximity. People came to see a performance and asked: "When is it starting?" And I'd respond: "It already started." People watched their own bodies carefully because they moved around the dancers. If the dancers went upstairs, the audience followed them. Or if the dancers came towards the audience, they would move.

But in other moments of the performance, you're seeing the dancers' labor and fatigue, you're seeing them breathe and hearing them exhale. Or, if the dancer was in a device, holding a position, the audience saw how the dancer was shaking or moving. That is a really important moment in which to confront a body. And that, for me, also comes out of the notion of kink and the idea of fetishization, because as ballet dancers we do crazy things to our body.

The Master and Form came from my personal narrative—the ballet world didn't like my feet. I used a wooden device—a foot stretcher—to bind my feet and give me arches. For *The Master and Form* I wanted to make full-body structures to affect the whole body; an idea that reminded me of BDSM furniture.

Once, someone in the audience was watching me direct. As I looked at one of the dancers, I noticed they weren't in full turnout, but I didn't say anything. The dancer saw me looking, and then slowly corrected.

It's such a ballet thing. And the audience is there to experience that moment of discipline in action. It's that dynamic that led to the piece being called *The Master and Form*. But who is the master? There were so many kinds of masters within the collaborative space.

TK: That proximity and durational experience creates discomfort within the audience. Personally, I felt awkward staring too long when I would notice someone else looking at me, while I was looking at a dancer, when in reality, they were probably looking beyond me, at another dancer. It subverts the subject-object relationship when you allow an audience member to spend time so close.

SH: There is intimacy in these experiences, because these are moments that you are actually not supposed to see. Here, the dancer is seen training for a pose. The audience does not typically have access to that. It also changes the expectations of viewing dance, an exhibition, or a performance, I think.

BF: The expectations of the audience were absolutely challenged. We had questions like: "Are there tickets?" or "I can't stay the whole time. Is that okay?" We built this installation throughout the house, but every time the dancers went into a space and started to perform, the audience gathered as if around a stage. There was almost always space between the dancers and the audience, especially at the Whitney. The audience had the invitation to enter the space and walk around, but no one did. As soon as the dancers left, the audience would start to walk around the objects, like sculptures.

TK: And that's where I would say the architecture of the Graham impacted the sensibility of the performance. We looked very closely at the Madlener House as a specific point of departure for Brendan—thinking about the way the dancers could use the space. We extruded molding into open space, shifting the existing architecture to become appendages for the dancers. That's how kink became more crucial to the context, allowing us to transplant elements from other contexts into the Graham. Like a cage that was meant to, yes, resemble the kind of cage you might find in a kink club, but also proportioned in a way that mimics a ballet barre in a studio. It was about experimenting with other forms, while quoting the house and the context.

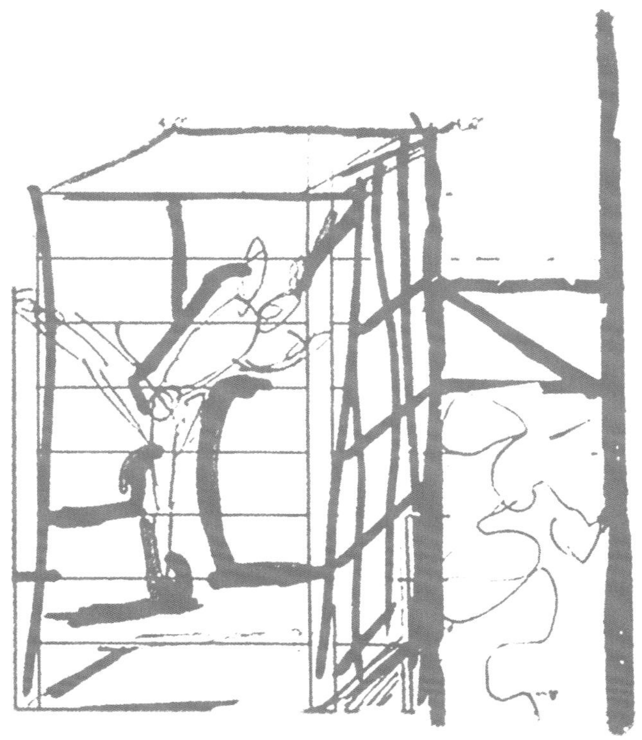

BF: The idea of repeating thresholds, for example, to create rhythm, which became dance scores, was like a form of notation. I think that was really beautiful.

TK: We brought that into the Whitney as well, by repeating the mullion spacing across the walls.

BF: And that gave the walls a rhythm. It created repetition and movement in the space by engaging elements of architecture. You could say that it's a feeling of the score through the architectural devices. It really gave the dancers another moment to think: "Oh, I can play with the space in a different way." This idea of play is central; I called the structures playgrounds, which of course references Noguchi. But they were also like BDSM playgrounds, which relates to the idea of furniture intimacy. With BDSM furniture, when the body and the device (typically made of leather) engage, it's skin to skin contact. It suggests that the device is collaborating with the body; it's an extension of the body. This became something that dancers really took on as a concept in the process. Also, the sounds of the performance were captured by an audio recording and played back through speakers, representing the ghostly residue of the bodies in the space when they were gone. The recording followed the score and moved throughout the space as the live performance did. For me, it was another chance to play with the intimacy of the space.

SH: Though the institutional setting differed between Graham and Whitney, both shared in the experience of everybody—dancers, audience, collaborators, staff—working it out together, negotiating how it would unfold. Confidence grew as the performance progressed.

BF: Absolutely. I love the natural progression. Adapting and presenting *The Master and Form* from the Graham for the Whitney, developing *Contract and Release* for Noguchi, I know this is just the beginning. I'm so thankful for the collaboration, especially its continuation. It has definitely affected the way I make art. It is something I'm striving for within my work—ways to be more collaborative, more generous. Ways of working that are more based on exchanges; where it's not about me, or you, it's about us. I am so excited because we found this synergy and kept going! For me, the continuation is essential. Even now, this book becomes another extension of the ideas we've shared.

1 Charles Aubin, Carlos Mínguez Carrasco, and Roselee Goldberg, *Bodybuilding: Architecture and Performance* (New York: Artbook | D.A.P., 2019).

2 Shannon Anderson, ed., *Brendan Fernandes: Lost Bodies* (Kingston: Agnes Etherington Art Centre, 2016).

3 Crystal Mowry, ed., *Still Move: Brendan Fernandes* (London: Black Dog Publishing, 2017).

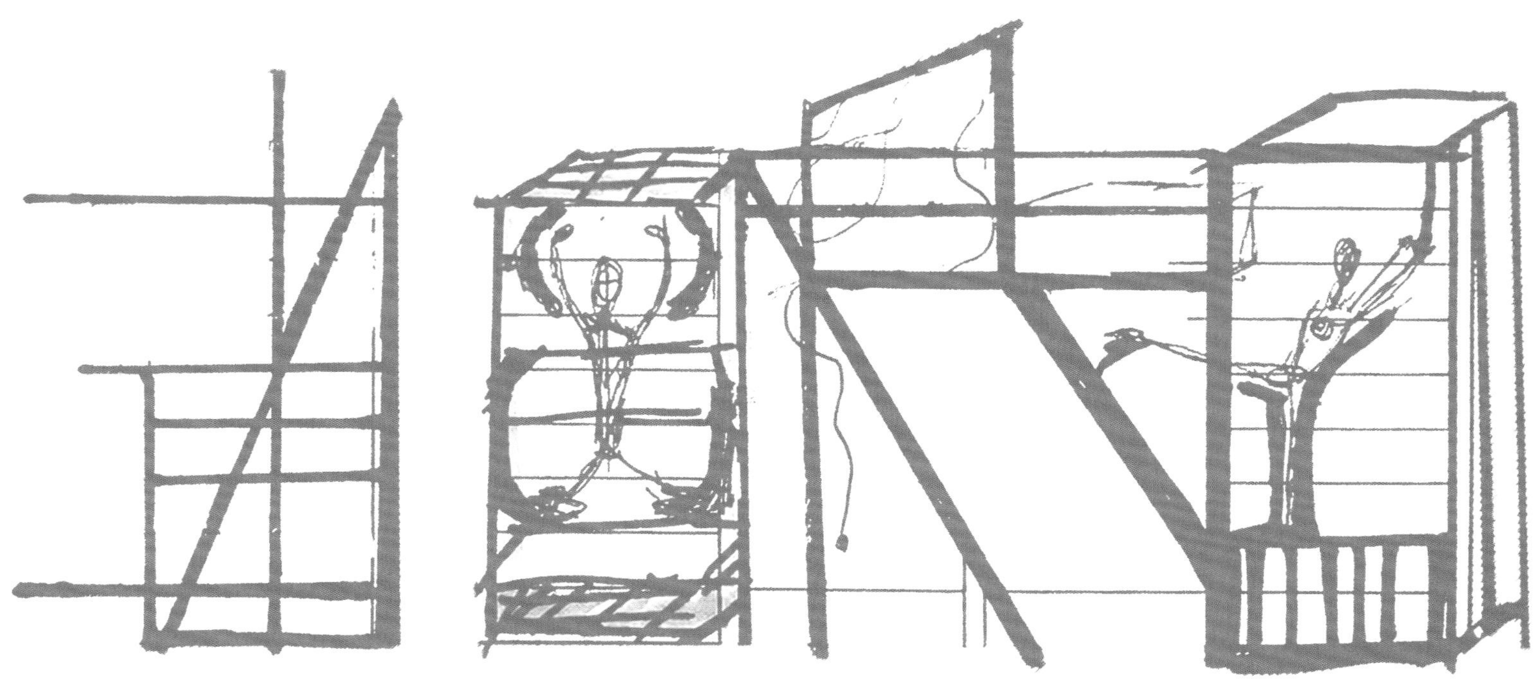

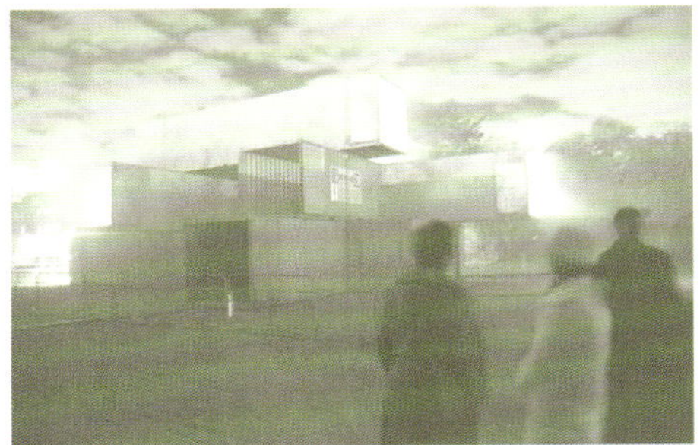

A

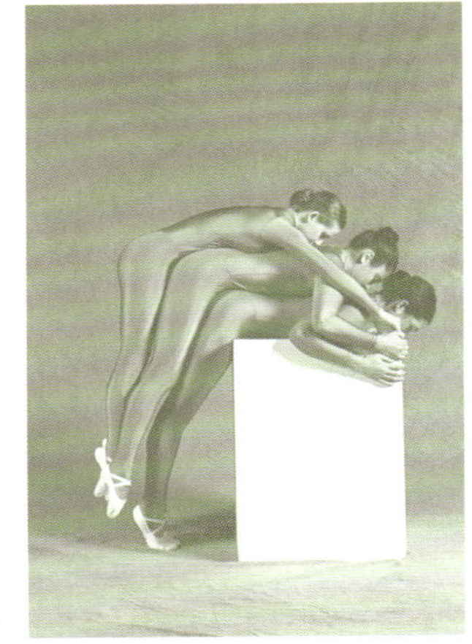

B

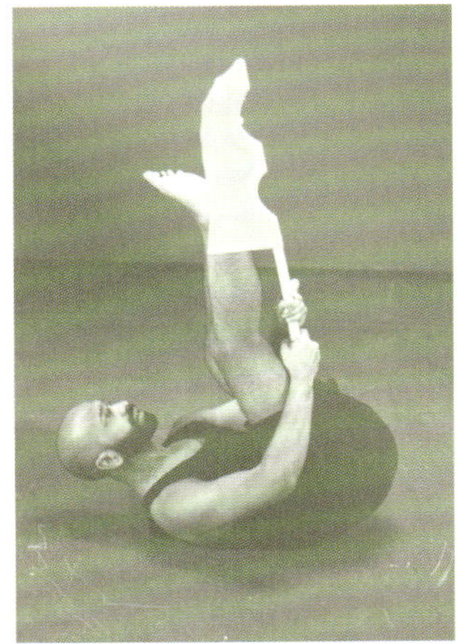

C

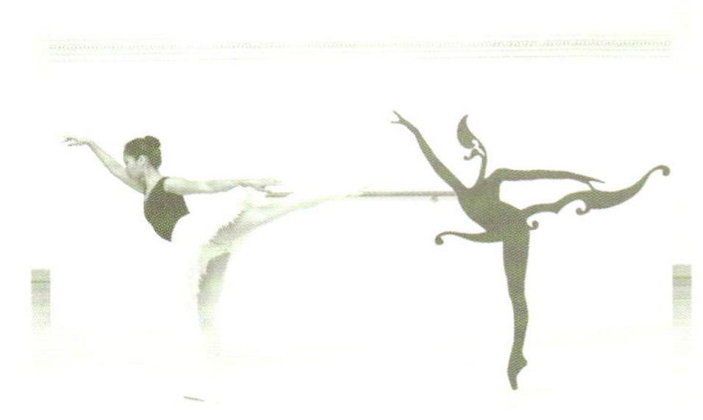

D

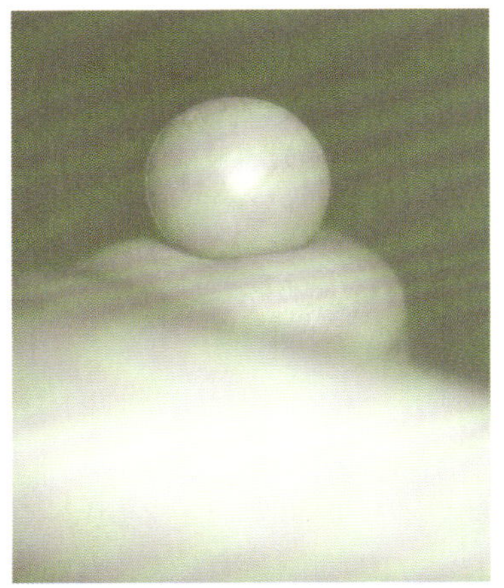

E

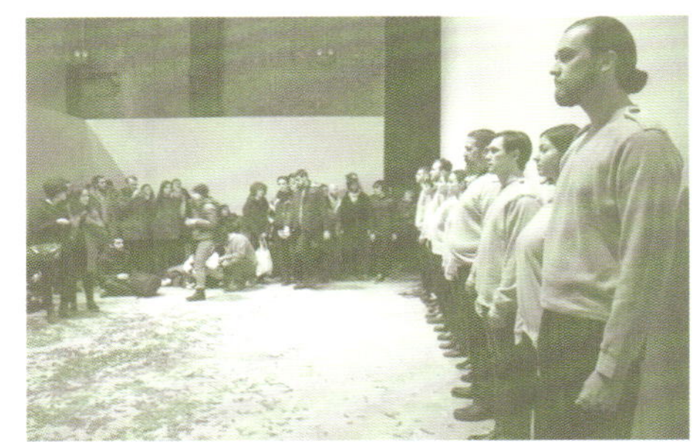

F

A

Future (. . . - - - . . .) Perfect, 2008
Image courtesy of the artist
Photo by Brendan Fernandes

B

The Working Move, 2012
Digital print,
48 × 34 inches
Edition of 3 + 2 AP

C

Standing Leg, 2014
Performance still
Dancer: Brendan Fernandes
Videographer: Felix Chan
Image courtesy of Kitchener-Waterloo Art Gallery

D

Inverted Pyramid, 2014
Installation view, mixed media installation, dimensions variable
Dancer: Jenna Savella, soloist with the National Ballet of Canada
Image courtesy Varley Art Gallery of Markham
Photo by Toni Hafkenscheid

E

Still Move, 2014
Digital print,
20 × 16 inches
Edition of 3 + 2 AP

F

Closing Line, 2014
Performance still
Dancers: Angela Freiberger, Katie McQueston, Ethan David Wilson Lester, Timothy Hospodar, Moira Williams, Michael Mahalchick, Natalie Galpern, Jessica Karuhanga, Suzan D. Polat, Chris Boiga, Jorge Sanchez, Brendan Mahoney
Original score: Thomas Ian Campbell
Original costumes: Brendan Fernandes
Images courtesy of The Sculpture Center
Photo by Megan Mantina

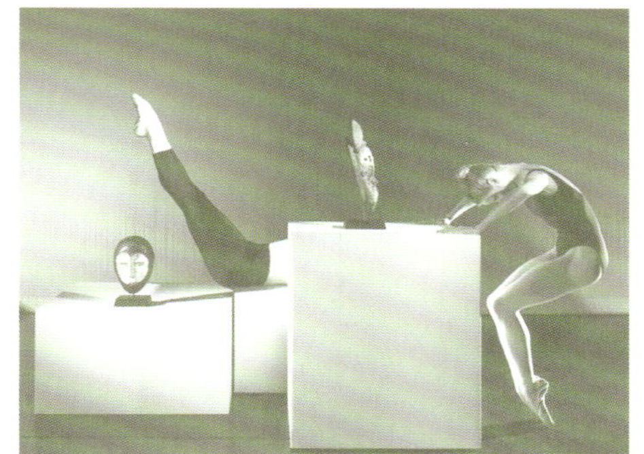

G

H

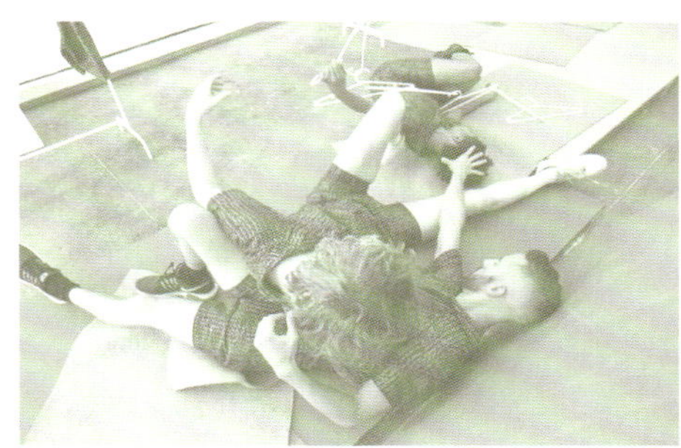

I

J

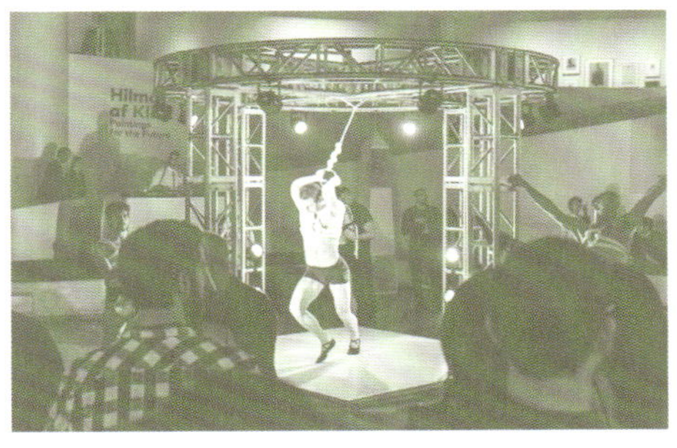

K

G

As One, 2015
Digital print,
34 × 48 inches
Edition of 3 + 2 AP

H

In Touch, 2015
Performance stills
Dancer: Etienne Capko of Gansango Dance, Seattle
Original costume: Anna Rose Telcs in collaboration with Brendan Fernandes
Commissioned by the Seattle Art Museum

I

Steady Pulse, 2017
Dancers: John Alix, Khadija Griffith, Oisín Monaghan
Uniforms: Rational Dress Society
Image courtesy of Recess
Photo by Wendy Ploger

J

Stand Tall, 2017
Performances by University at Buffalo Dance Students: Ginger Page, Savannah Sigmon, Maggie Hansen, Taylor Heaphy, Mary Pappagallo, Laura Nasca
Images courtesy of the University of Buffalo Art Galleries
Photo by Studio Avli

K

Ballet Kink, 2019
Performance staged as part of the Solomon R. Guggenheim's Young Collector's Party in April 2019
Dancers: Abigail H. Simon, Allison Walsh, Elina Miettinen, Violetta Komyshan, Nico Brown, Tyler Zydel, Jonatan Lujan, Josep Maria Monreal Vidal, Mauricio Vera Nuńez
Rope bondage: Master Ming (Ming Chang) assisted by Vincent Tiley
DJ: Karsten Sollors
Image courtesy of the Guggenheim Museum
Photo by Scott Rudd Events

The Master and Form (2018–19)
The Graham Foundation, Chicago,
January 25 – April 7, 2018

The exhibition at the Graham Foundation included an installation of steel scaffolding, "training device" sculptures, ropes, audio recording, and performance.

List of training devices:

In First, in Fifth (2018)
Stained ash wood, leather, and carpet

In Passé, in Fourth (2018)
Stained ash wood, leather, and carpet

In Cambré à Terre (2018)
Stained ash wood, leather, and carpet

In Second (2018)
Stained ash wood, leather, and carpet

In Arabesque (2018)
Stained ash wood, leather, and carpet

Cast List
The five dancers who performed *The Master and Form* at the Graham Foundation are:

Satoru Iwasaki
Yuha Kamoto
Andrea de León Rivera
Antonio Mannino
Leah Upchurch

Costumes: Dancer's own dance wear

Scaffolding by and exhibition design developed in collaboration with Norman Kelley. The training devices were fabricated by Jason Lewis.

Score created in collaboration with Amanda Jane Graham.

The Master and Form (2018–19)
The Whitney Museum of American Art,
New York, May 17 – September 22, 2019

The installation of *The Master and Form* at the 2019 Whitney Biennial included steel scaffolding, "training device" sculptures, ropes, audio recording, and performance.

List of training devices:

In First, in Fifth (2018)
Stained ash wood, leather, and carpet

In Passé, in Fourth (2018)
Stained ash wood, leather, and carpet

In Cambré à Terre (2018)
Stained ash wood, leather, and carpet

In Second (2018)
Stained ash wood, leather, and carpet

In Arabesque (2018)
Stained ash wood, leather, and carpet

Cast List
The twelve dancers who performed *The Master and Form* during the Whitney Biennial are:

Héctor Cerna
Charles Gowin
Violetta Komyshan
Tiffany Mangulabnan
Jordan Miller
Josep Maria Monreal Vidal
Mykel Nairne
Amy Saunder
Mauricia Vera
Allison Walsh
Jennifer Whalen
Tyler Zydel

Costumes: Johana Davenport Calica

Scaffolding by and exhibition design developed in collaboration with Norman Kelley. The training devices were fabricated by Jason Lewis.

Score created in collaboration with Amanda Jane Graham.

The Master and Form installation is co-owned by The Joyner/Giuffrida Collection, San Francisco and the Rennie Collection, Vancouver.

Brendan Fernandes: Contract and Release (2019)
The Noguchi Museum, New York,
September 11 – March 8, 2020

The exhibition at The Noguchi Museum included an installation of steel scaffolding, "training device" sculptures, and performance.

Still Release I (2019)
Walnut
(identifying features: two prongs, wide-spread, knobs on underside)

Still Release II (2019)
Walnut
(identifying features: two prongs with crossbar)

Still Release III (2019)
Walnut
(identifying features: two prongs, close-set with knobs on outside)

Still Release IV (2019)
Walnut
(identifying features: two prongs, close-set, only chair with knobs on seat)

Still Release V (2019)
Walnut
(identifying features: single prong, three knobs on prong)

Still Release VI (2019)
Walnut
(identifying features: single prong with crossbar)

Cast List
The six dancers who performed *Contract and Release* at The Noguchi Museum are:

Héctor Cerna
Violetta Komyshan
Victor Lozano
Tiffany Mangulabnan
Oisín Monaghan
Amy Saunder

Score created in collaboration with Amanda Jane Graham.

The works included in *Contract and Release* are courtesy of the artist and Monique Meloche Gallery, Chicago.

p. 21
The Master and Form (2018–19)
Dancer: Andrea de León Rivera
Image courtesy of the Graham Foundation, Chicago
Photo by Brendan Leo Meara

p. 29
The Master and Form (2018–19)
Dancer: Satoru Iwasaki
Image courtesy of the Graham Foundation, Chicago
Photo by RCH

p. 30
The Master and Form (2018–19)
Dancer: Antonio Mannino
Image courtesy of the Graham Foundation, Chicago
Photo by RCH

p. 31
The Master and Form (2018–19)
Dancer: Yuha Kamoto
Image courtesy of the Graham Foundation, Chicago
Photo by RCH

p. 33
The Master and Form (2018–19)
Dancers: Satoru Iwasaki, Yuha Kamoto, Andrea de León Rivera, Antonio Mannino, Leah Upchurch
Image courtesy of the Graham Foundation, Chicago
Photo by RCH

pp. 34–35
The Master and Form (2018–19)
Dancers: Satoru Iwasaki, Yuha Kamoto, Andrea de León Rivera, Antonio Mannino, Leah Upchurch
Image courtesy of the Graham Foundation, Chicago
Photo by Brendan Leo Meara

pp. 50–51
The Master and Form (2018–19)
Dancers: Charles Gowin, Héctor Cerna, Josep Maria Monreal Vidal, Tiffany Mangulabnan, Violetta Komyshan
Image courtesy of the Whitney Museum of American Art
Photo by Matthew Carasella

p. 52
The Master and Form (2018–19)
Dancers: Amy Saunder, Mauricio Vera, Tiffany Mangulabnan
Image courtesy of the Whitney Museum of American Art
Photo © 2019 Paula Court

p. 53
Both images:
The Master and Form (2018–19)
Dancers (top): Charles Gowin, Héctor Cerna, Josep Maria Monreal Vidal, Violetta Komyshan
Dancers (bottom): Charles Gowin, Violetta Komyshan
Images courtesy of the Whitney Museum of American Art
Photo by Matthew Carasella

pp. 54–55
The Master and Form (2018–19)
Dancer: Héctor Cerna
Image courtesy of the Whitney Museum of American Art
Photo by Matthew Carasella

pp. 66–67
The Master and Form (2018–19)
Dancers: Josep Maria Monreal Vidal, Mauricio Vera, Tiffany Mangulabnan, Tyler Zydel, Violetta Komyshan
Image courtesy of the Whitney Museum of American Art
Photo © 2019 Paula Court

pp. 88–89
Contract and Release (2019)
Dancer: Tiffany Mangulabnan
© The Isamu Noguchi Foundation and Garden Museum, NY / ARS
Photo by Nicholas Knight

p. 90
Contract and Release (2019)
Dancers: Tiffany Mangulabnan, Oisín Monaghan, Victor Lozano
© The Isamu Noguchi Foundation and Garden Museum, NY / ARS
Photo by Nicholas Knight

p. 91
Contract and Release (2019)
Dancers: Tiffany Mangulabnan, Oisín Monaghan, Victor Lozano
© The Isamu Noguchi Foundation and Garden Museum, NY / ARS
Photo by Nicholas Knight

pp. 92–93
Contract and Release (2019)
© The Isamu Noguchi Foundation and Garden Museum, NY / ARS
Photo by Nicholas Knight

p. 94
Contract and Release (2019)
Dancer: Victor Lozano
© The Isamu Noguchi Foundation and Garden Museum, NY / ARS
Photo by Nicholas Knight

p. 95
Contract and Release (2019)
Dancer: Oisín Monaghan
© The Isamu Noguchi Foundation and Garden Museum, NY / ARS
Photo by Nicholas Knight

pp. 96–97
Contract and Release (2019)
© The Isamu Noguchi Foundation and Garden Museum, NY / ARS
Photo by Nicholas Knight

pp. 98–99
Both images:
Contract and Release (2019)
Dancers: Oisín Monaghan, Victor Lozano
© The Isamu Noguchi Foundation and Garden Museum, NY / ARS
Photo by Nicholas Knight

pp. 100–01
Contract and Release (2019)
Dancers: Tiffany Mangulabnan, Oisín Monaghan, Victor Lozano
© The Isamu Noguchi Foundation and Garden Museum, NY / ARS
Photo by Nicholas Knight

pp. 111–19
All images:
Contract and Release (2019)
Dancers:
p. 111 Oisín Monaghan
p. 112 Victor Lozano
p. 113 Victor Lozano
p. 114 Héctor Cerna
p. 115 Violetta Komyshan
p. 116 Violetta Komyshan
p. 117 Victor Lozano
p. 118 Héctor Cerna
p. 119 Oisín Monaghan, Violetta Komyshan
Images courtesy of The Isamu Noguchi Foundation and Garden Museum, NY / ARS
Photo by Neige Thebault

Juliet Bellow

Juliet Bellow is Associate Professor of Art History at American University. Her book *Modernism on Stage: The Ballets Russes and the Parisian Avant-Garde* was published by Ashgate Press in 2013, and she served as a Consulting Scholar for the 2013 exhibition *Diaghilev and the Ballets Russes, 1909-1929: When Art Danced With Music*. Her other publications include articles in *Art Bulletin*, *Art Journal*, *American Art*, and *Modernism/modernity*; chapters in edited volumes including *The Cambridge Companion to Ballet*, *The Modernist World*, *Arabesque without End: Across Music and the Arts*, and *Foreign Artists and Communities in Modern Paris, 1870–1914*; and contributions to exhibition catalogs on Sonia Delaunay (Tate Modern/Musée d'Art Moderne de la Ville de Paris), Merce Cunningham (Walker Art Center), and Auguste Rodin (Courtauld Institute of Art/Musée Rodin, Paris).

Andy Campbell

Andy Campbell is an art historian, critic, and curator working in Los Angeles, where he is Assistant Professor of Critical Studies at USC-Roski School of Art and Design. He is the author of *Bound Together: Leather, Sex, Archives, and Contemporary Art* (Manchester University Press, 2020), *Queer X Design: 50 Years of Signs, Symbols, Banners, Logos, and Graphic Art of LGBTQ* (Black Dog & Leventhal, 2019), and the co-editor (along with Amelia Jones) of the catalog *Queer Communion: Ron Athey* (Intellect, 2020). His art writing can be found in *Artforum*, *The Invisible Archive*, *X-Tra*, and *Aperture*.

Hendrik Folkerts

Hendrik Folkerts is the Dittmer Curator of Contemporary Art at the Art Institute of Chicago. There, he has organized solo exhibitions and presentations of Igshaan Adams (2022), Mounira Al Solh (2018, with Jordan Carter), Vaginal Davis (2019, with Solveig Nelson), Anne Imhof, Naeem Mohaiemen (2019, with Robyn Farrell), Malangatana Ngwenya (2020, with Felicia Mings and Constantine Petridis), and Vivian Suter, as well as *Iterations*, a series of large-scale performance commissions that presented new works by Alexandra Bachzetsis, Cevdet Erek, Ralph Lemon, Paulina Olowska, and Cally Spooner, among others. Folkerts was curator at documenta 14 from 2014 until 2017. Together with the team led by artistic director Adam Szymczyk, he was responsible for the exhibitions in Athens, Greece and Kassel, Germany. Prior, Folkerts was Curator of Performance, Film, and Discursive Programs at the Stedelijk Museum in Amsterdam (2010 until 2015). His texts have been published in journals and magazines such as *South as a State of Mind, Mousse Magazine, Artforum International, The Exhibitionist*, *Metropolis M*, *Art & the Public Sphere*, as well as numerous exhibition catalogs. Most recently, he contributed to monographs on Andy Warhol, Carlos Motta, Anne Imhof, Mounira Al Solh, Vivian Suter, Bouchra Khalili, Alexandra Bachzetsis, and Samson Young.

Dakin Hart

Dakin Hart is Senior Curator at The Isamu Noguchi Foundation and Garden Museum (Long Island City, NY), where he oversees the Museum's exhibitions, collections, catalogue raisonné, archives, and public programming, and has the daily good fortune of collaborating with Isamu Noguchi in absentia. His previous positions include Assistant Director at the Nasher Sculpture Center (Dallas), Artistic Director and Director of Artists in Residence at Montalvo Center for the Arts (Saratoga, CA), and Assistant to the Director of the Fine Arts Museums of San Francisco. He has also worked as an independent curator and writer.

Sarah Herda

Sarah Herda is Director of the Graham Foundation for Advanced Studies in the Fine Arts. Founded in 1956, the Graham fosters the development and exchange of diverse and challenging ideas about architecture and its role in the arts, culture, and society. As part of her leadership of the organization, Herda oversees an international grantmaking program to individuals and organizations, and curates exhibitions and public programs at the Foundation's headquarters, the historic Madlener House in Chicago. She served as an Artistic Director of the inaugural Chicago Architecture Biennial in 2015 and was Director and Curator at Storefront for Art and Architecture, New York.

Brett Littman

Brett Littman has been the Director of The Isamu Noguchi Foundation and Garden Museum in Long Island City, New York since May 2018. He was Executive Director of The Drawing Center from 2007–2018; Deputy Director of MoMA PS1 from 2003–2007; Co-Director of Dieu Donné Papermill from 2001–2003, and Associate Director of Urban Glass from 1996–2001. Littman's interests are multi-disciplinary: he personally curated more than thirty exhibitions over the last decade, dealing with visual art, outsider art, craft, design, architecture, poetry, music, science, and literature. He was named the curator of Frieze Sculpture at Rockefeller Center (2019–2020) and is also an art critic, lecturer, and an active essayist for museum and gallery catalogs, in addition to writing articles for a wide range of U.S. and international art, fashion, and design magazines. A native New Yorker, Brett Littman received a Chevalier of the Order of Arts and Letters from France in 2017 and his B.A. in Philosophy from the University of California, San Diego.

RÉVÉRENCE

To extend one's body in a bow or curtsy position at the end of a ballet class is called *révérence*. This grand gesture is a way to acknowledge and give respect to the people you have just collaborated with—other dancers, your teachers, your pianist, and your audience. Conceptually, collaboration is a major part of how I search for community while fostering political solidarity. In my work there are many "moving" parts where I am working with groups of people to achieve an ongoing production, in order to make dance and art. I am very grateful to these people for coming with me on my journey and for sharing their contributions.

To my dancers, I am ever grateful to you all; you give me your body, your minds, and your souls. Without you, my work would not exist. Specifically, I want to thank the following performers: Héctor Cerna, Charles Gowin, Yuha Kamoto, Lloyd Knight, Violetta Komyshan, Andrea de León Rivera, Victor Lozano, Tiffany Mangulabnan, Antonio Mannino, Jordan Miller, Josep Maria Monreal Vidal, Oisín Monaghan, Mykel Nairne, Amy Saunder, Leah Upchurch, Mauricia Vera, Allison Walsh, Jennifer Whalen, and Tyler Zydel. You all were vital parts to *The Master and Form* and *Contract and Release*.

In these processes I began to work together for the first time with an architectural firm, which allowed me to grow and develop my ideas. I am indebted to Norman and Kelley, you gave me insight into my process and allowed me to grow and expand the ways my installations manifest. Thank you to Jason Lewis and Daniel Sullivan for fabricating my sculptures and installations with such care. To Rad Hourani for your genderless and non-binary costumes, you made each dancer feel individual, but also part of a community. Thank you to Amanda Jane Graham, my friend and dramaturg, for listening to my ideas and helping me edit them to become nuanced and rich.

Without the generous support of the Graham Foundation, The Whitney Museum of American Art, and The Noguchi Museum, these two projects would not have had space to manifest. The incredible teams of people at each institution made this all come to be, and I would especially like to thank Ellen Hartwell Alderman, Nora Daly, Carly Fischer, Melissa Gatz, Dakin Hart, Sarah Herda, Rujeko Hockley, Ramsay Kolber, Brett Littman, Jennifer Lorch, Jane Panetta, Laura Pfeffer, Scott Rothkopf, Alexandra Lee Small, Kate Wiener, and Raul Zbengheci.

I am so grateful that these ephemeral moments of making dance and art, these manifestations, can now live on in book form and become archived. Thank you to Platform: Jacob Lindgren and Paul Zdon for designing a conceptually sound and aesthetically beautiful book.

Each page is a dance and I love how you have created movement to honor my work. Thank you to Juliet Bellow, Andrew Campbell, Hendrik Folkerts, Dakin Hart, Sarah Herda, Brett Littman, and Thomas Kelley for sharing words, insights, and ideas to make me think harder about my practice. I am so excited to see how your words make me grow and develop. With gratitude to Alhena Katsof, you made this book flow through your editing skills, it is simply a better publication because of you. And to Edoardo Ghizzoni and the team at Skira, I am grateful for our partnership and all of the generosity you have given me in the process of making this book and as it enters into this world.

I am ever so grateful to my team, Ryan Josey and Bianca Marks, you are my pillars of support and I look forward to us growing together. To the Monique Meloche Gallery team I am grateful for the support and dedication you give to me as an artist. To my community at Northwestern University and in the Department of Art, Theory and Practice I am grateful for your continued support of my research and work. Thank you as well to Artadia for your fiscal sponsorship and ongoing support.

To my family: Hazel Fernandes, Rudy Fernandes, Lisa-Marie Fernandes, Aamir Fazil, Noah Fazil, Tamara Fernandes, Bruce Schumann, and Zahra Schumann—this pandemic has kept us apart, but I always know you love and support me. I look forward to being able to share myself (and my art) with you. This is coming!!!!!

And last but not least, my chosen family and comrades, you make life adventurous and fun, but most importantly, together we create community. Kurt Balder, Aniko Berman, Ian Bourland, Tom Campbell, Domenic Del Carmine, Ellen-Blair Chube, Amanda Chudak, Christin Comper, Matt Congdon, Shaun Dacey, Jordan Eagles, Tad Freese, Madeleine Grynsztejn, Deana Haggag, Saxon Harr, Brook Hartzell, Donny Hodge, Pamela J. Joyner, Parambir Keila, Jacob Korczynski, Tom Krell, Kyle Krietemeyer, Heather Nadine Lake, Alida & Christopher Latham, Alphonse Lembo, Melissa Levin, Joseph Liatela, Mary-Beth Liberatore, Warren Lobo, Greg Malinowski, Trista E. Mallory, Evan Moffitt, Christine Negus, Karen Ng, Becky DiPasquale, January Parkos Arnall, Anjli Patel, Abby Pucker, Bob Rennie, Julie Rodrigues Widholm, Francey Rusell, Jane Saks, Devyani Saltzman, Eric Shiner, Chris Skovron, Karsten Sollors, Travis Stasney, Nat Trotman, Janna Van Grunsen, and Ashley Wynn: thank you for your past, present, and future love.

With gratitude and in *révérence*,
Brendan

Design
Platform

Editor
Alhena Katsof

Copy editor
Carlotta Santuccio

Digital imaging preparation
Ryan Josey

First published in Italy in 2021 by
Skira editore S.p.A.
Palazzo Casati Stampa
via Torino 61
20123 Milano
Italy
www.skira.net

Printed and bound in Italy. First edition
ISBN: 978-88-572-4559-1

Distributed in USA, Canada, Central & South America by ARTBOOK | D.A.P. 75, Broad Street Suite 630, New York, NY 10004, USA.
Distributed elsewhere in the world by Thames and Hudson Ltd., 181A High Holborn, London WC1V 7QX, United Kingdom.

Published in partnership with

Graham Foundation

noguchi

Fiscal sponsor

ARTADIA
NON-PROFIT
ORGANIZATION
501(c)(3)
EST 1999

Graham Foundation for
Advanced Studies in the Fine Arts
4 W Burton Pl, Chicago, IL 60610

The Noguchi Museum
9-01 33rd Rd, Queens, NY 11106